FREEDOM IS NOT ENOUGH

FREEDOM IS NOT ENOUGH

The War on Poverty and the Civil Rights Movement in Texas

WILLIAM S. CLAYSON

UNIVERSITY OF TEXAS PRESS, AUSTIN

The publication of this book was supported in part by a gift from Lowell Lebermann.

COPYRIGHT © 2010 BY THE UNIVERSITY OF TEXAS PRESS

Printed in the United States of America

First edition, 2010

Requests for permission to reproduce material from this work should be sent to:
   Permissions
   University of Texas Press
   P.O. Box 7819
   Austin, TX 78713-7819
   www.utexas.edu/utpress/about/bpermission.html

♾ The paper used in this book meets the minimum requirements of ANSI/NISO
Z39.48-1992 (R1997) (Permanence of Paper).

LIBRARY OF CONGRESS CATALOGING-IN-PUBLICATION DATA

Clayson, William S. (William Stephen), 1970–
   Freedom is not enough : the war on poverty and the civil rights movement in
Texas / William S. Clayson. — 1st ed.
   p.   cm.
   Includes bibliographical references and index.
   ISBN 978-0-292-72898-1
   1. Poverty—Government policy—Texas—History—20th century.   2. Economic
assistance, Domestic—Texas—History—20th century.   3. Civil rights movements—
Texas—History—20th century.   4. Texas—Social conditions—20th century.
5. Texas—Economic conditions—20th century.   6. Texas—Politics and
government—1951–   I. Title.
HC107.T43P63115   2010
362.5′56109764—dc22

                                                                    2009023608

TO MOM AND DAD

Somehow you never forget what poverty and hatred can do when you see its scars on the face of a young child.

— LYNDON JOHNSON, 1965 SPEECH INTRODUCING
THE VOTING RIGHTS ACT

CONTENTS

A section of photographs follows page 64.

ACKNOWLEDGMENTS

When I began studying the War on Poverty deep in the recesses of the library at Texas Tech, my wife and I were expecting our first child. Now we have four kids, a ten-year-old boy and his three little sisters. We spent seven years bouncing around the country while my wife, Darby, finished her residency and a service obligation to the Air Force. I worked at six colleges in four states. I spent a miserable year in Kuwait mobilized as an Army reservist. Darby is out of the Air Force now, and we have settled into a relatively pleasant suburb in Las Vegas, a lifetime away from the government documents section in Lubbock. That this book got published in spite of all those complications owes less to my own perseverance than to the help and encouragement of family and colleagues.

I would not have completed this book without my wife, Dr. Darby Clayson. For the past fifteen years, Darb has been my best friend and role model. Other than my parents, she is the only person in my life whose confidence in me has never wavered. I owe Joey, Sarah, Elisabeth, and Emily an apology for the fact that the laptop screen has gotten more face time with their dad than they have over the past few years.

I also would like to thank my War on Poverty cronies. In the fall of 2003 I received an email out of the blue from Marc Rodriguez, who invited me to a conference at Princeton University. The scholars at that conference reshaped my thinking and have transformed the historiography of the War on Poverty. Along with Marc, the attendees included Annelise Orleck, Bob Bauman, Tom Kiffmeyer, and Rhonda Williams, all of whom have published books on the poverty fight in communities around the country. Professor Orleck has become our collective mentor, and as a Las Vegan I am especially thankful for her *Storming Caesar's Palace*. After the Princeton conference we took the show on the road and did the 2005 American Historical Association conference in Seattle. In 2007 Lisa Hazirijan and Guian McKee brought an even larger group together at the Miller Center for Public Affairs at the University of Virginia. Along with the scholars mentioned above, the Charlottesville conference included Susan Ashmore, Dan Cobb, Kent Germany, Laurie Green, Ivy Holliman, Amy Jordan, Thomas Jackson, and Wesley Phelps. In 2009 many from the same group took the War on Poverty tour back to Seattle for the Organization of American Historians conference. Wes and I also did a panel at the Texas State Historical Association conference in Austin that year. These collaborations moved my work into new and unexpected directions, and I am so grateful to the group for its professionalism.

My mentors at Texas Tech deserve recognition. Alwyn Barr, a fine scholar who has worked with Tech graduate students through four decades, took great care guiding me through my dissertation. Although George Flynn retired the year before I defended my dissertation, he convinced me that good scholarship is not merely a means to an end but rather the historian's *raison d'être*.

I am grateful to others who contributed toward this book's publication. The staff at the Institute of Texan Cultures in San Antonio, especially Tom Shelton and Patrick Lemelle, went above and beyond on short notice to help with photos. And the caring professionals of the editorial staff at the University of Texas Press deserve credit for their part in bringing the project to fruition.

When I took my current position at the College of Southern Nevada, it was with the understanding that my scholarly ambition would be secondary to teaching and service responsibilities at the college. Scholarship is not part of the job description for community college historians. Yet my fellow historians at CSN—John Hollitz and Mike Green—have shown me that it is possible to remain professionally engaged while teaching ten sections a year. I like to think that what we community college professionals do is part of the solution to poverty in America. I have taught about 3,500 students in my career, most of whom would have been excluded from higher education without a community college. To these students I offer my sincere thanks for keeping me employed and my apologies for taking too long to grade their papers while I worked on this book.

FREEDOM IS NOT ENOUGH

INTRODUCTION

In March 1965 television audiences got a jarring glimpse of the violence that enforced segregation in the Jim Crow South. Mounted sheriff's deputies and Alabama state troopers, menacing in protective masks, trampled and beat young marchers in a cloud of tear gas on the Edmund Pettus Bridge in Selma. Such brazen racist violence captured on the television news seemed to discredit the recent legislative triumph of the Civil Rights Act and pending voting rights legislation for southern blacks. To reaffirm the nation's commitment to civil rights, Lyndon Johnson responded with a speech that compared the bravery of the marchers, who risked their lives for the right to vote, to the Minutemen at Lexington and Concord. The speech endeared him to civil rights activists across the nation. Martin Luther King Jr. admitted that he shed tears when the president echoed the clarion of the civil rights movement: "We *shall* overcome." Richard Goodwin, who wrote the speech, recalled, "God, how I loved Lyndon Johnson at that moment."[1]

Later in the speech the president reflected on his brief career as a teacher at the "Mexican" school in the small South Texas town of Cotulla. Johnson's tenure at Cotulla gave him firsthand experience with the effects of racism and poverty on children.[2] First to his speechwriter Goodwin and then to the nation, Johnson recollected his time in Cotulla with a sense of commitment to his former students:

> Somehow you never forget what poverty and hatred can do when you
> see its scars on the face of a young child . . . It never occurred to me in

my wildest dreams that I might have the chance to help the sons and daughters of those students . . . But now I have that chance—and I'll let you in on a secret—I mean to use it.[3]

The president's pledge to heal the wounds of poverty and hatred intimated more than civil rights legislation. He also alluded to his War on Poverty, begun the previous year under the Economic Opportunity Act (EOA). The EOA had the most ambitious agenda of all the legislation introduced in the Great Society. Johnson proposed to accomplish nothing less than an end to poverty in the United States.

Following Johnson's speech, a reporter for the *San Antonio News* traveled to Cotulla to check on progress since the president's time at the school. Cotulla remained a "picture of poverty" more than three decades after politics lured LBJ to Washington.[4] School Superintendent Roy Landrum, a classmate of Johnson at Southwest Texas State Teachers College, explained that La Salle County still had "children that go to school without breakfast." The county had one of the highest illiteracy rates in Texas. The *Express-News* article cited a study that placed the average income for families in Cotulla at $1,585, half the national poverty rate, and the average level of schooling at 1.4 years.

Despite such grim conditions, Johnson gave Cotullans hope in 1965. The War on Poverty offered impoverished communities like Cotulla funding to build their own antipoverty programs. When LBJ gave his speech after Selma, the Office of Economic Opportunity (OEO), the executive agency created to fight the War on Poverty, had already financed the development of a locally operated Community Action Program (CAP). The Tri-County Community Action Committee headquartered in Cotulla was one of more than a thousand local Community Action Agencies (CAAs) nationwide. The Cotulla effort began with a literacy program for poor citizens of the area.[5] The head of the program was Dan Garcia, one of LBJ's former students. When the Cotulla literacy program began, Johnson called Garcia and the mayors of Cotulla and neighboring Pearsall to congratulate them. Mayor J. W. Collins of Pearsall told the president that people in the community looked forward to the program because "there was great interest among Latin-Americans to learn English and Anglo-Americans to learn Spanish."[6] Such optimism and cooperation in his program, especially between whites and disadvantaged Mexican Americans, certainly pleased LBJ as the racial strife of the decade began to escalate.

By the end of the 1960s, after Johnson left office and a full-scale retreat from the War on Poverty was well under way, the effort had done little to improve the social and economic conditions of Mexican Americans in Cotulla. They remained far below the town's white minority in income, employment, and economic opportunity. The educational discrepancies underscored the continuing legacy of segregation. The "Mexican" school where LBJ worked, Wellhausen School, was dilapidated and had facilities and programs far inferior to those of the school on the Anglo side of town. Wellhausen had no cafeteria and no gym, and the school's restrooms were in a different building from the classrooms. Instruction included little Spanish-language material. Mexican American students started off behind their Anglo counterparts, and few caught up. An estimated 80 percent of Mexican Americans in Cotulla dropped out of school before the age of eighteen.[7]

While the War on Poverty did little to counteract the economic inequalities of Cotulla, the effort coincided with a dramatic political transformation. A political revolution came to South Texas in the sixties, forced on the region's Anglo establishment under the sway of the militant Chicano youth movement. Through the Mexican American Youth Organization (MAYO) and its political outgrowth, La Raza Unida Party, young Chicano activists took the mantle of leadership in the Texas civil rights movement by the end of the 1960s. In 1970 La Raza Unida Party organized the election of Cotulla's first Mexican American mayor, Alfredo Zamora, along with two city councilmen and two members of the school board. La Raza Unida organized similar takeovers elsewhere in the Winter Garden region of South Texas, most notably in Crystal City. The unprecedented electoral success of La Raza Unida shocked Cotulla's Anglo minority, just eight hundred of more than four thousand residents, who had controlled the town and systematically limited Mexican American voting and office holding since the turn of the twentieth century. The new school board members realized the worst fears of the Anglo old guard when they desegregated Cotulla's schools. In 1970 Anglo and Mexican American students went to Wellhausen for first and second grade and to the "white" school on the other side of town for third and fourth.[8]

The Anglo leadership of South Texas traditionally voted Democratic and supported Lyndon Johnson since his days as a congressman. Yet Johnson's War on Poverty contributed to the mobilization of political groups like MAYO that sought to wrest control of local politics from Anglos. Workers from Volunteers in Service to America (VISTA), an OEO program, formed organizations in Cotulla's neighborhoods that generated interest in voting and in supporting La Raza candidates.[9] Beyond Cotulla, VISTA provided funding and staff for MAYO to organize in communities across the state.[10] VISTA became enmeshed in controversies over school administration when VISTA volunteers received funding from the Cotulla CAA to begin a bilingual education program. With the help of lawyers from the Mexican American Legal Defense and Education Fund, VISTA community organizers began a petition drive to abolish the Inter-American Test of Oral English in Cotulla schools, a hurdle that held back many of Cotulla's Mexican American students.[11]

The relationship between Chicano activists and VISTA in Cotulla exemplified a connection that few historians of either the civil rights movement or the Great Society have addressed. The body of scholarship on the civil rights movement gives little indication of either the great hope the War on Poverty initially held out to activists or the sense of resentment that emerged when results failed to measure up to expectations. Neither does the historiography clarify the extent to which OEO programs subsidized civil rights activism. The extensive literature on the Johnson administration also fails to measure how the changing values of the civil rights movement informed the implementation of War on Poverty policy, especially on the state and local levels.

For civil rights activists and segregationists as well as the OEO's antipoverty warriors and their opponents, the connections between the civil rights movement and the War on Poverty were salient. African Americans saw the OEO as a potential ally in the civil rights agenda. Most black Texans surely would have agreed with Martin Luther King Jr. in ranking the inclusion of African Americans in the War on Poverty among his top priorities:

> If our demonstrations are to stop, there must be some equality in terms of grappling with the problem of poverty. We have a poverty bill which has been nobly initiated by the President of our nation and the Congress, but in the South so often Negroes are denied the opportunity to be a part of the administration of them, and we feel that if demonstrations are to stop, Negroes must be brought into the very central structure of the whole poverty program.[12]

Further, the reduction in poverty was as important a goal for minority groups as desegregation. The 1963 March on Washington was, after all, a March for *Jobs* and Freedom. In his seminal Howard University commencement speech in June 1965, Johnson seemed to agree that economic equality should be the next goal of the civil rights struggle:

> [T]his is the next and more profound stage of the battle of civil rights. We seek . . . not just equality as a right and a theory but equality as a

fact and equality as a result . . . Freedom is not enough . . . You do not take a person who, for years, has been hobbled by chains and liberate him, bring him up to the starting line of a race and then say, "you are free to compete with all the others," and still justly believe you have been completely fair.[13]

Regardless of what Johnson intended, both supporters and opponents of the civil rights movement considered the War on Poverty that "next and more profound stage."

The history of the War on Poverty provides valuable lessons on the nexus between liberalism and the civil rights movement in the later 1960s. Post–World War II liberalism, as epitomized by Johnson and the Great Society, remained faithful to the idea that the purpose of government was to create and defend equality of opportunity. In the mid–twentieth century, the primary obstacles to this goal were racial segregation and chronic poverty—hence Johnson's two major domestic policy efforts entailed civil rights legislation and programs to combat poverty. Politics and principle required the separation of these efforts. Johnson and his antipoverty warriors understood the political consequences of an antipoverty program targeted at minorities. More importantly, a War on Poverty centered around racial inequities would have seemed a retreat from a fundamental goal of postwar liberalism—a society in which race had no bearing on opportunity. Yet, as the growing body of literature on the OEO suggests, race and civil rights issues suffused the War on Poverty.[14]

The purpose of this book is to trace the connections between the War on Poverty and the civil rights movement using Texas as a statewide case study. Texas provides an excellent setting to study the OEO and the movement. The state had the nation's largest poor population when the War on Poverty began. Among the states, Texas was second only to California in the amount of OEO funding received.[15] As a state that is both southern and western, Texas exemplifies the complexities of race politics in the 1960s. Mexican Americans formed the state's largest minority and struggled to overcome a system of segregation as entrenched as that of the Jim Crow South. The state had the concentrated urban poverty on which the OEO focused and the stubborn rural poverty that the OEO sorely neglected. Texas also illustrates the emergence of the Sunbelt as a force on the national political stage.

Any discussion of antipoverty policy in Texas first requires a clear understanding of the depth of the problem in the state. In the mid–twentieth century, poverty in Texas was real and pervasive, not simply relative material depravation. Poverty left thousands of Texans malnourished, illiterate, unhealthy, underemployed, and politically powerless. This was especially true among nonwhites. Mexican American and African American Texans remained in an economic stasis similar to the conditions the nation endured during the Great Depression.

An important objective of the book is to demonstrate how significant the War on Poverty was to Texans in the 1960s. We might consider the idea ridiculous or naïve in the early twenty-first century, but in 1964 Texans across the political spectrum took seriously Lyndon Johnson's proposal to end poverty through government action. Critics on the far left saw the budget and concluded from the beginning that it would not be enough, but liberals and civil rights activists around the state had high hopes for the War on Poverty. As the Civil Rights Act tore down the barriers of legalized segregation, the Economic Opportunity Act promised a society free from chronic poverty. On the right, conservatives feared a new tax-consuming bureaucracy emanating from Washington. Like other Great Society initiatives, the OEO seemed an imposition on local and state authority that would threaten the status quo. Worse yet, in a deeply segregated state like Texas it appeared to give financial teeth to integration. To Goldwater Republicans, a new force in state politics, the War on Poverty seemed the brainchild of left-leaning sociologists intent on installing socialism.

As the centerpiece and most controversial feature of the War on Poverty, the Community Action Program occupies most of the attention of this study. More than one hundred Community Action Agencies operated in Texas. These local agencies administered a variety of other OEO programs on the local level, including the Neighborhood Youth Corps (NYC), Legal Services, and Head Start. This book focuses on San Antonio, El Paso, and Houston as the cities with the most extensive and controversial CAAs in the state. The Dallas–Fort Worth region developed CAAs later, after the OEO had ironed out the more politically controversial elements of CAP, and local political leaders steered them in an uncontentious, service-oriented direction. Other cities and towns from the Panhandle-Plains region to the Rio Grande Valley are included. I explore the issue of rural poverty, but the OEO's "almost exclusively urban cast" makes poverty in the cities by necessity the focus of the study.[16]

I have integrated the Job Corps and VISTA into the broader picture of the War on Poverty in Texas as well. The Job Corps, implemented in the Johnson administration, continues to this day, though in a much more limited capacity than originally envisaged. Opponents of the War on Poverty opposed the establishment of Job Corps programs on the local level, primarily because they feared large concentrations of young black males in their communities. Civil rights leaders at first championed the Job Corps as a great opportunity to train young men and women for jobs. As the civil rights movement changed tone in the later sixties, many African American leaders came to criticize the Job Corps as little more than a convenient method to keep a leash on young black men and the centers as akin to prisons. Coming to a similar conclusion from the inverse perspective, conservative opponents viewed the Job Corps as more or less a bribe to appease potential rioters and criminals.

VISTA volunteers came to the state infused with the liberal optimism of the early sixties. Like their counterparts in the international Peace Corps, domestic VISTA volunteers were mostly young white idealists who believed in the transformative power of progressive government. As early as 1967 VISTA in Texas reflected the influence of the New Left and militant civil rights groups. Volunteers organized boycotts, school walkouts, and angry demonstrations. White leaders in East and South Texas labeled the VISTA volunteers "outside agitators" and petitioned the governor to have them removed. Significantly, VISTA subsidized the expansion of MAYO in its early stages. A marked change in VISTA tactics clearly shows how the Nixon administration reoriented the War on Poverty after LBJ left office.

Beyond explaining the contextual significance of the War on Poverty, the story of the OEO in Texas helps elucidate the transformation of state politics (and, in the long run, national politics) that began in the sixties. By the time OEO programs came to Texas in 1965, the Democratic Party in the state was split into conservative and liberal factions. Conservative Democrats, led by Governor John Connally, were the primary opponents of the War on Poverty in Texas. While the governor was solidly in the mainstream of the national party prior to 1964, his opposition to the Civil Rights Act distanced him from LBJ, his political mentor. From 1964 on, Connally and a majority of white Texans began a steady march to the political right. To the surprise of OEO officials in Washington, Connally became a major obstacle in the implementation of OEO programs in Texas. Connally opposed the War on Poverty for much the same reason he opposed the Civil Rights Act. From the governor's point of view, the OEO bypassed state authority, and most of his constituents opposed it as another liberal spending program targeted at minorities.

In opposition to the conservatives, a liberal coalition comprised of minorities, organized labor, and white progressives emerged within the Democratic Party by the early 1960s. The liberal coalition, led by Senator Ralph Yarborough, showed a remarkable degree of solidarity across race lines. Defense of OEO programs became a strong impetus for this solidarity as liberals squared off against establishment politicians like Connally and entrenched political cliques on the local level. The solidarity of the liberal coalition waned as the decade came to a close. Leading figures from minority communities, including staunch allies of LBJ, chastised the OEO for its failures to include minority groups in the administration of the War on Poverty.

On the local level, CAAs came under fire for failing to live up to the OEO's call for the "maximum feasible participation of the poor." Civil rights leaders translated the OEO's guiding principle into participation by Mexican Americans or African Americans. They also thought it feasible for the poor, or at least civil rights organizations as representatives of the poor, to participate in War on Poverty programs by running them and controlling the budgets. It is evident that lower-income Anglos likewise thought of the War on Poverty in racial terms, as few white Texans showed interest in OEO programs, while Mexican American and African American Texans competed for limited federal antipoverty funds in major cities across the state.

Tensions between black and Chicano Texans reflected the ascension of militant values among activists, a trend that coincided with and was heightened by the launch of the War on Poverty. As employees or clients of local CAAs in cities across Texas, many future militant leaders gained a degree of political education from the War on Poverty. As CAP employees, nascent militants witnessed or participated in political confrontations with entrenched, Anglo-dominated local establishments over CAP funding. Further, OEO programs provided access to residents of lower-income communities, a benefit that proved instrumental in political organizing. With budgets and salaried workers, the OEO also subsidized the development of political organizations led by militants. The influence of militant movements became evident in OEO programs early on, as both clients and employees of various agencies began to question the commitment of Anglos to advancing the cause of the Chicano and black freedom struggles.

Chicano and Chicana youth formed the most fully developed militant civil rights groups in Texas.[17] The Chicano movement began with small groups of angry students, centered primarily in San Antonio and spearheaded by MAYO. It rapidly matured into a dynamic political force in Texas politics under La Raza Unida Party, a third party that challenged Democratic control over the Mexican American electorate. While only a minority of Mexican Americans in Texas embraced Chicano radicalism, the values of the movement had a broad influence in barrios throughout the state.

OEO programs became scenes of confrontation between LBJ liberals and the Chicano militants. The primary source of this tension involved OEO officials' insistence on the need to fight a "colorblind" War on Poverty.[18] Although sensitive to the realities of racism and discrimination, liberal leaders and local antipoverty administrators largely embraced the colorblind ideal in regard to the War on Poverty not only because the majority of poor Texans happened to be Anglo but also because they kept faith with the liberal ideal of integration. Chicano militants, however, had a clear and angry understanding of the racially disproportionate nature of poverty in Texas. They knew that young people from the barrios had less hope of pulling themselves out of poverty than poor whites. Besides disregard of such disparities, the colorblind principle of the OEO clashed with the values that defined the Chicano movement: political empowerment, economic self-determination, and cultural nationalism. Because of their commitment to these values, Chicanos counted among their adversaries Anglos as well as Mexican American liberals like San Antonio Congressman Henry B. Gonzalez. The conflict with the older generation of Mexican American leaders indicates that the rift was about racial ideology, not simply about overcoming white supremacy. In executing the War on Poverty, Chicano movement leaders wanted the money the OEO offered but wanted Chicanos to administer the programs in keeping with the values of the Chicano movement.

Black Power fell short of the Chicano movement in Texas in terms of political development, but the values of black nationalism made deep inroads in the state by the close of the sixties. Like their Chicano counterparts, militant African American leaders in Houston who were associated with the Student Non-violent Coordinating Committee (SNCC) attempted to form their own independent community action organization and applied for funding from the OEO in contention with the city's CAA. The story became more complex in Houston, however, because of the potential for urban violence. While minor in comparison to riots in the North and the West, significant violence flared in Houston as tensions between law enforcement and the black community reached a fever pitch in the summer of 1967. The city's political leadership, with Mayor Louis Welch at the forefront, placed some of the blame for the tension on the OEO for financing militant groups, while local African American leaders blamed the OEO for failing to do enough to fight poverty in the city.

When these various elements are put together, the history of the War on Poverty traces the rise and fall of postwar liberalism in the Lone Star State. The liberals had momentum in Texas politics when the War on Poverty began in 1964. The election of Johnson, liberal Senator Ralph Yarborough's defeat of Congressman George H. W. Bush in the 1964 Senate campaign, and the undeniable successes of the civil rights movement all seemed to point toward a future defined by the values of liberalism, even in Texas. Yet by the end of the decade Chicano militants and black nationalists began to question these values. The militants considered integration, the fundamental value and goal of postwar liberalism, tantamount to assimilation, a rejection of their unique cultures. They could not be convinced of the distinction between the historically racist, conservative Democratic Party of Texas and the pro–civil rights, liberal Democratic Party of Lyndon Johnson. Of course, Johnson did not help matters by escalating the war in Vietnam, fueling the resentment of militants as minority soldiers died in disproportionate numbers.

At the same time, the essential conservatism of the white electorate manifested itself in state politics. Republican leaders like Senator John Tower and George H. W. Bush cited the War on Poverty as an example of a program that ignored the concerns of the "silent majority." The new conservative thrust in Texas politics, however, began to distance itself from an overt concern with segregation, the overriding concern of southern politics in the postwar decades. Although the legal barriers fell, Texas became more deeply segregated after the collapse of Jim Crow as mostly white suburbs sprawled into the piney woods, hills, and prairies surrounding the state's cities. With a booming economy and a greater portion of the electorate distanced, both geographically and economically, from the realities of poverty, politicians had little motive for defending liberal efforts like the War on Poverty. The Democratic Party was already losing ground as white moderates started voting Republican. All the Democrats seemed to offer affluent white suburbanites was higher taxes to fund social programs like the OEO, apparently to benefit minorities. The GOP began to court the votes of Mexican Americans, citing the War on Poverty as a liberal spending program that neglected their concerns in favor of lawbreaking blacks. By the time Johnson left office in 1969, Democratic leaders, threatened by Republican successes, began to work against the War on Poverty. Meanwhile, the Nixon administration, with a young Donald Rumsfeld at the helm of the OEO, scaled back the effort and reoriented its ideological underpinnings.

Finally, I offer this work to answer a call made more than twenty-five years ago by Allen J. Matusow in *The Unraveling of America*. In that book, still a touchstone in the historiography of the period, Matusow sharply criticized Johnson and the OEO for the flaws and foibles of community action. Yet Matusow proffered that no "final judgment" could be made on CAP and, by extension, the rest of the War on Poverty "until an army of local historians recovers the program's lost fragments."[19] While not exactly an army, I consider myself a member in good standing of a small cadre of historians committed to telling the tale of the War on Poverty as it was fought in ghettos and barrios, on farms and in mining towns, in migrant camps and on Indian reservations, by men and women across the nation. It is only fitting to tell the story where it all began for LBJ—in Texas.

Poverty, Race, and Politics
in Postwar Texas

ONE

Michael Harrington's *The Other America* may have sparked a "rediscovery" of poverty in the 1960s, but chronic poverty was no revelation in the Lone Star State. Texas had more poor people than any other state when Lyndon Johnson took office.[1] Yet poverty in Texas had been on the decline since 1945 as the state followed the nation into the dramatic economic and social transformation of the postwar decades. By the time the War on Poverty began in 1964, many more Texans had moved into John Kenneth Galbraith's affluent society than remained in Harrington's other America.

Much of the change and the growing affluence resulted from national demographic shifts. Texas had begun to integrate into the economic milieu that Kevin Phillips first dubbed the Sunbelt, a region of growing affluence based on inmigration for better weather, sprawling homogeneous suburbs, and high levels of federal spending, especially for defense. The state's population skyrocketed from 6.4 million in 1940 to nearly 10 million in 1960. The population of Texas went from more than half rural before World War II to two-thirds urban by 1960. Given the state's historically rural personality, it is likely that few Texans realized that the state had a higher proportion of city dwellers in 1960 than the nation as a whole.[2]

But, as many Texans say, Texas is different. As much as it reflected national trends, the state remained unique. In great part native Anglos identified with the past, clinging to memories of the Republic of Texas and the old Confederacy. Many also remained committed to the racialist preoccupations of the Jim Crow South. Yet Texas was also part of the West, sketched in the popular imagination by the rugged individualism of ranchers and roughnecks. Texas was also different from the rest of the South because it did not have a predominantly biracial society. Mexican Americans comprised the state's largest minority group, making Texas ethnically more akin to California than Georgia. Texas' ties to the old South kept its African American and Mexican American populations, comprising nearly a third of the whole, subordinate to the demands of legalized segregation and racism.

In many ways, a struggle between Texas' unique position and the pressure to integrate into the socioeconomic mainstream defined the history of the state in the postwar period. Conservative Texans sought to maintain the social status quo even as they advanced into a new economic era defined by higher incomes and greater material advantage. They clung to western ideals like rugged individualism as southern racial values outlined by Jim Crow left the state's minority populations behind. Although the majority of poor Texans in 1960 were white, only about one in five whites lived in poverty. Among Mexican Americans and African Americans the figure was closer to one in two. The racially disproportionate nature of Texas poverty in the postwar period, when combined with the momentum of the civil rights movement, made the War on Poverty a politically divisive issue when it came to the state in 1964.

RACE AND POVERTY IN POSTWAR TEXAS

Despite the rapid economic growth of Texas in the postwar decades, the state's economy continued to rank behind national averages in most indices in the early sixties. Nearly a third of Texans lived on incomes below the poverty line, compared to the fifth so lamented by Harrington and other observers nationally. The median income of $4,433 was $600 less than the national average.[3] Census takers defined 28 percent of Texas homes as "deteriorated" or "dilapidated," compared to 19 percent nationally.[4]

If the statistics are analyzed according to race, however, it is evident that white Texans kept pace with and even surpassed national averages in some categories. The median annual income of white men in Texas, $3,728, ranked almost $400 higher than the national average for male workers. The poverty rate of whites in Texas was slightly lower than the national average (20 versus 22 percent). The proportion of white-owned homes census takers deemed deteriorated or dilapidated fell 2 percent below the national average. White Texans, in short, shared in the boom that characterized the postwar economy.[5]

Texas trailed behind the national pace of economic change because the state's 1.4 million Mexican Americans and 1.2 million African Americans did not participate equally with whites in the postwar boom. Nearly half of all Mexican Americans and African Americans in the state in 1960 lived on incomes below the federal poverty line, compared to about 20 percent of whites. The boom times delivered black and Mexican Texans from living conditions that had not changed since the 1930s. The majority of both populations still worked as farm laborers or debt peons in 1930. By 1960 Texas' largest minority groups reached an economic status that was statistically similar to Great Depression–era standards for the nation as a whole. Nonwhites in Texas undoubtedly advanced in the postwar years, but they remained in a state of economic depression similar to the conditions that prompted the creation of the American welfare state three decades prior.[6]

A brief summary of the statistics makes it difficult to apply a term like "postwar boom" to black and Chicano Texans. The median annual income of Mexican American families in Texas stood at $3,000, equal with the national poverty line. The unemployment rate among Mexican Americans, nearly 8 percent, was twice that of whites. Mexican Americans in Texas averaged just six years of school, two fewer than the national average for Latinos and five fewer than the state average for Texas.[7] Only thirty thousand of the nearly million and a half Mexican Americans in the state graduated from high school, and just six thousand completed four years of college.[8] The median annual income for black families in Texas reached just $2,520 by 1960. Unemployment among blacks was double the rate for whites. Only 31 percent of blacks finished high school, and 8.4 percent had attended at least one year of college, both 10 percent behind the average educational attainment of whites.[9]

These statistics do not account for the hundreds of thousands of undocumented Mexican immigrants coming into Texas during the period. Illegal immigration exceeded the total number of documented Mexican immigrants by tenfold in most years. The segregated social order of Texas excluded the state from the Bracero Program, a "guest worker" program instituted by agreement between Mexico and the United States to fill the demand for agricultural laborers. Designed as a wartime solution to labor shortages, the Bracero Program continued into the postwar decades due to pressure from corporate growers for cheap labor. The Mexican government, however, excluded South Texas farm counties because of legalized segregation and white supremacism in the state. Despite these conditions, undocumented laborers became the norm on the state's increasingly corporatized farms. Thousands of Mexican farm laborers remained trapped in lives defined by tentative and temporary conditions as they migrated with the seasons from fields in Texas to fields elsewhere in the United States or, depending on inconsistent immigration enforcement, back to Mexico.[10]

Most Mexican Americans and African Americans in the state worked at low-paying jobs. On San Antonio's west side, for example, more than half of all residents lived on incomes below federal poverty standards. A Labor Department study concluded that San Antonio had the nation's highest "subemployment rate," a figure that combined unemployment, underemployment, job turnover, and other factors into a single statistic. Expressed as a percentage of working-age adults, subemployment described a lack of worthwhile jobs that created chronic poverty within a community. San Antonio's subemployment rate of 47.4 percent ranked higher than notoriously poor communities in Harlem or New Orleans.[11] El Paso's south side had similar job problems. One OEO study found that 81 percent of employed residents in El Paso's southside barrios earned incomes below the poverty line.[12] Low-paying farmwork and chronic underemployment made Laredo, according to an OEO report, the "poorest city in the nation."[13] When informed that the federal government considered $3,000 per year the poverty line, one resident of Houston's Third Ward, the city's poorest neighborhood, told a reporter for the *Texas Observer:* "Man, who makes close to $3,000 a year? That's more'n $55 every week of the year, they ain't a whole lot makes that much every week."[14]

High unemployment, underemployment, and low incomes meant that many nonwhite Texans lived without conveniences that most Americans had come to consider necessities of life. Among nonwhites in the state, 45 percent had no car, 43 percent had no hot and cold running water in their homes, 32 percent had no television, and 29 percent lacked flush toilets. Census takers considered more than half of all homes occupied by nonwhites in the state dilapidated or deteriorating.[15] While the census failed to tally housing statistics on Mexican Americans for the state as a whole, local conditions provided some indication of living standards. In the 1960 census, 70 percent of all homes in El Paso's El Segundo Barrio, most rented from absentee "slumlords," were considered dilapidated or deteriorating.[16] Half of all Mexican Americans in Houston rented their homes, and half of those homes were recorded as deteriorating or dilapidated. In Eagle Pass, nearly half of all Mexican American homes had no flush toilets or hot and cold running water.[17]

But poverty in the 1960s still meant more than a lack of modern conveniences or even of money. Malnutrition and death from a lack of basic health and sanitation infrastructure remained common. In San Antonio two-thirds of residents in the city's westside barrios were malnourished. The west side had the nation's highest infant death rates from dehydration caused by diarrhea.[18] And a report on public health in El Paso indicated that "for many years the great majority of deaths among children from typhoid fever, smallpox, scarlet fever, whooping cough, diphtheria, enteritis, and diarrhea have been reported from South El Paso, where most of the Mexicans live."[19]

Poverty remained pervasive in rural Texas, but the problem largely moved into the city along with the bulk of the population. The mechanization of agriculture required fewer farm laborers. The farm economy pushed people away as the city pulled them in with low-paying blue-collar jobs. Along with mechanization, the corporatization of agriculture drove small-farm owners off the land as larger and larger farms became the norm in the state. The overall number of Texas farms decreased. These trends in agriculture had their most deleterious effects on nonwhite farmers. The number of African American farm owners in the state declined from more than 50,000 in 1940 to about 15,000 in 1960. The number of tenants and sharecroppers also declined dramatically, to just over 3,000 in 1960, while there were ten times that number two decades earlier. Among Mexican Americans, independent *patrones*, local owner-operators of small farms, all but disappeared from the landscape to be replaced by absentee owners and local managers who treated laborers as interchangeable parts on ever-expanding factory farms. By 1960 nearly 75 percent of Mexican Americans and African Americans lived in cities, and about half of these lived on incomes below the poverty line. This amounted to an urban underclass of about a million black and Latino poor in the segregated neighborhoods of the state's cities and larger towns.[20]

SEGREGATION

Well before Congress passed the Civil Rights Act, all but the most die-hard white supremacists recognized the impending demise of Jim Crow following the U.S. Supreme Court's *Brown v. Board of Education* decision in 1954. Yet with the economy gaining strength among Anglo Texans, segregation became more pronounced as the suburbs sprawled farther away from city centers. The trend known as "white flight" often conjures images of urban dwellers fleeing proximity to ghettos in the Northeast, but it also fueled the growth of the suburban Sunbelt. White flight reinforced segregated living arrangements even as the legal barriers of Jim Crow seemed on their way out. The Houston suburb of Pasadena, for example, had only twenty-nine blacks out of nearly sixty thousand residents in 1960. In Dallas, which was 25 percent African American in 1960, thirty-six of its two hundred census tracts had no black residents. White flight accelerated through the sixties. By the end of the decade, Dallas had fourteen census tracts, almost all to the southeast of the central city, that were 95–100 percent black. Houston had ten that fell into the same category. The census shows that the inverse was the case in the sprawling suburbs of both cities, with white majorities in dozens of tracts. In the suburb of Arlington, all but one census tract were at least 80 percent white. In cities like El Paso and San Antonio where Mexican Americans formed majorities or near-majorities, similar trends of white flight were apparent. Segregation was even more complete in smaller cities. In 1960 the census determined that Odessa was 98 percent segregated, among the most segregated cities in the country. Lubbock had one census tract that was 95–100 percent black and another that was 50–80 percent Hispanic, while the rest of the city was at least 80 percent white. Two of Waco's census tracts were 80 percent black and the balance predominantly white.[21]

Segregation in the cities made the disproportionate poverty all the more apparent. Each city had black and/or Mexican "sides" that became defined not just by a prevailing ethnicity but by chronic poverty and higher population densities. On a short drive through any city or large town in the state, one could move from a largely white and affluent neighborhood with good schools and plenty of shopping to economically stagnant barrios or ghettos with neglected infrastructure, struggling businesses, and poor housing. Dallas had four census tracts in which 40 percent of the population lived on poverty wages or less. All four were also 80 percent black. More than half of the predominantly Mexican American neighborhoods in Corpus Christi had poverty rates of 40 percent. In cities where whites were in the minority, census maps show small islands of white population. Only one census tract in Laredo had a population that was predominantly white, and that tract happened to be the only one in the city in which less than one-fifth of the families lived in poverty.[22] At the same time, poor African American and Mexican American communities had denser populations. Black neighborhoods in Dallas and Houston began to look more like the inner-city ghettos of the North and the West.[23] Barrios in the state's larger cities became similarly crowded; Rodolfo Acuña describes San Antonio's west side as "nothing but rural shacks packed together in an urban ghetto."[24]

The economic contrast between segregated neighborhoods was obvious to black and Chicano Texans in the cities. These inequalities made poverty an aspect of the social and political identity of minority groups in the state. At the same time, Texas featured little class consciousness across race lines based on similar economic circumstances. Poor whites were dispersed in smaller urban clusters. Born into a racist culture, poor whites showed little desire to ally themselves politically with poor blacks or Chicanos in the state. Poor whites often resisted identifying themselves as poor. R. U. Maddox, a native of rural Texas who migrated to Dallas for work, defiantly informed Sargent Shriver in 1964 that "based on the $3,000 yearly income as a definition of poverty, adjusted back . . . I was born and reared in poverty but didn't realize it."[25] A lack of white participation presented a basic problem of the OEO once the War on Poverty got off the ground in 1964.

CIVIL RIGHTS AND TEXAS POLITICS

As they swelled the ranks of the urban poor, Chicanos and blacks became politically mobilized in the postwar decades. The proximity of city life fostered political activism. Organizations such as the National Association for the Advancement of Colored People (NAACP) and the League of United Latin American Citizens (LULAC) expanded their memberships in the postwar years. The leaders of these organizations came mostly from the middle and upper classes of society, including professionals, businesspeople, and clergy. They shared the values prevalent in the African American civil rights movement in the early sixties, values that were in keeping with what historian Gary Gerstle has defined as "civic nationalism." The idea of civic nationalism encompassed a belief in "the fundamental equality of all human beings, in every individual's inalienable rights to life, liberty, and the pursuit of happiness, and in a democratic government that derives its legitimacy from the people's consent."[26] The rhetoric of Martin Luther King Jr. exemplified the loyalty of postwar civil rights activists to these ideals. The goal of civil rights activism in the postwar decades was to make civic nationalist ideals a reality.

In Texas, Mexican American civil rights activists in the postwar decades most clearly identified with the ideals of civic nationalism. Historian Mario Garcia dubbed the leadership of this period the "Mexican American generation," a term that has come to describe the cohort of leaders who emerged from the struggles of the Great Depression and World War II. This generation remained proud of its roots but emphasized integration into mainstream American society and believed in the ideals of U.S. citizenship. The members of this Mexican American generation objected to the use of the term "Mexican" to categorize them as a separate race, preferring the terms "Mexican American" or "Latin American" to describe themselves as another loyal and proud immigrant group, like Italian Americans or Polish Americans. They encouraged their children to learn English, get a good education, and achieve middle-class ideals of economic security and comfort. They worked primarily

in the courts and in the political arena to put an end to a system of segregation that was, in the words of David Montejano, "as complete—and as 'de
jure'—as any in the Jim Crow South."[27] Hector P. García of Corpus Christi
exemplified the leadership of this period. García founded the American GI
Forum, a veterans service organization that ranked among the most politically
influential in the state by the 1960s.

A similar cadre of leaders emerged among African American Texans during
the postwar years. Like the Mexican American generation's leadership, black
civil rights leaders emphasized ending segregation, equal access to education,
office holding, and voting rights. James Farmer was the most famous movement leader to come out of Texas in the postwar decades. A founding member
and national director for the Congress of Racial Equality (CORE), Farmer
grew up in Marshall, where his father served on the faculty of Wiley College.
For the most part, the African American leadership of the postwar period
came from the small but growing middle class.[28]

Service in the armed forces during World War II very much informed
the ideology of the postwar generation. After risking life and limb to defend
their country, returning veterans found it difficult to accept the status quo of
segregation and discrimination. Like many other returning veterans, Hector
García recognized the irony of returning home from a war against fascism to
face discrimination in the "land of the free." García later explained, "We were
Americans, not 'spics' or 'greasers,' because when you fight for your country
in a World War, against an alien philosophy, fascism, you are an American and
proud to be an American."[29]

The postwar generation of civil rights activists made major strides toward
greater equality for minority groups in Texas, especially in education. Both
Mexican American and African American Texans made gains toward integrating schools in the state before *Brown v. Board of Education*. The American
GI Forum and LULAC led efforts in the courts to integrate and improve the
schools in areas with large Mexican American populations. The decision of
the U.S. district court in *Delgado v. Bastrop Independent School District* (1948)
prohibited state school districts "from, in any manner, directly or indirectly,
participating in the custom, usage or practice of segregating pupils of Mexican
or other Latin American descent in separate schools or classes." The NAACP
used *Delgado* as a precedent in the *Brown* case.[30] In 1946 Houston postman
Herman Sweatt sued the University of Texas for refusing his application to
law school on the basis of race. Despite state lawmakers' establishment of segregated law schools for blacks, the U.S. Supreme Court's favorable decision
in *Sweatt v. Painter* (1950) signaled the end of de jure segregation in American

higher education and forced the state's colleges to integrate their graduate and professional schools. By the mid-sixties, pressure from civil rights activists forced the end of legal segregation in most Texas school districts and colleges. Continued segregation caused by housing discrimination or white flight should not overshadow the end of legally sanctioned segregation in education as a major accomplishment.

The successes of the postwar generation in drives for integration and equality inspired both communities to action in electoral politics. In 1957 El Paso elected its first Mexican American mayor, Raymond L. Telles. Henry B. Gonzalez became the first Mexican American elected to the Texas congressional delegation. In South Texas the Political Association of Spanish Speaking Organizations (PASSO), with the help of the International Brotherhood of Teamsters, organized a bloc voting drive that elected the first all–Mexican American city council in the United States, in Crystal City, Texas. This so-called "first uprising" far outweighed its impact on Crystal City, a town of about nine thousand. Montejano contends that the Crystal City uprising "symbolized the overthrow" of Jim Crow in South Texas.[31] It also introduced Albert Peña Jr. into Texas politics. As the leader of PASSO, Peña influenced the younger generation of Mexican American civil rights activists in the state, those who would lead the Chicano movement in the later 1960s. While Peña entered politics with the rest of the Mexican American generation, his dynamic, aggressive style deviated from the more moderate tactics of most of his contemporaries.

The legacy of Jim Crow continued to inhibit black advancement in electoral politics until after the passage of the Voting Rights Act in 1965 and the Supreme Court's abolition of the poll tax in 1966. Yet black involvement prior to these accomplishments had a significant impact on politics in Texas. Nearly 40 percent of potential black voters in the state had registered by 1958, in comparison to 49 percent of whites. The Democrats and the GOP placed African Americans on their executive committees. In Houston, Democrat City Councilman Louis Welch responded to the growing strength of the black vote by participating in a sit-in at city hall. Welch's later election to the mayor's office owed much to the support of African Americans in the city.[32]

The civil rights movement and the politicization of minority groups transformed Texas politics. Since the New Deal, the Democratic Party and state politics had been controlled by "the Establishment," which George Norris Green defined in 1979 as a "loosely knit plutocracy comprised mostly of Anglo businessmen, oilmen, bankers, and lawyers."[33] The Establishment had largely been opposed to the New Deal during the Depression and into the war, but the electorate overwhelmingly supported Roosevelt. Like other southerners, Texans overall supported liberal federal spending programs. The tax base in the state remained low, so Texans gained far more from New Deal programs than they sent to the Internal Revenue Service.[34] Many Establishment politicians, including Lyndon Johnson, made their careers by fostering federal spending programs in the state. Federal subsidies and the economic might of the Establishment kept Texas in the Democratic fold. The loyalties of the South began to wane in the postwar years, however, primarily because of the Democratic Party's association with race issues.

Franklin Roosevelt ducked making a firm commitment to civil rights for blacks but instituted limited programs during the Depression and the war to ensure their political support without alienating southern whites. Harry Truman did more and broke an "unwritten understanding" that the party had maintained with southern whites since the Wilson administration.[35] When Truman integrated the armed forces and sent a modest civil rights bill to Congress with the Fair Deal package of 1948, he violated "an understanding that [southern] support of the party in its decided leftward movement since 1912 would be repaid by a willingness to permit the South to maintain the existing patterns of race relations and, to a lesser degree, those characterizing the relationship between capital and labor."[36] Truman's civil rights policies led to the Dixiecrat revolt in the 1948 election, costing Truman four Deep South states.

Truman's continued support of New Deal programs and the loyalty of most rank-and-file Democrats allowed him to win Texas comfortably, yet the Establishment began to drift toward the GOP in the postwar period for two reasons: oil and civil rights. In 1947 the Supreme Court ruled that the federal government, not the states, controlled "tidelands" waters near the coast that contained rich reserves of oil. Led by Governor Alan Shivers, Establishment Democrats in Texas began moving their support to the GOP in the 1950s because Eisenhower came down on the side of the states in the tideland issues. The "Shivercrats" endorsed Eisenhower for president in the 1952 and 1956 elections.

Oil was a major factor in the Shivercrat revolt, but electoral trends within the state leading up to the sixties suggest that race remained foremost in the minds of many voters. Those Texans who followed Strom Thurmond into the Dixiecrats in 1948 also largely came out for Eisenhower in the 1950s. Knowing the potency of race issues, even Lyndon Johnson voted to maintain the poll tax four times as a congressman. He voted against the establishment of the Fair Employment Practices Commission during the war as well. During his 1948 senatorial campaign, Johnson "lambasted Truman's whole civil rights program as worthy of a police state."[37]

The 1954 race for the governor's office reveals the weight of race issues in state politics. In his failed 1954 bid for the governor's office, Ralph Yarborough, whose record was otherwise more liberal than Johnson's, came out as opposing the "forced commingling" of the races in the wake of the *Brown* decision. Shivers, Yarborough's opponent, came out as a vocal, if privately troubled, supporter of continued segregation. "All of my instincts," Shivers said, "my political philosophy, my experiences and my common sense revolt against this Supreme Court decision."[38] When the 1954 gubernatorial primary went into a runoff, Yarborough sought to weaken Shivers' support in East Texas by playing the race card. Yarborough's team publicized the fact that Shivers paid for his kids to attend St. Edward's High School in Austin, the only integrated school in the city, and informed voters that Shivers had supported the integration of the University of Texas. Worse yet, Yarborough's campaign distributed pictures of Shivers eating with African American troops from Texas in Korea. The Shivers campaign went further, sending several newspaper editors an altered photo of Yarborough with darker skin and a flat nose to make him look black.[39] Shivers' victory owed much to red-baiting related to Yarborough's Congress of Industrial Organizations (CIO) connections, but such ugly campaign shenanigans clarify the significance of race in Texas politics. The Texas electorate, which included only a small fraction of minority racial populations up until the sixties, had a choice not between segregation and integration but between varying degrees of continued white supremacy.

The defection of the Shivercrats from the national party in the two Eisenhower-Stevenson contests had significant repercussions for the future of the Democratic Party in the state. Painting the Shivercrats as disloyal, liberal Democrats fought against Shivers and the Democratic establishment to move the state party into step with the national party.

The liberals formed a coalition made up of minorities, organized labor, and Anglo progressives, primarily from the cities, to challenge the conservative dominance of the state party. The liberal coalition, often referred to as the "labor liberals," gained strength in the early 1960s. Occasionally the factions in the Democratic Party were referred to as "state" and "national" Democrats to allow the liberals to distinguish their values from those of the conservatives. Given that Eisenhower had carried the state in the two previous elections, Kennedy's success in the 1960 election reveals the strength of the liberal coalition at the beginning of the decade. Scholars have argued that both the Mexican American vote, mobilized in Viva Kennedy clubs, and the African American vote delivered Texas, and the White House, to Kennedy. With a margin of victory of less than 1 percent, the Kennedy campaign needed the full participation of the entire coalition to win.[40]

As the Democrats split and the national party became more associated with civil rights, the Republican Party became more attractive to Texas conservatives. The successes of Eisenhower revealed this growing strength. The GOP began to influence electoral outcomes. The split in the conservative vote allowed Ralph Yarborough's Senate victory in 1957. The election of Republican John Tower in 1961 to fill the seat vacated by Lyndon Johnson and again in 1966 highlighted the growing strength of the GOP in the state. Tower, closely tied with the neoconservative movement of Barry Goldwater, became the first Republican elected to the Texas congressional delegation since Reconstruction.[41]

Besides gaining conservative votes from the split among Democrats, the GOP also benefited from race politics in Texas because of the continuation of discriminatory voting practices. A Republican Party pamphlet titled "Texas Republican Precinct Plan" explained how the GOP, even with just 20 percent of voters, could win statewide elections because of the poll tax. According to the pamphlet, "Adults comprise approximately 60 percent of the population. 60 percent of ten million is 6 million. 20 percent of six million is 1.2 million people—enough Republican votes to win practically every election ever held in Texas (only 2,050,000 people paid poll taxes in 1961)."[42]

The OEO entered Texas in a time of dramatic change. The postwar economic boom had moved whites in the state and the nation into a new era of affluence. The affluent society left black and Mexican Texans behind, but the civil rights movement promised a revolutionary change in race relations in the state. The Civil Rights Act tore down the legal barriers of Jim Crow, and many Texans were confident that the Economic Opportunity Act promised to accomplish the same for chronic poverty.

Postwar Liberalism, Civil Rights, and the Origins of the War on Poverty

TWO

The vitriol of political talk in recent decades has clouded historical understanding of liberalism in the twentieth century. Conservatives have largely driven the political discourse in America since LBJ left office, defining liberal Democrats as, more or less, feminist proponents of abortion and gay rights who are soft on defense and cater to minorities with affirmative action and welfare programs. Ronald Reagan made "liberal" an epithet—"the L word"— and made "big government" liberalism nearly synonymous with "socialism." Reaganite myth held that government of the New Deal and the Great Society intruded on individual liberties, stole from working families with oppressive taxes, made people hopelessly dependent, weakened the national defense in the face of mortal threats, and sought to erase the moral codes that defined American society.[1]

During the first quarter-century of the cold war, American liberals stood in sharp contrast to the values later ascribed to them by Reagan. The women's movement was in its infancy, and social issues like abortion and gay rights had barely appeared on the radar screen. Prior to the escalation of U.S. involvement in the Vietnam War, liberals stood among the staunchest anticommunists and advocates of a strong national defense. The concept of affirmative action had not yet coalesced as a policy option and, if it had, would have offended the racial egalitarianism to which most liberals subscribed. Postwar liberals began to distance themselves from the radical or socialistic ideas with which many had toyed during the New Deal. As Henry Wallace's abortive

1948 campaign showed, the old ideals of progressivism rang hollow in the midst of a booming economy and the shadow of a communist menace.[2]

This is not to say that postwar liberalism lacked an agenda or a coherent set of values. Thinkers like Reinhold Niebhur and others associated with Americans for Democratic Action (ADA), the primary liberal lobbying group of the era, redefined liberalism in the postwar years to meet the demands of the cold war. Liberal thinkers recognized that the nation was, according to the policy declaration of the ADA, in a "two front fight for democracy, both at home and abroad." To win the battle between democracy and communism, the liberals argued, government must first recognize and work to overcome what remained undemocratic about American society.[3] No cause affected this process more than civil rights, and no politician influenced what liberal government would become more than Lyndon Johnson.

LYNDON JOHNSON AND CIVIL RIGHTS

Johnson's personal political philosophy is hard to pin down. His view of politics was all about compromise, electioneering, and finding consensus in disputes. He objected to labels like "liberal" and "conservative." He disliked ideologues and politicians who voted according to a dogmatic set of principles or prejudices. In an article published in the winter 1958 *Texas Quarterly* titled "My Political Philosophy," Johnson classified himself as "a free man, American, United States Senator, Democrat, liberal, conservative, Texan, taxpayer, rancher, businessman, consumer, parent, and voter." Johnson believed "that everyone has something to say, that a national answer exists for every national problem, that the highest purpose of government is to help Americans reach the fullest potential of their physical and human resources, and that waste of these resources is the major enemy of our society." Paul Conkin called Johnson's list of principles nothing more than a "series of clichés,"[4] but a brief look at LBJ's postwar career suggests that the values he expressed in 1958 were in tune with the evolving ideology of postwar liberalism.

Two primary concerns shaped Johnson's tenure in the Senate: his presidential ambitions and the issue of civil rights. With the support and tutelage of Richard Russell of Georgia, Johnson became Senate minority leader in 1954, moving into the majority leader's chair the following January when the Democrats gained control after the midterm elections. Up to that point Johnson had stayed in step with other southerners on civil rights issues. To do otherwise would have killed his electoral chances in Texas. After his decisive reelection victory in 1954, Johnson's presidential ambitions required him to distance himself from the southern bloc. Along with two other southern senators, Albert Gore Sr. and Estes Kefauver of Tennessee, Johnson refused to sign the Southern Manifesto, which condemned the Supreme Court's decision in *Brown v. Board of Education* as an unconstitutional violation of states' rights. Russell, as the leader of the southerners, evidently did not feel betrayed by his protégé. Russell and the southern bloc assumed the loyal Texan would slow down civil rights legislation once he entered the Oval Office.[5]

By the late 1950s liberals had embraced civil rights as a primary cause because the Republican leadership had, for the most part, acquiesced to the surviving institutions of the New Deal. Eisenhower signed legislation to expand Social Security and the minimum wage. Welfare spending increased throughout his administration. Although Red Scare tactics often painted the New Deal as encroaching socialism, the Republican leadership developed a hands-off policy toward the welfare state. "Should any political party attempt," Ike once prophesied, "to abolish Social Security, unemployment insurance, and eliminate labor laws and farms programs, you would not hear of that party again in our political history."[6] Eisenhower, a devotee of balanced budgets, even allowed Keynesian economic adjustments when the economy seemed in need of assistance. The red-baiting of the cold war, along with a growing economy, made it difficult for liberals to champion new progressive welfare or labor policies. With Republicans acquiescing to liberal causes and Democrats resisting identification with progressive policy, civil rights assumed center stage on the liberal agenda. This was not merely by default; the growing momentum of the southern struggle against Jim Crow compelled the ascension of civil rights in the national discourse. More than his southern colleagues, LBJ recognized the significance of civil rights to the future of American politics.

Johnson deserves much of the credit for the passage of the Civil Rights Act of 1957. As Russell and the other southerners gave doomful speeches about a second Reconstruction enforced by federal arms, Johnson brought leaders from both parties to compromises that enabled the bill's passage. These compromises weakened many of the original bill's more dramatic features, including a renewal of a Reconstruction-era law that allowed the use of troops to enforce voting rights. Johnson had a stipulation removed that gave power to federal judges to try violations of the law without juries. Most observers considered the revised bill an empty gesture or a cynical move by Johnson to curry favor with northern liberals. Nevertheless, some important liberal stalwarts, including most prominently Minnesota Senator Hubert Humphrey, thought it an important step forward—the first federal civil rights legislation in more than three-quarters of a century. Once passed, the act did little for southern blacks, but it demonstrated Johnson's grasp of the significance of civil rights.[7]

Despite his efforts as majority leader, doubts about Johnson's liberal credentials emerged when John F. Kennedy, after beating LBJ in the 1960 primaries, invited him to join the ticket. CORE leader James Farmer considered Johnson's nomination for vice president a "disaster, because of his southern background and his voting record on civil rights." Joseph Rauh of Americans for Democratic Action, in front of a national television audience at the party convention, called for Kennedy to reconsider Johnson's nomination. Liberals feared, Oklahoma Senator A. S. Monroney explained, that Johnson was "Simon Legree" in disguise and, "at any moment, would walk on stage with his big black snake whip to beat back any civil rights legislation." Despite such doubts among Democrats, Johnson made sense as a running mate for Kennedy. He could deliver Texas, which Kennedy needed to win, but he had moved away from the southern bloc through his tenure as majority leader. Conservative southerners considered him a "counterfeit Confederate" and a "scalawag." Having enemies among conservative southerners bolstered LBJ's liberal credentials. "By changing Lyndon Johnson from a Texas to a national politician," a *New Republic* editorial writer argued, "Kennedy frees him to take more liberal positions if, as Johnson's old friends in Washington have always vowed, those are the true beliefs of the inner man."[8]

What the inner man really believed mattered little. The proof of Johnson's liberal credentials lies in the legislation of the Great Society, though Johnson's many biographers tend to place credit or blame for the Great Society on his personal motivations. One of the problems with trying to understand Johnson's place in American political history involves what Paul Conkin has called the "growth industry" of LBJ biographies. The overwhelming detail of biographies like those written by Robert Dallek and Robert Caro makes it difficult to find any coherence in Johnson's career. From the vast literature on Johnson emerges a man of ultimate ambition and arrogance, of remarkable optimism bordering on hubris, with sometimes shocking behavior and crude mannerisms. Most of Johnson's biographers depict the Great Society as a creation of this complex personality. Some, including Dallek and Doris Kearns, describe the Great Society as a product of Johnson's optimism and idealism. Others paint a portrait of the Great Society as an extension of Johnson's political opportunism on a national scale. "It is hard to identify," Conkin explains in his own treatment of LBJ, "any one focus or find any controlling priorities [in the Great Society] because, in a sense, Johnson never adopted any save those related to political opportunities."[9]

Multivolume biographies of a man who spent more than three decades in a dirty business like politics naturally will reveal complexities and contradictions, but the Great Society should not be viewed as merely a product of Johnson's grand utopian vision for the future of America or his personal ambition. The Great Society kept faith with the developing agenda of postwar liberalism. Most of the major bills had roots in earlier liberal failures. Truman introduced the idea of medical care for the aged; Kennedy developed a tentative antipoverty campaign and introduced a broad civil rights bill. Rather than a departure based on Johnson's ambition or personal need to achieve greatness, one should view the Great Society as the culmination of postwar liberalism.

Johnson did more than his predecessors because of the national mood following the Kennedy assassination and the electoral mandate he received in 1964 and apparently because he seems to have had a conviction that more needed to be done. Liberals up until the 1960s viewed the economy as "an ever-expanding economic pie" that helped to prevent recessions and brought affluence to most of the population. With basic Keynesian tools the liberals believed they could not only prevent another depression but also maintain a relatively constant rate of growth. Johnson seemed committed to this "new economics," including the need for tax cuts to induce economic activity, but he lacked faith in the ability of economic growth to reach everyone. After nearly two decades of continuous growth, one in five Americans remained in poverty. LBJ strove to do something historic and revolutionary, like his mentor's New Deal, for those Americans left out of the general affluence of the postwar years.[10]

Because the administration unleashed so many bills, proposals, and task forces, it is difficult to find any ideological coherence to the Great Society, but much of the major legislation indicates that Johnson and his advisers focused on inequality of opportunity as the primary obstacle to broader social and economic progress. The Elementary and Secondary Education Act upheld the traditional faith in education to enhance equal opportunity. A revised immigration bill was intended to equalize access to American opportunities among potential immigrants. A host of health care bills, culminating with the creation of Medicare and Medicaid, were sought to equalize access to health care. The Voting Rights Act of 1965 achieved what no other piece of legislation, including the Fifteenth Amendment to the Constitution, did in expanding black voter participation.

In an emphasis on equality of opportunity, the Great Society reflected the prevailing tradition of individualism in American history. American society historically placed the onus of success or failure on the individual; it was not up to the state to compensate for an individual's personal failings. The progressive tradition that emerged in the early twentieth century and was cemented during the New Deal never raised questions about this basic premise. With the Great Society, liberals led by Johnson merely sought to eliminate legal barriers and compensate for the failure of the economy to provide for competent, hard-working individuals. This broad outline for governmental action represented a coherent ethos that historian Gareth Davies has best labeled "liberal individualism."[11] Under the values of liberal individualism, the Great Society was meant to create a level playing field on which individuals could succeed regardless of their race or economic standing at birth. A fundamental problem with the concept of a level playing field was that it focused on race and economic standing to the exclusion of gender. Postwar liberals narrowly focused on working men, when within lower-income and many non-white households women were often the primary breadwinners. Translated into federal policy, the exclusion of women handicapped the War on Poverty from the start.

The Great Society reflected the desire of liberals to recognize and overcome barriers to equality of opportunity. Other than gender discrimination, which did not seem to register as a serious problem with LBJ and his cohorts, the two greatest barriers to equality remained racial discrimination and chronic poverty. Minority groups could not advance on an equal footing if the law allowed for their subordination. Similarly, the poor remained stuck in a vicious cycle of deprivation because they lacked equal access to education, training, health care, and quality jobs. Without these vital benefits, poverty passed from one generation to the next.[12] The bills Johnson introduced to overcome these barriers represented the greatest triumphs of liberalism since the New Deal. The Civil Rights Act (CRA) was intended as a mechanism to accomplish the full meaning and potential of the Fourteenth Amendment to the Constitution. The Economic Opportunity Act (EOA) was nothing less than a law designed to end poverty in the United States. Although the Johnson administration endeavored to disassociate the two, the CRA and EOA each portended the achievement of equal opportunity that lay at the center of the liberal agenda in postwar America. He may not have known it, but

when speaker Newt Gingrich declared in 1994 that "we simply must abandon the welfare state and move to an opportunity society," he echoed much
of what liberals had argued to advance an antipoverty program three decades
earlier.[13]

THE ECONOMIC OPPORTUNITY ACT

The EOA, like much of the Great Society agenda, had roots in the Kennedy
administration. An antipoverty bill for Kennedy's 1964 legislative package
was being put together when the president was assassinated. David Hackett,
Robert Kennedy's nominee to run the antipoverty campaign, prepared many
of the proposals in the bill. Hackett first proposed to learn more about why
chronic poverty occurred more in certain groups and geographic regions. He
did not recommend that anyone "announce to anybody that we're going to
solve poverty." Instead, he suggested the development of federally supported
demonstration programs in select communities. In this way, kinks in the program could be worked out before launching a national program.[14]

The Kennedy and Johnson antipoverty efforts came from a similar ideological perspective and employed similar tactics, but they differed based on
the ambitions and political situation of each administration. Kennedy, after
a narrow electoral victory in 1960, stood in no position to remake America
with many bold domestic initiatives. Passing a tax cut remained his main domestic goal. Wanting the New Frontier, his domestic program, to have some
substance in relation to poverty, Kennedy presented a series of piecemeal
efforts targeted at particular groups or problems, most of which the Johnson
administration later integrated into the broader War on Poverty under the
EOA. In May 1961 Kennedy sponsored the Area Redevelopment Act (ARA)
to assist depressed pockets such as the southern Appalachians. By 1964, $300
million had been spent under the ARA. The 1962 Manpower Development
and Training Act (MDTA) provided $3.2 billion over the next decade; much
of this money was spent under Johnson's Job Corps program for youth job
training in high-poverty areas.[15] The National Service Corps, a domestic version of the popular Peace Corps, was an idea introduced by Robert Kennedy
and continued under the Johnson administration as VISTA.[16]

The groundwork for the War on Poverty laid by the Kennedy administration began from the fundamental assumption that poverty resulted from a
lack of opportunity for individual initiative to flourish. From this perspective,
the economy required no restructuring but only corrective measures to ensure equal opportunity. The bulk of the effort, then, kept faith with the liberal

individualist values that would underlie the Great Society. The one aspect of the War on Poverty that did not fit into the ideology of liberal individualism—and the antipoverty tactic that would draw the most criticism—was community action.

Community action was an avant-garde sociological concept to include the poor in their own rehabilitation. Chicago activist Saul Alinsky pioneered community action as a method of mobilizing the poor to organize politically to confront unresponsive local establishments. Community action promised to build a foundation to bring about broad institutional change. None of the existing institutions that affected ghetto life—schools, welfare programs, local government, housing agencies, or law enforcement—provided the poor with substantive benefits. Community action promised to reform these existing institutions through political activism. One poor person had little voice, but organized into voting blocs the urban poor could get results. Community action theory held that professional organizers would play a temporary role. Once community leadership developed, government officials would step back and allow local people to run the programs.[17]

Community action crept into federal antipoverty policy through Kennedy's juvenile delinquency program. Matusow contends that early in his term Kennedy came to understand "the true dimensions of poverty in America, the linkage between joblessness and race, and the dangerous discontent festering in big-city slums."[18] Because of these concerns, juvenile delinquency emerged as a major focus of the Kennedy program, especially in black ghettos. Although no major outbursts of urban violence had occurred since the 1940s, youth gang violence in the cities was on the rise. Juvenile delinquency in the 1950s became a more serious problem than *Rebel Without a Cause* or *West Side Story* suggest. In Harlem, 248 fighting gangs roamed the streets by the late 1950s. The gangs were not yet associated with organized crime or drug dealing, but the protection of turf led to routine violence. In New York City the adolescent homicide rate tripled in the 1950s (from 2 to 6 deaths per 100,000), and the number of adolescents convicted of homicide rose from zero in 1955 to 200 in 1964.[19] Urban violence began to shift away from historical patterns. Wartime riots in Detroit, Los Angeles, and other cities tended to feature whites targeting black communities. By the sixties, authorities feared that a reversal of that pattern might bring violence to white communities.

The Juvenile Delinquency Act, which Kennedy signed into law in September 1961, provided the Department of Health, Education, and Welfare (HEW) with $30 million to finance locally run delinquency control programs. Hackett designed his program around the ideas of the best-known scholar in the field of juvenile delinquency, Lloyd Ohlin of the Columbia University School of Social Work. Ohlin and Richard Cloward had published a book titled *Delinquency and Opportunity: A Theory of Juvenile Gangs* in which they spelled out ideas that would be fundamental to the War on Poverty. While at Columbia, Ohlin began a delinquency project called Mobilization for Youth (MFY) in Harlem. Hackett convinced HEW directors to provide $2.1 million for MFY with the hope that a model might be developed for other communities to follow. MFY, in many ways the first federally sponsored community action program, offered neighborhood service centers that provided information on existing welfare services, which were unfamiliar to many people in slum communities, along with public service jobs for young people, job information, some employment for neighborhood residents, and a forum for political organizing. Although MFY would serve as a model, HEW required local governments to develop their own programs. Eventually, sixteen cities received funding to establish community action projects.[20] Because community action as developed for the delinquency program remained the main effort of the War on Poverty once Johnson took office, the association between federal antipoverty programs and urban blacks persisted despite the battery of other programs begun under Kennedy and continued by Johnson.

Once Johnson established himself in office, he determined to go further on poverty than Kennedy even considered. Poverty provided him with a domestic platform plank for the 1964 election. A full-scale "unconditional War on Poverty" offered a cause that, in the wake of the assassination, would befit the "Kennedy legacy" and would allow LBJ, in his words, to put his "own stamp on this administration in order to run for office."[21] When Walter Heller of the Council of Economic Advisors (CEA) briefed Johnson on the progress of Kennedy's program in December 1963, LBJ reacted coldly to the idea of demonstration programs. He wanted federal antipoverty assistance made available to all localities, not just a select few.[22] A comprehensive national War on Poverty, which it thenceforth became, "excited Johnson's attraction to grand visionary plans."[23]

Like the limited New Frontier antipoverty initiatives, the War on Poverty was focused on employment training and educational programs to give individuals the means to pull themselves up by their own bootstraps. Johnson wanted to abandon traditional welfare systems and insisted that the War on Poverty not be waged by handing out "doles."[24] Indeed, the administration presented the antipoverty campaign as a measure to save on welfare costs, which had expanded in the 1950s. The number of families receiving benefits through Aid to Families with Dependent Children (AFDC) rose from

710,000 to 3 million between 1945 and 1960. AFDC provided 40 percent of the income of the average family living below the poverty line.[25] If poverty could be reduced in the short run, then the long-term cost of welfare would be reduced. A 1964 report of the CEA explained this line of reasoning: "We pay twice for poverty: once in the production lost in wasted human potential, again in the resources diverted to coping with poverty's social by-products. Humanity compels our action, but it is sound economics as well."[26] LBJ also avoided the staggering cost associated with make-work job programs.

To administer his War on Poverty, Johnson selected R. Sargent Shriver, the director of the Peace Corps and a Kennedy brother-in-law. LBJ chose Shriver because he wanted to maintain an association between the Kennedy administration and the poverty program. Shriver reluctantly accepted the charge (though Johnson gave him little choice) and publicly shared the president's belief that if the antipoverty effort was "effectively and energetically carried forward, [it] will in the end eliminate poverty from the United States."[27] To meet this daunting goal, he received little guidance from his new boss. According to rumor, LBJ told him little more than to keep out "crooks, Communists, and cocksuckers." These proved the least of Shriver's problems.[28]

Writing the legislation and getting it through Congress presented the first problem. Not knowing where to begin, Shriver consulted Michael Harrington. The author told him straight off that the plan to request $1 billion for the poverty war was "nickels and dimes."[29] Most informed people understood that a billion dollars per year would not end poverty. The A. Philip Randolph Institute prepared a "freedom budget" in 1966 that recommended $185 billion to eliminate poverty in a decade. But Shriver, like Johnson, had little interest in new taxes or unbalanced budgets to fight the poverty war. Both rejected Labor Secretary Willard Wirtz' suggestion to alleviate poverty with a $3 billion to $5 billion jobs program financed by a cigarette tax.[30] Shriver had no affinity for doles, either. It was the director who coined the phrase that the War on Poverty was a "hand up, not a hand out."[31] In this sense, Shriver shared Johnson's belief in equalizing opportunity as the main tactic for overcoming poverty.

Nor did Shriver show enthusiasm for community action. When briefed on community action the first time, Shriver concluded abruptly, "It'll never fly."[32] He doubted the capacity of community action programs to coordinate local institutions. The new "poverty czar" wanted to center the legislation on a jobs training program. The economic opportunity bill that he and his staff sent to Congress placed the Community Action Program in a secondary role to Shriver's favorite proposal—the Job Corps. Despite this, CAP became the centerpiece and the most controversial program of the War on Poverty. Shriver would later tout CAP as "the boldest of OEO's inventions."[33]

How CAP got past Johnson is a bit of a mystery. The president may have seen CAP as a more efficient way to channel federal funds into extant services for the poor. He may have warmed to the CAP requirement for the maximum feasible participation of the poor—seeing the poor working in the program like the young Texans he mentored in the National Youth Administration during the Depression. Daniel Patrick Moynihan argued that Johnson treated CAP with "instant suspicion and dislike" because he foresaw the problems that CAP eventually caused: "He had no sympathy whatever for financing a conflict of the Democratic poor against the Democrat mayors of the nation."[34] Matusow, on the other hand, concludes that Johnson simply failed to understand the broad purposes of community action. Johnson did not grasp that the program was designed to give the poor the means to politically organize against unresponsive local establishments. The evolution of community action over the next few years holds up Matusow's conclusion that "Johnson's usually reliable political antennae failed to sense in community action a threat to the harmony and political consensus he so valued."[35]

Congress passed the EOA at the end of July 1964. Shriver's team altered much of the original legislative package to attract votes in Congress. Title I established the Job Corps to develop job training centers for underprivileged youth, primarily from urban areas, as an expansion of Kennedy's MDTA. Along with industrial training, the Job Corps would operate conservation camps, a nod to the still revered Civilian Conservation Corps (CCC) of the New Deal period. Title II established CAP, an Adult Basic Education program, and Head Start. Title III set up rural poverty and Migrant Opportunities programs. Title IV established a small-business opportunities program. Title V instituted work experience programs including the Neighborhood Youth Corps. Title VI established VISTA as an expansion of JFK's National Service program and as a domestic version of the Peace Corps. Johnson's sense of fiscal prudence placed severe limitations on spending. The appropriation for OEO came in October when Congress authorized $800 million.[36]

The act established the Office of Economic Opportunity in the executive branch. Johnson appointed Shriver as the director of the OEO and as his assistant Adam Yarmolinsky, who had been working under Robert McNamara in the Defense Department. The OEO would not run the effort independently. Shriver would direct the Job Corps, VISTA, CAP, and the Migrant Opportunities program. The Labor Department would assist with the Neighborhood Youth Corps. The Agriculture Department, Small Business Administration, and HEW worked on various other programs.[37] This hodgepodge of bureaucracies became a basic problem of the OEO throughout its history. Little coordination developed among agencies to manage limited funds spread over far too many programs. Instead of choosing a single method to attack poverty, the OEO covered as many methods as possible.[38] Because LBJ offered an open-ended invitation for communities to develop CAPs, however, the administration of CAP used up a large share of OEO funds (three-eighths of all funds for the first fiscal year), and community action became the dominant strategy for fighting poverty.[39]

Even as the EOA made its way through Congress, how the War on Poverty, especially CAP, would be administered remained a source of confusion in Washington. As an undersecretary of labor, Moynihan recognized that "the Bureau of Budget's understanding of what CAP was going to be like was probably not what OEO was thinking, and almost certainly not what was going to happen, regardless of the wishes of anyone in Washington."[40] The act clearly spelled out the goal—the elimination of poverty sometime in the future. But the realization of that goal depended upon the largely untested theory of community action. Not even Ohlin or Hackett wanted to do more than set up a few demonstration projects to test the theory before it went national. They offered no promises about the end of poverty. In their short-sighted quest to get the legislation passed, Johnson and Shriver made national policy of an untested sociological theory that few people fully understood.[41]

THE ECONOMIC OPPORTUNITY ACT AND THE CIVIL RIGHTS ACT

Along with community action, the relationship between the EOA and race generated most of the controversy surrounding the emerging War on Poverty. Implicit in some arguments about the War on Poverty is the idea that the effort was more or less a smokescreen for deeper, more Machiavellian political motives. The unspoken motives, the argument went, were to quell the discontent seething in the nation's ghettos and maintain black support for the Democratic Party. The starting point for this critique of the War on Poverty, and indeed for all discourse about the relationship between race and the Great Society, is the work of sociologists Frances Fox Piven and Richard A. Cloward. They couched a critique of the War on Poverty within a broader critique of the role of welfare in capitalist regimes. Essentially, they argued that capitalist regimes employ welfare schemes only to quiet social unrest; otherwise governmental support is kept deliberately sparse in order to maintain a cheap labor force. Leading historians dismiss the Piven and Cloward thesis in relation to the War on Poverty. James Patterson correctly argues that Piven and Cloward "misread" history in their conclusions about the antipoverty effort of the 1960s because there had been no riots before the War on Poverty began, and the Civil Rights Act ensured black political support.[42]

Because Congress passed the Civil Rights Act a month before the EOA, local and state political leaders, civil rights activists, and segregationists assumed that the two acts were related. At least through 1964 and early 1965, the OEO and the Johnson administration insisted that the War on Poverty was a "colorblind" effort, separate from the civil rights movement or the Civil Rights Act.[43] A comprehensive national attack on poverty had to derive from acknowledgment, as was often repeated by Johnson's policy makers, that "most poor people are not black, [and] most black people are not poor."[44] No civil rights groups or leaders were directly involved in drafting the legislation. "Of all the people in the civil rights business," assistant director Yarmolinsky once explained, "none of them were involved in this business."[45]

Predictably, conservative southern Democrats viewed the War on Poverty as a "help the blacks" effort. For example, when one of LBJ's spokesmen went to Representative Wilbur Mills of Arkansas to ask support for the EOA, Mills threw the proposal across the room and said that he was "not going to be involved in any program to help a bunch of niggers."[46] In the OEO southern Democrats foresaw, Taylor Branch notes, "integrated job training programs, newfangled Head Start classes, perhaps even federal grants to the NAACP."[47] Considering that southerners historically benefited from federal largesse, there can be little doubt that their opposition to the War on Poverty was rooted in the association between the effort and civil rights. Congressman Howard Smith of Virginia laid bare this association prior to the House vote on the EOA: "I want to say to the Members from the South who are going to vote for this bill—and I know that there are a lot of them—that they are voting to implement the civil rights bill that they opposed and voted against."[48]

Shriver worked to limit the connection between civil rights and the poverty war to appease southern members of Congress. In 1965 he attempted to console a joint session of the Arkansas legislature:

> I've heard the arguments . . . This war against poverty is just a device
> for forcing integration in the South. That is wrong. No program of
> ours can be initiated if any state governor says no, but our programs
> must conform to the nation's laws and therefore will be administered
> without discrimination as to race, color, or creed.[49]

To further appease southerners, Shriver even dismissed Adam Yarmolinsky from his staff. Yarmolinsky, called to the OEO from the Defense Department, had a background that made him suspicious to southern conservatives. While working for McNamara, Yarmolinksy, the son of Russian-speaking New Yorkers, ordered that segregated housing be off limits to troops stationed in the South. Johnson agreed to have Yarmolinsky dismissed as a quid pro quo for the support of North Carolina Democrat Harold Cooley and his state's congressional delegation. LBJ attempted to cover up his dismissal by stating that Yarmolinsky had not been released from the Defense Department, but the message seemed clear to most observers.[50]

Johnson was a calculating politician, but the War on Poverty should not be viewed as just a political scheme. It was not an effort to appease urban blacks, despite the roots of community action in Kennedy's juvenile delinquency program. Neither should one view the colorblind commitment of the OEO as a device to appease southern conservatives. More importantly, one can see in the OEO the ideological values of postwar liberalism at work. The design of the War on Poverty came from an ideological perspective central to Johnson's conception of liberalism, which held that the purpose of government was to create progressive legislation to advance equality of economic and political opportunity for individuals. Davies has explained this idea best: "The authors of the Economic Opportunity Act explicitly repudiated notions of racial targeting in favor of a highly optimistic social philosophy predicated on the notion that all the poor needed was individual opportunity."[51]

Yet it is misleading to argue that the CRA and EOA were unrelated. It is important to understand that the colorblindness of the OEO emerged from the goals Johnson's civil rights legislation was meant to achieve—a society in which race had no effect on individual advancement. The CRA was not designed to give special advantage to minorities but, like the EOA, to remove obstacles that impeded equal opportunity.

Despite the best efforts of the administration, once OEO programs arrived in local areas, the association between poverty and race shaped the effort as it evolved. When OEO programs first arrived in Texas, opponents and supporters alike viewed the War on Poverty as an economic extension of the Civil Rights Act. Riding on the crest of LBJ's legislative wave, the War on Poverty seemed to represent a triumph of liberalism. Liberal Texans of all races came together to enthusiastically support the OEO and defend it against entrenched conservative opposition. In 1964 and 1965, few recognized that beneath the solidarity lay strong differences of opinion over what role race should play in the antipoverty crusade.

The War on Poverty
and Texas Politics

THREE

The Democratic Party in Texas began to unravel in the postwar period. No other state, George Norris Green asserts, "could boast of a governor (conservative John Connally) and a senator (liberal Ralph Yarborough) in the same party who hardly spoke to each other and who took every opportunity to undermine each other for six years."[1] No other issue informed this enmity more than civil rights. Conservatives who identified with Governor Connally maintained that civil rights legislation violated states' rights. Liberals, represented through the sixties by Senator Yarborough, firmed up their commitment to civil rights with a strengthening coalition of African American and Mexican American voters. The newly emergent Republicans, led by Senator John Tower, became the primary beneficiaries of the civil war among the state's Democrats. Tower renounced the Johnson administration's civil rights initiatives and drew many Texas voters who could not disassociate Connally's state Democratic Party from the party of LBJ.

Support for or opposition to the Civil Rights Act of 1964 coincided with support for or opposition to the OEO and the War on Poverty. As a protégé of LBJ, Connally favored progressive policy and supported the OEO when it began, but liberal programs like the War on Poverty placed him in a difficult position. The governor found himself at odds with the national party leadership and his conservative Democrat constituents who opposed the program due to its associations with race. By 1965 Connally became a vocal critic of the War on Poverty, using, as he had with the 1964 Civil Rights Act, the issues of states' rights and local control to justify his opposition. Yarborough, backed by the civil rights coalition in the state, became the strongest advocate of the OEO among the state's leading politicians. Although Democrats comprised a majority of Texans throughout the 1960s, the party split, and its association with civil rights issues made Senator Tower and the Republicans that much more attractive to conservative whites. For his part, Tower categorized the War on Poverty as another unnecessary federal bureaucracy that pandered to lazy tax parasites. In language reminiscent of the Red Scare, Tower informed his constituents that the Civil Rights and Economic Opportunity Acts were nothing less than encroaching socialism.

GOVERNOR CONNALLY AND THE STATE ROLE IN THE WAR ON POVERTY

The antipoverty warriors had intentionally limited the role of governors and state legislators in the War on Poverty. The local emphasis of CAP aimed the effort at the county and municipal levels because states "didn't fit into the CAP concept."[2] The EOA provided the states with only limited influence over the shape of the War on Poverty. First, the EOA fixed funding for CAP programs according to the number of poor people in each state's population. According to OEO estimates, the poor in Texas comprised 5.68 percent of all the poor people in the United States, so Texas received a statutory allotment of 5.68 percent of all CAP funds. The federal government assisted all fifty state governments in forming their War on Poverty administrations by 1967, but these state OEOs played minor roles. The Texas Office of Economic Opportunity (Texas OEO) was administered by Governor Connally's office but did not formally fit into the OEO's chain of command.[3] The role of the Texas OEO, according to director Terrell Blodgett, was "that of a hybrid—neither fish nor fowl. We are not completely bypassed . . . and at the same time we are not the approving authority on community action programs."[4] Blodgett predicted "difficulties and misunderstanding between state offices and the national headquarters of the OEO" if Shriver did not clarify the role of the state.[5]

To add more substance to state authority in the antipoverty effort, Titles I and II of the EOA required that all local antipoverty agencies submit proposals to the governor's office for approval. Each governor had veto authority over CAP, VISTA, Job Corps, and NYC programs and over contracts with nongovernmental agencies (including CAAs).[6] Johnson included the governor's veto in the legislation as a conciliatory measure. The president did not want southern governors to view the War on Poverty, like the civil rights legislation of 1964 and 1965, as a circumvention of state authority. Still, Shriver and most of the OEO staff had trepidations about the governor's veto. Officials worried specifically about Alabama Governor George Wallace, who they feared might use the veto power to maintain control of War on Poverty funds in Alabama. If the governor vetoed antipoverty plans drafted by his political opponents, the War on Poverty in Alabama would function, according to Bill Moyers, Johnson's special assistant and later press secretary, as "a Wallace political machine financed with federal funds."[7] Moyers argued that, if this came to pass, the OEO "would be better off in Alabama not to have a poverty program."[8]

Because of his personal relationship with LBJ, it seemed unlikely in 1965 that Connally would interfere with the War on Poverty. Connally had worked as campaign manager on LBJ's 1946 House campaign, the failed 1941 Senate campaign, the dubious victory in the 1948 campaign, and the unsuccessful bid for the Democratic nomination in 1960.[9] Vice President Johnson arranged a behind-the-scenes appointment of Connally as the secretary of the Navy during the Kennedy administration.[10] Connally, who was not elected to political office until he won the governorship in 1962, spent most of his political career as "Lyndon's boy."[11]

The two began to differ on key issues when Johnson became president. No issue defined the split more than their divergent positions on the Civil Rights Act of 1964. Unlike Johnson, the governor still had to win elections in a state in which few minorities could vote and civil rights legislation was widely opposed by whites. Connally argued that "voluntary desegregation" had made "dramatic progress," so he refused to acquiesce to "extreme elements" who sought a federal law to "tell us how we ought to do things . . . we're doing them already."[12] Connally's opposition to the Civil Rights Act did not reach the same level of vociferousness as that of other southern governors, but it clearly moved him away from the mainstream of the party.[13]

Governor Connally surprised most of the OEO staff in Washington and Austin when he became the first governor to exercise his veto power under the EOA. In May 1965 an application for a Neighborhood Youth Corps project in the Rio Grande Valley crossed Connally's desk in Austin. The project, organized by the Texas Farmers Union, a state affiliate of the United Farm Workers (UFW), planned to employ 790 youths from migrant families in thirty-three counties in a variety of public service jobs. Connally informed Shriver that he vetoed the project because the salaries for the two top administrators, $15,000 per year for the director and $5,400 for the deputy director, seemed excessive.[14] The governor also objected to the $1.25 minimum wage that the OEO provided NYC enrollees. Connally argued that the wage, at twenty-five cents above the federal minimum, was unfair because it would provide NYC enrollees with higher wages than those earned by their parents.[15] In a political satire in the *Texas Observer*, Connally argued that a youth earning $1.25 "makes too much. Certainly more than his mother and father. A dollar and twenty-five cents an hour would ruin the economy of Texas!"[16]

Connally's action served as a major catalyst for a move in the Senate to eliminate the governor's veto power in the EOA. Once the proposed repeal came to his attention, Connally sent a telegram to Johnson to inform the president that he was "gravely concerned."[17] Connally attributed the success of the OEO up to that point "to the fact that there has been a sensible partnership between the federal government and the states. If this cooperation is destroyed by impulsive action . . . the needy and unemployed youth of our nation will be the unfortunate losers."[18] Johnson assured Connally privately that the governor's veto would remain in the EOA.[19] In July 1965, however, Congress gave Shriver, as director of the OEO, the power to override a governor's veto. Congress amended the EOA to limit the governor's veto power primarily to protect programs from George Wallace, however, not Connally or other governors. The governors would still have a veto power, but Shriver could override a veto "based on racial discrimination, political manipulation, or 'some other kind of undue influence.'"[20]

Connally visited Shriver's office in Washington in summer 1965 to discuss the veto power and the War on Poverty in general. Connally once again informed the director that the governor's office should run the whole program. To illustrate the failures of the bureaucracy, Connally chastised the OEO for appointing a felon to head one of the CAAs.[21] Shriver, expecting the criticism, informed the governor that the former felon had been out of jail for nearly fifteen years and in the interim became a well-respected member of the community. Firing him, Shriver informed the governor, would have been "morally irresponsible."[22] Little came from the meeting and, in the end, Connally's opposition to the War on Poverty came to naught.

Connally biographer James Reston has argued that defense of "simple turf" caused the governor to veto the program.[23] The governor vetoed the measure, according to Reston, because he felt that the president should dismantle the OEO bureaucracy and operate the War on Poverty "exclusively through the governor's office."[24] It is evident, however, that Connally objected to the War on Poverty because his conservative Democratic constituency opposed the program. After his meeting with Shriver, Connally attempted to smooth things over with LBJ by explaining his position and the objections of his constituents. The governor explained to Marvin Watson, LBJ's chief of staff, that "most of the people down here dislike the program . . . reporters [in Texas], every one of them, thinks this program is a big boondog."[25] Connally argued that education provided the best hope of fighting poverty. The governor declared that what Texas was going to do for the poor, despite the OEO, was "give 'em education. Once they get that, they're going to be in a position to become productive taxpaying citizens of the state. That's a good investment."[26]

Unable to shape the direction of the OEO programs in Texas, Connally lost interest in the War on Poverty. Even Walter Richter, who became the director of the Texas OEO in December 1966, was uncertain what Connally wanted him to do. After directing the Texas OEO for six months, Richter still "felt the need for a better understanding of your [Connally's] feelings and philosophies which, I am fully aware, the program should reflect."[27] In truth, there was not much left for the Texas OEO to do once Congress circumvented the veto power. The only function that the Texas OEO provided was "technical assistance" to local communities in the development of CAAs. The federal OEO expected that state War on Poverty agencies would place "emphasis on providing aid to small communities" because rural areas lacked the technical know-how and resources of large cities.[28]

YARBOROUGH AND THE LIBERAL COALITION

As Connally distanced himself from LBJ, the OEO's primary ally in Texas became Senator Ralph Yarborough, a political adversary of both the president and the governor in the 1950s.[29] Throughout the 1950s the liberal wing of the Democratic Party expanded continuously as an urban coalition of middle-class Mexican Americans and African Americans, labor unionists, and church organizations gathered to oppose the traditional priorities of conservatives. Historians have sometimes referred to this coalition as the "labor liberals" because much of the leadership entered politics by way of careers in organized labor.[30]

As a congressman and a senator, LBJ tended to side with the conservative faction of the party in Texas, primarily due to the liberal identification with the labor movement. Johnson's political career owed much to support from antilabor corporations such as Brown and Root Construction. He made an effort to disassociate himself from the labor movement to avoid alienating the conservatives or his financial backers.[31] Once Johnson moved into national politics as a presidential candidate, his old loyalties to the Texas establishment no longer made sense, especially in terms of their continued focus on segregation and states' rights. For their part, the liberals in the state party were able to look past Johnson's antilabor history in Texas. Johnson's clear support for civil rights and the War on Poverty made the choice between the president and Governor Connally easy.

Connally's opposition to the War on Poverty provided Senator Yarborough and the liberals with ammunition to "deepen Connally's reputation as backward on social issues."[32] As a member of the Senate Labor Committee, Yarborough ranked among the strongest opponents of the governor's veto because he feared that Connally would use it to "frustrate the purposes of the War on Poverty."[33] Yarborough blamed the need to override the veto on "the crippling actions of a few governors who caused this veto power to be taken away from the governors of all fifty states, most of whom did not abuse this power."[34] The senator never mentioned Connally by name, but he cited Connally's veto of the Rio Grande Valley NYC project, which was "said to be the best planned rural antipoverty project in America," as the "irresponsible action that forced me to devote much time to aid in eliminating the governors' unrestricted veto power over poverty projects, which has now been done."[35]

Although Yarborough served as the leader of the liberal wing of the Texas Democratic Party in the 1960s, the rank-and-file strength of the coalition came largely from the Mexican American and African American communities of the state's large urban centers. These groups already had mobilized politically for the civil rights movement and maintained influential political organizations. Across the nation, civil rights organizations embraced the OEO as a way to circumvent intransigent state and local officials and move beyond civil rights and segregation toward economic justice.

Few Texans showed more support for the OEO than black civil rights and community leaders. The *Houston Informer,* the leading newspaper in the state's largest African American community, ran regular stories explaining the benefits of the OEO. The War on Poverty, the *Informer* proclaimed on Christmas Day 1965, offered "hope to the poor and jobless."[36] The *Informer* expressed especially high praise for the Job Corps. The paper announced Job Corps recruiting drives and gave addresses and telephone numbers to help potential corpsmen and corpswomen obtain application materials. Before any assessment of the Job Corps emerged, the *Informer* explained that the program offered training that "will greatly increase the enrollees' chances of getting a job."[37] Beyond the vocational training offered, the *Informer* recommended the Job Corps as an invaluable opportunity for young people to mature and develop. The Job Corps, another story proclaimed, was "aimed at those who need a change of environment and individual help to develop talents, self confidence, and motivation to improve themselves. The Job Corps will provide a total learning experience."[38] The *Informer* provided the Job Corps with so much good press that administrators at Camp Gary, the largest Job Corps project in the state, awarded the paper a special letter of commendation in 1967.[39]

Mexican American leaders also stood among the effort's strongest supporters in the state.[40] Organizations like the American GI Forum and LULAC viewed the Great Society as "the Big Chance" to raise Texas' largest minority from deprivation.[41] Bringing War on Poverty funds to Mexican American communities became a major priority for Mexican American civil rights groups and leaders. As Arnoldo De León has explained in reference to Houston, Mexican American groups continued to lead drives to improve employment and education but "most importantly to secure a share of the poverty program funds for the Mexican-American neighborhoods."[42] Prominent Mexican American political figures like San Antonio Congressman Henry B. Gonzalez and GI Forum leader Hector García of Corpus Christi worked actively on behalf of local War on Poverty efforts.[43]

The governor's attempt to thwart the War on Poverty deepened his unpopularity with Mexican Americans. Connally's opposition to OEO programs came to symbolize the insensitivity of conservative Democrats to the economic plight of Mexican American communities in the state. The most vociferous Mexican American opponent of Connally in Texas was Albert Peña, a Bexar County commissioner and PASSO leader. When Connally vetoed the Rio Grande Valley NYC program, Peña attacked the governor:

> Connally argued that the Mexicans in Texas shouldn't rely so much on the national government to solve their socio-economic problems, they should pull themselves up by their own boot straps. This is all well and good, but we do not wear boots. And they stole our huaraches. But we got some good shoes made with strong American leather in American factories and we are going to pound the pavement in the barrios until the soles of our shoes are worn thin . . . Our feet may blister, our toes may break out the side of our shoes, but Mr. Governor we are going to do everything we can to make the War on Poverty a reality in Texas.[44]

Connally's opposition to the War on Poverty was the underlying cause of a dramatic moment of solidarity within the state's liberal coalition. On

Labor Day 1966 the United Farm Workers organized a 490-mile march from the Rio Grande Valley to Austin to protest the governor's "disparaging remarks about $1.25 as the minimum wage for poverty program workers."[45] Ultimately, the UFW moved beyond the War on Poverty to demand a raise in the minimum wage for all workers in Texas. That they initiated the march to defend a War on Poverty program illustrates the great hope that liberals had for OEO programs.

Connally made every effort to ignore the marchers. To avoid a showdown in Austin on Labor Day, Connally met the marchers in New Braunfels, forty miles north of San Antonio. The governor pulled into New Braunfels in a limousine to meet the dusty marchers. He informed the leaders of the march that they would not find him in Austin on Labor Day and that he was unwilling to call a special session of the legislature to vote on a minimum-wage measure because, he said, "I don't think the urgency of it is of such a character that it [is] compelling." To solve the problems of the poor all at once, Connally explained to the marchers, was to "expect the impossible." Labor leader George Nelson, one of the organizers of the march, explained to the governor, "We're not expecting the impossible, Governor . . . just the possible, a minimum wage of $1.25, which is only reasonable."[46]

Yarborough took full advantage of the march to contrast the values of the liberal coalition with those of the governor and other conservative Democrats. In San Antonio the senator met with the marchers at the San Fernando Cathedral to show his support and announce his plan to introduce a motion in the Senate to increase the federal minimum wage to $1.60 an hour. When the marchers reached Austin, Yarborough gave a passionate speech to commend the effort. The speech revealed the great hope liberals had for federal antipoverty efforts. With tears in his eyes, Yarborough addressed the marchers:

> Amigos, compadres—fellow marchers . . . as our senior U.S. Senator,
> I *hold* the highest elective office and with all the power and good will
> which the people of Texas can give . . . I welcome you with open arms
> . . . A hundred years ago we ended physical slavery. We are here to end
> poverty and economic slavery.[47]

Through the rest of the sixties, Connally's apparent insensitivity to civil rights and poverty continued to damage his standing with Mexican Americans and further divided the Democratic Party in the state. In 1967 the governor unleashed the Texas Rangers on striking migrant workers in the Rio Grande Valley and lost more Mexican Americans' support because of the "bruising excesses" of the Rangers in breaking the strike.[48] State Senator Joe Bernal said Connally became increasingly viewed as a "hate figure" among Mexican American Texans.[49]

JOHN TOWER AND THE REPUBLICAN RESPONSE TO THE WAR ON POVERTY

As the Democratic Party became more associated with civil rights and liberal programs like the War on Poverty, white Texans began defecting to the Republican Party. Senator Tower and other Texas Republicans included the War on Poverty on their long list of complaints against the federal bureaucracy. Tower attacked the War on Poverty as "a mess of unworkable, discarded depression era ideas laced into badly written legislation founded on hypocritically used statistics and administered by a poverty czar."[50] The senator categorized the War on Poverty as "socialistic" and another liberal attempt to circumvent the power of local government. When the Kennedy administration began planning for a "domestic Peace Corps" in early 1963, Tower described the program with a blend of Texas provincialism and Goldwater-esque anticommunism:

> This domestic Peace Corps proposal calls to mind the old CCC of depression days. It is amusing to consider it could send graduates of eastern finishing schools to Texas to teach Texans how to raise peanuts or cotton . . . This socialistic scheme is just one more step in preparing our young people for collectivization.[51]

Tower's constituents opposed the War on Poverty as another federal measure that bypassed state and local sovereignty. The correspondence files in Tower's papers from 1964 bulge with letters from constituents angry about the proposed EOA. George T. Abell from Midland labeled the poverty program "another mortal millstone around the necks of the American people . . . The function of looking after the people who are *really* in need should be handled by the states, all of which are capable and qualified to look after the citizens who are in *real* need."[52] Such objections became so common that Tower's staff created a boilerplate response sent to scores of constituents:

> Of course nobody is in favor of poverty . . . but we should attack poverty not by creating a new tax absorbing bureaucracy, but by encouraging the creation of new jobs in private industry and business.

Catchy political slogans and expensive federal programs won't create jobs. The more logical route would be for the federal government to withdraw its interference in, and harassment of private initiative and private investment, allowing the private sector of the economy to create new jobs required to effectively attack poverty.[53]

Further, Tower concluded that the War on Poverty amounted to nothing more than an expensive resurrection of "discredited" New Deal programs: "We already have tried and found wanting the CCC and the WPA [Works Progress Administration] and the perpetuation of tiny farms without the resource to compete." Since the Depression years, according to Tower's figures, the government had spent "$44 billion a year for welfare. There is no reason to try these things again."[54]

Once the EOA passed, Tower argued that the greatest danger the expensive bureaucracy posed was that it bypassed state and local government. The OEO represented "a new and unjustified course of government responsibility and of federal action in particular . . . it tells local groups they can no longer deal with city councils and state government."[55] Like Governor Connally, Tower particularly objected to the $1.25 minimum wage proposed for NYC enrollees. The senator said it was another case of the federal government imposing its standards on local communities.[56] Tower defended the governors' veto power as their "only means of obtaining [the] cooperation of federal bureaucrats."[57] With the OEO, the senator concluded, the states had been "brushed aside, and the federal government blunders ahead anyway."[58]

As might be expected, much of Tower's criticism focused on the bureaucratic expense of the OEO: "Federal poverty czars are getting rich while the poor get poorer."[59] The senator considered the Job Corps "a costly and temporary aid for a very small number of young men and women . . . the Job Corps could cost $190 million the first year for 40,000 enrollees."[60] Such an expense, the senator calculated, amounted to $5,000 per enrollee, or seven times the average per pupil expense in American public schools. Tower sought to dismantle the OEO in order to "take the bureaucratic profit out of 'poverty.'"[61]

Senator Tower and other Texas Republicans knew that many of their constituents opposed the War on Poverty because the OEO seemed to favor minority groups. A 1964 letter from one of Tower's constituents, a man named D. H. Edge, suggests the association of Texas Republicans between the War on Poverty and civil rights legislation:

I am writing you about two bills before congress, namely, the civil rights bill and President Johnson's proposed War on Poverty. I feel if these two bills are passed, Americans will lose a great many of their freedoms, and the free enterprise system will be in existence only a short while.[62]

Tower understood that Edge was not alone in his complaint. Millions of white Americans had grown tired of civil rights activism and federal legislation on the behalf of minority groups. Texas Republicans took notice when George Wallace polled well in the Democratic primary in 1964.[63] Tower, the leading Republican in Texas during the 1960s, opposed the Civil Rights Act of 1964 and the Voting Rights Act of 1965. George H. W. Bush, who lost a Senate race to Yarborough in 1964, "emphatically opposed [the] civil rights legislation."[64] Opposition to federal welfare measures like the War on Poverty went hand in hand with opposition to federal civil rights initiatives. As elsewhere in the South the Republican Party began to attract those whites in Texas who came to associate the Democratic Party with "taxes and civil rights and give-away programs that both cost them money and favored minorities."[65]

In spite of Johnson's admirable intentions, the effort became one more source of political conflict in Texas. The contentiousness would be even more pronounced on the local level, especially in urban areas where large sums of OEO dollars were at stake. But before they started fighting over the money, local people first had to navigate the OEO bureaucracy to figure out what community action was all about.

Launching the War on Poverty in Texas

FOUR

The battery of programs introduced by the OEO, presented as a bewildering list of acronyms, confused local officials when the War on Poverty came to the Lone Star State. In Brownsville the Cameron County Commissioners' Court invited the local press to a discussion of the unfolding fight on poverty. County Judge Oscar C. Dancy's understanding of the OEO's role reflected that of many local officials in Texas: "I'm in favor of cooperating with the President and the governor as far as we can on this poverty thing . . . The beautification of highways, parks, seems to be the first on the President's program."[1] Dancy and many others seemed to believe that LBJ intended more or less to revive the New Deal. When a reporter asked the judge, "Is it a make work program, like the WPA was?" Dancy replied, "Yes, I would say it is, at least I think."[2]

In March 1965 Texas Congressman Wright Patman wrote to Shriver to find out what the OEO was up to. Gillis Long, who had replaced Yarmolinsky as Shriver's assistant, informed Patman that "the problems and range of alternative actions in waging a successful War against Poverty are infinite," but the OEO proposed to "provide the opportunities for that one-fifth of our population who are not now capable of maintaining even a minimum standard of living, to participate in the economic growth of the nation—at least to the extent that their basic needs can be satisfied."[3] Long went on to explain each title of the Economic Opportunity Act specifically, emphasizing the provisions in the act that created opportunities for youth.

Patman, a longtime member of the House of Representatives who had voted for the EOA, probably already knew everything Long told him. Most likely, Patman wrote Shriver to learn more about the mechanics of the War on Poverty. The director's assistant avoided answering nuts-and-bolts questions. How much money would be available? How would the money be distributed? What role would local and state government have in the poverty war? What was community action? Would members of Congress have any input? It would have been difficult, however, for Long to address such questions in early 1965 because no one could foresee how the OEO would function on the local level.

A HOMETOWN FIGHT

Most local officials learned about the War on Poverty from the newspapers. In late 1964 and 1965 the OEO issued press releases to explain how to apply for War on Poverty funds. A press release titled "The War on Poverty—A Hometown Fight" stated that "individual communities will do the job with private and public resources that will be augmented by this new federal assistance."[4] Communities received guidance on how to measure poverty in their areas, on what sort of programs might be developed, on what programs the OEO was developing in Washington, and on the application process for CAP grants.[5] This began what Matusow called a "wild scramble" to develop local Community Action Agencies.[6] The theorists who had conceived community action during the Kennedy administration cautioned local groups to spend at least one year in program development.[7] Wanting to get the money before LBJ or members of Congress changed their minds, local officials devoted little time to developing an understanding of the subtleties of community action. By June 1965 more than four hundred CAAs had been established. By 1966 there were more than one thousand.[8]

The OEO gave communities some leeway on program development but required local CAAs to follow a few directives. The most famous and controversial requirement was that CAAs employ the "maximum feasible participation" of the poor. For Johnson and the OEO, maximum feasible participation simply meant self-help. Shriver wrote in 1964 that the War on Poverty was founded on a "commitment to ensure that the poor themselves actively participate in the planning, implementation, and administration."[9] The OEO's annual report for 1965, *The Quiet Revolution*, indicates that CAP policy makers envisioned the poor offering input in the development of "a wide variety of services generated locally to help the poor help themselves."[10] Beyond such vague notions, the OEO provided few specifics on what maximum feasible participation meant.

Nevertheless, many cities that applied in 1965 had at least one CAP application rejected because it did not fulfill this guideline to the satisfaction of OEO administrators. "Maximum feasible participation" became for the OEO what "all deliberate speed" was to the *Brown* decision. Each constituency involved—the OEO, state and local governments, and the poor themselves—had a different definition of "maximum feasible participation." The vagueness of the doctrine attracted the attention of historians more than any other aspect of the War on Poverty, beginning with *Maximum Feasible Misunderstanding*, Daniel P. Moynihan's well-known 1970 condemnation of CAP.

Along with deciphering the intent of maximum feasible participation, locals had to negotiate the OEO bureaucracy. Those who criticized the OEO for being overly bureaucratic had a point. Shriver's office in Washington employed a platoon of bureaucrats, among them a deputy director, an executive secretary, three assistant directors for each major program (CAP, Job Corps, VISTA), an assistant director for management, and ten other assistant directors with specific duties, such as congressional liaison and head of the OEO inspection service.[11]

Below the federal level in Washington, the OEO had seven regional offices. The Southwest regional office in Austin oversaw OEO operations in Arkansas, Oklahoma, New Mexico, and Texas. Each region had a director, responsible to Shriver, to carry out the executive functions of the region. Bill Crook, a political ally of LBJ from Texas, served as regional director in Austin until he became the national director of VISTA in 1967. Walter Richter, who had been the director of the Texas OEO, became the regional director when Crook left. The regional director's staff consisted of an assistant regional director to match each assistant director under Shriver. By September 1965 the regional offices handled most paperwork processing, including the approval of CAP grants.[12] OEO directives failed to communicate this effectively, however, leaving communities confused about where to send funding requests. Members of Congress, the governor, Shriver, and even LBJ himself received proposals directly from confused local officials unaware of the responsibilities, or perhaps even the existence, of the regional office.

Once local officials sorted out the bureaucracy of the OEO, municipalities across the state took the first step toward CAA development by holding public meetings to discuss the antipoverty effort. Low attendance at public meetings indicates that the poor knew little about the war that the president pledged to wage on their behalf. In Fort Worth, the Tarrant County Community Council, an established community service agency, became the city's CAA. The council held meetings from July to October 1965 in fifteen "target areas," neighborhoods with high concentrations of poverty, to discuss how the CAA would work. Between 6 and 350 people attended each meeting, though the average attendance was between 20 and 40 people.[13] Such small turnouts must have disappointed the CAA staff, considering that 100,000 people in Fort Worth lived on incomes below the poverty line.[14]

After local officials held public meetings, each antipoverty agency formed a CAA board of directors. Boards normally included officials from city and county governments, members of local school boards, representatives of prominent business interests, and leaders of church groups. The EOA required the inclusion of poor people on CAA boards. In most cases, local CAA boards worked closely with city hall or county commissioners to develop the CAAs, but the regional office required that city governments recognize the autonomy of CAA boards.[15]

Once formed, a CAA board submitted a proposal for a program to the regional office in Austin. The proposals explained the antipoverty plan the CAA members had in mind, how much programs would cost, how they would be administered, whom they would help, and how the poor would be involved. Most proposals specified who would serve on a CAA's board of directors. Each funding proposal had to include a CAP Form 1 itemizing the costs of the proposal, provide an official name for the CAA, and be signed by the head of the CAA board of directors. If a CAA failed to include the form or filled it out improperly, the OEO staff would not act on the proposal. In Robstown, Texas, the local CAA board prepared a proposal for a summer job training program for seventy boys and girls. The proposal thoroughly explained how the program would function. The enrollees were to work in local schools and hospitals, in "study centers," as coaches' assistants, at the library, or in a variety of other capacities as the need arose. The Robstown CAA board complained to Senator Yarborough after weeks passed and the regional office took no action on the proposal. The senator received a response from the OEO regional office explaining that even though the proposal was in order, the Robstown CAA neglected to include CAP Form 1, so the proposal sat on the regional director's desk in Austin.[16]

The OEO regional office scrutinized urban applications very carefully. Because CAA board membership represented the apogee of maximum feasible participation, the OEO office in Washington rejected many urban CAP grants in early 1965 for lack of participation by poor people on CAA boards.[17] The regional director rejected the first application of the Lubbock County CAA because it included only three representatives of the poor on its eighteen-member board.[18] The Fort Worth proposal had only three board members from low-income groups but also a "CAP Committee" with 175 members who lived in low-income areas. The Fort Worth CAP grant application did not specify the committee's responsibilities, but it is clear that the board proposed it to enhance the CAA's maximum feasible participation credentials.[19] Cities often developed elaborate CAP proposals that featured a variety of programs all administered by an umbrella CAA. In Austin, the Travis County Community Action Agency administered sixteen programs, including those funded in conjunction with the Labor Department, such as NYC and the Work Experience Program.[20]

The conservative political culture of the state often made urban politicians hesitant to begin War on Poverty programs. In February 1968 Dallas Congressman Earle Cabell complained directly to Sargent Shriver that the Dallas program received far less War on Poverty funding than other Texas cities. Although Dallas had approximately as many poor citizens as Houston (estimated at 356,000 and 357,000, respectively), Dallas received $3.6 million for fiscal year 1968 compared to $13.5 million for Houston. For the same year El Paso received $5.1 million, though the estimated poor population in that city stood at 125,000.[21] Cabell's district received less funding, according to Shriver, because Dallas got "into the program late, started slowly, and has proceeded conservatively, and as a result is not funded as fully as other cities."[22] The Dallas program "was not well established" when most big-city CAAs expanded their programs in fiscal year 1966. Budget limitations forced many urban CAAs to cut funding in 1967, when the Dallas County Community Action Committee (DCCAC) had just begun.[23]

In an effort to overcome opposition, Dallas antipoverty warriors launched an advertising campaign in fall 1966. The DCCAC targeted the campaign at "the folks who needed convincing—the affluent Dallas stratum."[24] The high-end Neiman Marcus department store chain headquartered in Dallas agreed to pay for ads on posters and in full-page newspaper layouts. The ad campaign contrasted assumptions about federal antipoverty funds with the OEO philosophy of "a hand up, not a hand out." One ad featured a bumper sticker on the back of a 1965 Mustang that read, "I fight poverty 'I work.'" The text of the ad, under the banner headline "Big Joke," explained that the driver of the Mustang simply misunderstood community action:

Harry doesn't know it but the people who run the War on Poverty in Dallas County agree . . . Harry calls the War on Poverty a worthless giveaway program. That's because he doesn't know that DCCAC has no money, food, or clothing to give away. DCCAC can only give the poor the tools they need to help themselves: opportunity and motivation . . . Poverty is expensive when you treat it halfway with handouts. Four out of five children brought up on welfare raise their own families on welfare. And taxpayers, including you, Harry, must support them. Laugh that off.[25]

Another ad featured a photo of a black youngster named Harold to characterize the expense of intergenerational welfare dependence:

Meet Harold . . . Harold's grandfather never learned to read or write. Harold's father never learned that school was important so he dropped out. The same thing will probably happen to Harold. Last year Harold's immediate family cost the taxpayers about $3,500, not including the expense of arresting, detaining, and trying Harold's father for a felony. There are a lot of Harold's in Dallas County. Most of them will sire children themselves . . . The Dallas Community Action Committee has programs aimed at children Harold's age, the age at which the poverty cycle can best be broken . . . Harold can be something his ancestors never were—a taxpayer . . . The 1960s are a wonderful time. Automation and the computer age enrich our lives in a thousand ways . . . The only thing a computer can do for Harold is keep track of his growing family . . . and make out their welfare checks.[26]

The DCCAC advertising campaign drew praise from Shriver as an "imaginative, daring [approach] for many American communities where Community Action is being undertaken."[27] The stress on reducing welfare costs cohered well with the OEO's emphasis on reducing long-term welfare costs. It also illustrates the difficulties CAAs faced in overcoming assumptions about federal welfare initiatives and the poor themselves. DCCAC antipoverty workers understood that many Texans presumed that the OEO was just giving money to people who preferred not to work.

THE CHALLENGE OF COMMUNITY
ACTION IN RURAL TEXAS

While nearly 40 percent of poor Americans in 1965 lived in rural areas, the OEO spent 79 percent of its allocations the first two years in urban areas and most of this proportion in the nation's one hundred largest cities.[28] The rural programs set up under EOA Title III remained continually ill financed. The OEO neglected rural areas because, as James Patterson has pointed out, the antipoverty warriors were "mesmerized by a vision of poverty in the cities."[29] Some scholars have argued that the administration neglected rural areas intentionally to focus on preventing crime and violence in the cities. The War on Poverty was waged mostly in urban areas, however, because larger cities had the "professional personnel and effective organizations" to develop CAAs.[30] After 1967, according to one report, the OEO worked diligently to "avoid any suggestion that it is being *unfair* to rural areas" and established the Office of Rural Affairs to better coordinate the development of CAPs in loosely organized rural areas.[31]

Because of the diffusion of the rural population, War on Poverty officials had even more trouble getting the rural poor involved. Jim Wells County in South Texas ranked among the state's poorest predominantly rural counties. More than 40 percent of the county's families lived on incomes below the federal poverty line.[32] Yet when the Jim Wells County CAA organized a meeting to explain the War on Poverty, none of the county's low-income families attended.[33] Joe Cardenas, a school principal and CAA board member, solved this problem when he organized a canvass of schools through the Parent-Teacher Association to determine family eligibility according to income, health, employment, and education.[34] Ultimately, few rural counties had local officials as active as Cardenas, and most rural Texans received no direct benefit from the OEO.

OEO officials recognized the neglect of the rural poor early on and maintained an intensive effort to dispel the perception of the War on Poverty as just an effort for the big cities. In his request for budget increases from the Bureau of the Budget (BOB), Shriver informed budget director Charles Schultze in December 1965 that a reduced budget meant "the War on Poverty cannot reach into the poverty stricken portion of rural America, which it is just beginning to reach."[35] OEO official publications began to place greater emphasis on the OEO's effort to counteract rural poverty. A 1967 issue of *Communities in Action*, the official CAP newsletter, cited an exclusively urban emphasis as one of the "ten biggest myths about the OEO."[36] To counter the myth that the "battle against poverty is limited to the big cities—where all the commotion is," the article listed several rural initiatives and pointed out that 21 percent of CAP funds were devoted to rural CAAs. When a budget cut threatened CAP funds for fiscal year 1969, Southwest regional director Walter Richter warned regional CAP administrator Fred Baldwin that because of Washington's "strong emphasis on services to rural areas . . . it is apparent that the larger cities must bear the burden of this cut."[37]

Nevertheless, spending on the rural poor declined between 1966 and 1968. Spending on the Migrant Opportunities program declined from $8.2 million to $3.6 million in fiscal years 1966 to 1968. Economic Opportunity Rural Loans dropped in Texas from $1.3 million to about $1.1 million in the same period.[38] Spending on rural CAAs was proportionately low during the same period. For fiscal year 1966 the OEO allocated $5 million of $7 million for CAA development to the state's five most populous counties alone (Bexar, Dallas, El Paso, Harris, Tarrant). By 1968 the proportion of OEO dollars going to rural areas increased but remained disproportionate with the number of rural poor in the state. The OEO allocated the five largest urban counties nearly $15 million of $34 million for CAP operations (excluding funds for specialty programs such as NYC, Job Corps, and VISTA). Smaller cities in the state developed CAPs by 1968. The next five most populous counties (Travis, Lubbock, Potter, Nueces, and Jefferson) spent nearly $6 million.[39] Overall, 62 percent of CAP funds went to the state's ten largest cities.[40] Urban CAAs controlled funds for programs that were unavailable in most rural communities, such as NYC, Work Experience, and other programs not included in the CAP budget.

A few rural community leaders lodged complaints about these inequities. Jerome Vacek, executive director of the Navarro County Community Action Committee, complained to Senator Yarborough that "the big cities got far more than their share of OEO funds last year and we understand they have considerable unexpended funds in their existing programs. Now they want to tie up more of the allocated funds at the expense of rural programs."[41] For the most part, however, few rural community leaders complained about the funding imbalance between rural and urban communities. The fact that only 55 of the 254 counties in Texas, most of which were rural, bothered to apply for War on Poverty funds suggests that most small-town political leaders had little interest in the program.[42]

Some rural CAAs operated exemplary programs. In fall 1968 the OEO funded a combination housing construction and job training program for the poor of Beeville, a small town on the South Texas coastal plain. Eliseo Sandoval, a high school football coach, directed the Community Council of Bee County, the Beeville CAA. According to *Communities in Action*, the Beeville program exemplified community action because it featured local involvement at a "fantastic level." Sandoval rented discounted office space from the local post office. Local businessman Jesse Garza donated warehouse space and a machine to make cinder blocks. Rancher George Dickinson provided stone from a quarry on his land. Sandoval advertised for a construction training program in which sixteen trainees would work for a $50 weekly stipend converting the stone into cinder blocks and building twenty-seven new homes for low-income families in Beeville. The people who would live in the homes assisted in the construction along with volunteers from the area. To accompany the on-the-job training, trainees and prospective residents also attended Adult Basic Education courses offered by the CAA. Other townspeople provided fixtures, everything from front doors to bathtubs, for the finished houses.[43]

Beeville, however, proved an exceptional case. Few rural CAAs designed their own programs or included the poor in planning. Most operated "national emphasis" programs like Head Start or Neighborhood Youth Corps. The Castro County CAA requested $112,290 from the federal government to run a remedial reading instruction and adult literacy program, an after-school study center for older children, and a Head Start center.[44]

Yielding to political pressure to reach out to the rural poor, the OEO eased expectations for maximum feasible participation in rural programs. The Jim Wells County CAA board members included the county attorney, county commissioner, school principal, mayor of Orange Grove, and superintendent of Concepcion Independent School District—but no members from the county's poor population.[45] Most small-town CAAs simply proposed to run one or more of the OEO's national-emphasis programs such as Head Start. In Castro County nearly half of all families had incomes below the poverty line.[46] Local officials formed, by invitation, the board of directors for the Castro County Community Action Committee to represent "various institutions in town."[47] These included school administrators, the pastor of the "Negro Christian Church," a medical doctor, and a farmer. The committee appointed Bob McLean, the head of the First State Bank of Dimmit, as board president. The board appointed McLean, according to the proposal, because he "represents the banking interests of the county."[48] The proposal limited participation of the poor from the Dimmit eastside target area to public meetings with the board of directors.

A racist sense of paternalism informed a proposal from the Texas Panhandle town of Wellington in Collingsworth County. Judge Zook Thomas wrote Senator Yarborough that he and other leaders in the community wanted OEO funds "to help our colored people improve their living area. We are of the opinion that with a little help and encouragement we could get them to clean up their premises."[49] Thomas sought a program despite the objections of the mayor of Wellington, who said the city should not participate because "the problem is getting the colored people to pay their bills."[50] The OEO never funded a CAA for Wellington or Collingsworth County.[51]

THE JOB CORPS AND VISTA

The two major OEO programs that operated in Texas separate from CAP were the Job Corps and VISTA. Unlike CAP programs designed on the local level and national-emphasis programs operated by the CAAs, the OEO administered Job Corps and VISTA programs through separate bureaucracies within Shriver's office. Shriver paid close attention to the Job Corps. From the beginning he argued that the Job Corps should supersede CAP as the main effort of the OEO. VISTA received special consideration due to its resemblance to the politically popular Peace Corps, which Shriver had directed in the Kennedy administration.

CAP cost more money than any other War on Poverty program nationally, but the Job Corps ranked as the most expensive program in Texas. By 1968 allocations for Job Corps centers in Texas amounted to $22 million, nearly 20 percent of all War on Poverty funds spent in the state. Texas stood second only to California in total funds spent for the Job Corps. Texas ranked first in number of Job Corps enrollees, with 3,282 training in the state. Young Texans took advantage of Job Corps opportunities more than people from any other state; 3,766 Texans were enrolled in Job Corps centers across the nation in 1968.[52]

Three Job Corps training centers opened in Texas during the Johnson administration. In the two urban centers the Job Corps stationed enrollees in abandoned federal facilities near cities, and in the one "conservation" camp enrollees received job training and worked in forestry projects on federal land. Shriver preferred to use private corporations to run the camps.[53] The director successfully lobbied companies including Westinghouse, Litton Systems, Packard Bell, and General Electric to participate in the Job Corps, and universities, local school systems, and established nonprofits like the YWCA also ran centers.[54] A nonprofit corporation established by Governor Connally, the Texas Educational Foundation (TEF), operated the two urban camps in Texas. Its establishment made Texas administratively unique in the Job Corps.

The TEF used the Texas Employment Commission to process applications and screen candidates.[55]

LBJ dedicated the first urban center in Texas, Camp Gary, at an abandoned Air Force base outside San Marcos in April 1965. Of the three Texas centers, Camp Gary received by far the most enrollees, money, and public attention. The OEO operated Camp Gary as the flagship center for the Job Corps. It became the largest Job Corps center in the country, housing more than three thousand trainees by 1966.[56] Camp Gary received two-thirds of all Job Corps funds allocated in Texas and ranked as the single most expensive War on Poverty project in the state. It also became the most popular of the three camps among potential clients. For the three thousand positions at Camp Gary in 1966, the Texas Employment Commission screened more than fifteen thousand applicants.[57]

The OEO opened the second urban center, the McKinney Job Corps Center for Women, at a vacant Veterans Administration hospital in the Dallas suburb of McKinney. The first enrollees did not arrive at the McKinney center until March 1967. Women remained a low priority for the Job Corps. While men's urban centers ranged from five hundred to more than three thousand corpsmen, women's centers averaged about four hundred enrollees. Women comprised no more than 20 percent of all enrollees.[58] The McKinney center, despite having just six hundred enrollees, was the largest women's center in the nation.[59] Shriver and his planners had not included a women's program in the original Job Corps blueprint. Early advertising for the Job Corps solicited applications from males specifically. The prevailing assumption that men would serve as the primary breadwinners of future families thwarted a women's program. Investment in a Job Corps program for women, the OEO's logic went, would be wasted when the female enrollees got married. The Job Corps included a women's program at the prodding of Oregon Congresswoman Edith Green, often viewed as one of the OEO's most formidable opponents. She demanded that a women's program be instituted because of the high rates of unemployment and poverty among unmarried women.[60]

Upon hearing a radio ad calling on young men to join the Job Corps, members of Congress reported to Shriver that the focus on males violated Title VII of the Civil Rights Act. In response to such concerns, Christopher Niehbur of the OEO Office of Inspection advised Shriver to change the ads because "maximum feasible participation should not be exclusive, I believe, of any significant group within a community. Women constitute a significant group in most communities."[61] Niehbur did not suggest that women "should be proportionately represented," but he concluded that the OEO "should strongly encourage greater inclusion."[62] The few programs offered to women trained enrollees mostly for subordinate, low-paying jobs as office clerks, nurses' aides, or other occupations categorized as "woman's work." The women's program was, in the words of Sar Levitan, "the stepchild of the Job Corps added as an afterthought in response to congressional pressure."[63] Indeed, the Job Corps example reflects the OEO's general failure to address poverty among women.

The Job Corps administered the only conservation camp in Texas, the New Waverly Civilian Conservation Center, in conjunction with the U.S. Forest Service on land within the Sam Houston National Forest north of Houston. The New Waverly camp opened in August 1965 and served 224 corpsmen when it reached its full capacity in 1967.[64] Conservation centers like New Waverly grew out of the attempt by the OEO to associate the Job Corps with the popularity of the CCC and the National Youth Administration (NYA) of the New Deal. Nostalgia for the CCC concept led many to join the Job Corps with the hope of working in conservation or forestry. Some corpsmen dropped out of Camp Gary when they realized that the Job Corps emphasized urban-industrial job training.[65] The popularity of conservation programs eventually compelled Shriver to allocate 40 percent of the Job Corps budget to conservation activities.[66] The training at New Waverly entailed more than conservation activities. New Waverly staff trained enrollees with skills of value to the expanding economy of the Houston area. Trainees at New Waverly spent much of their time on such tasks as "natural resource rehabilitation and forestation," but they also learned construction skills, auto mechanics, welding, and cooking. New Waverly corpsmen even had access to an apprenticeship program with the United Brotherhood of Carpenters and Joiners of America.[67]

Politically, the Job Corps enjoyed more popularity than other OEO programs in the initial stages of the War on Poverty. Governor Connally was particularly proud of Camp Gary.[68] Connally attended the dedication ceremony of the center with LBJ. In his dedication speech, the president cited Connally, who had worked in the NYA under Johnson during the 1930s, as an example of what a young man might achieve with a solid foundation in a program like the Job Corps. "I remember it was about thirty years ago," the president recalled, "that I had Governor Connally and a good many other people on this platform in the job corps of that day . . . So you fellows have something to shoot for here."[69]

As with CAP, opinion on the Job Corps varied among the state's political factions. Even beyond the governor's initial fondness for the program, Senator Yarborough remained the strongest political ally the Job Corps had in the state.[70] Conservative Democrats like Connally may not have opposed the Job Corps on ideological grounds but saw the program, like the rest of the War on Poverty, as an invasive federal bureaucracy that bypassed state and local government. A year after Connally attended the Camp Gary dedication ceremony, the *Washington Post* reported that he threatened to use his veto power to close the camp if the OEO did not grant his office more "policy making authority."[71] Houston Congressman Bush suggested the stance of Republicans when he explained to TEF director O. J. Baker that he had "serious reservations about the poverty program" and "fundamental disagreements with the Job Corps concept."[72]

The cost of the Job Corps provided critics with ammunition to attack the program. Detractors argued that the training of a Job Corps enrollee, about $8,000 per year by 1966, cost more than a year at Harvard. These costs seemed excessive to critics when, they argued, most of the job skills taught at Job Corps centers could be taught on the job by employers in a relatively short time.[73] Although the Job Corps proved expensive, critics tended to exaggerate the costs. The EOA amendments of 1967 placed a cap on annual Job Corps expenses at $7,500 per enrollee. Few enrollees cost this much because most stayed in the Job Corps for about nine months at an expense of about $5,625 each.[74] The OEO countered that while Camp Gary corpsmen enrolled between 1965 and 1970 cost on average about $6,000 to train, the job skills they gained would bring a lifetime tax revenue return of $11,200.[75]

VISTA remained the least expensive of the major War on Poverty efforts. In 1966 the OEO allocated about $16 million for VISTA, less than 5 percent of the cost for the Job Corps and about 2 percent of the cost for CAP. In Texas the program costs were similarly proportioned. Texas VISTA projects in 1966 cost $164,150. While VISTA costs in Texas expanded to a peak of $1.7 million in 1969, even this was negligible compared to the expenditures on other OEO programs.[76] VISTA was cheaper because it had few expenses beyond salaries for the volunteers. CAP, Job Corps, NYC, and other programs had extensive overhead costs, but VISTA, in the words of one historian, "was people."[77] VISTA maintained low overhead costs because volunteers used facilities provided by CAAs, local colleges, and other agencies associated with the poverty program. Perhaps because of VISTA's low costs, the program received more bipartisan support than CAP or the Job Corps. Although only 2,500 volunteers were at work by the end of the program's second year (1966), requests from local CAAs and other sponsoring groups for VISTA volunteers exceeded 15,000.[78] The total number of volunteers exceeded 4,600 by 1969.[79] At any time between 1967 and 1971, VISTA employed between 224 and 317 volunteers in the Lone Star State.

The number of VISTA projects in Texas peaked in 1968 at sixteen—eight rural and eight urban.[80] To conform to the local emphasis of the War on Poverty, VISTA established projects only at the request of local agencies. CAAs usually took the lead in developing projects, but occasionally local governments or private charities employed the volunteers as well. Local agencies used the VISTA volunteers as they saw fit, with the approval of the national VISTA office. As with all other War on Poverty programs, the governor had veto authority over VISTA projects.[81] Laredo maintained the largest VISTA project in Texas, with forty volunteers in 1969. Most VISTA projects in the state had fewer than twenty volunteers.[82]

For the most part, VISTA volunteers in Texas worked quietly within poor communities and achieved modest goals. The majority held to what VISTA director Bill Crook called "the silent service" image. They worked behind the scenes and, at least through the first year, generated relatively little antipathy from local political establishments. Because of the volunteers' enthusiasm and hard work, VISTA drew praise from the media as "the most generally admired of all the War on Poverty programs" through its first two years.[83]

VISTA made genuine progress in some communities—if the volunteers could find an advocate and an issue of interest to the neighborhood. Houston VISTA volunteers Jim Rayburn and Barry Kraut confronted neighborhood apathy when they established a project in "the Bottom," a slum of about eight hundred African American and Mexican American families along Buffalo Bayou. The two recalled spending their first few sleepless nights stifled by the living conditions and "listening to the creatures (rats)" crawl along the floors of their quarters.[84] Once they became more accustomed to their accommodations, Kraut and Rayburn had difficulty developing interest within the community. Fortunately for them, the owner of a local tavern, a woman whom Rayburn and Kraut simply called Ma Wright, befriended the VISTA volunteers. Ma Wright's endorsement apparently provided VISTA some credibility, as one volunteer recalled: "Things could have been a lot different if she hadn't been there to say, 'he's one of our VISTAs—he's alright.'"[85]

Rayburn and Kraut discovered a small park across a major freeway from the Bottom. The city had not equipped the park with any facilities or play equipment. Most children from the Bottom had no access to the park because of the freeway. To discuss the park, Rayburn and Kraut organized a series of meetings. While attendance at the meetings was irregular, Ma Wright's endorsement eventually brought in a core group of a few interested citizens. This core group agreed, with the encouragement of the volunteers, to form the People's Civic Club to serve as a political voice for the residents of the Bottom. With the help of the volunteers, the People's Civic Club wrote an urgent letter to the mayor's office about the park. City hall, in turn, installed some playground equipment and a fence in the park.[86]

The park improvement seemed to inspire more people to get involved. While the volunteers at first had difficulty getting more than four or five people to attend meetings, the People's Civic Club began having thirty or more people attend meetings regularly. Blair Justice, a Rice University sociologist and special assistant to Mayor Louis Welch, attended a meeting of the club to announce the opening of a special office called Project Partner as a liaison between the mayor and the residents of the Bottom. Project Partner facilitated substantive improvements for the Bottom, such as the installation of street lights, a tutoring project established in conjunction with local churches and Rice University, and, most substantially, the opening of a well-baby clinic in the neighborhood. The People's Civic Club, according to Justice, served as the "prime instigator" in achieving these improvements, and the volunteers had brought "many of the 'partners' together" to make the improvements happen.[87]

Kraut and Rayburn's effort exemplified how a VISTA project was supposed to work. The two organized local leadership, found an issue to mobilize the community, and successfully pressured local government to devote resources that improved poor neighborhoods. While few VISTA projects produced such exemplary results, the efforts rarely attracted criticism from community leaders. Houston residents did not stand alone in supporting VISTA volunteers. When the costs of the war in Vietnam caused Congress to temporarily suspend the subsistence allowance of VISTA volunteers in Cotulla, for example, local residents financially supported six volunteers so they could continue their preschool tutoring program for low-income Mexican American children.[88]

By mid-1967 the OEO funded three Job Corps centers, sixteen VISTA projects, and more than fifty CAAs in Texas. Most CAAs in the state operated with little controversy, but increased funding soon triggered wrangling between various interest groups, especially in larger cities where the stakes were highest. In urban Texas, as elsewhere in the nation, race politics motivated conflicts over OEO funding more than any other factor.

Juan Ortiz and Dan García were two of Lyndon Johnson's students during his years as an elementary school teacher in Cotulla, Texas, in the 1920s. Both men were in attendance when Johnson called the mayors of Cotulla and neighboring Pearsall to congratulate them on launching a joint Community Action Agency. García served as a city councilman and commissioner of streets and lights in Cotulla. San Antonio Express-News Collection, Institute of Texan Cultures, University of Texas at San Antonio, #E-0011-099-14. Courtesy of the Hearst Corporation.

Albert Peña was the leader of PASSO and one of a "new breed" of confrontational Mexican American activists in Texas. Peña was one of the strongest defenders of the War on Poverty in the state. San Antonio Express-News Collection, Institute of Texan Cultures, University of Texas at San Antonio, #E-001-088-9. Courtesy of the Hearst Corporation.

The headquarters of the Greater San Antonio Federation of Neighborhood Councils was in a building owned by the Catholic Church at 330 North Laredo Street near downtown. The federation, supported by SANYO and the OEO, became a political force in San Antonio during the later 1960s. Howell Collection, Institute of Texan Cultures, University of Texas at San Antonio, #H-1396-295. Courtesy of Ann Marie Howell.

The EODC's offices were on Houston Street on San Antonio's west side. Supporters of SANYO quarreled with city government for the financial and political limitations that officials from the EODC placed on SANYO and the Federation of Neighborhood Councils. A campaign sign for Albert Peña is on the truck parked in front. Howell Collection, Institute of Texan Cultures, University of Texas at San Antonio, #H-1376-89. Courtesy of Ann Marie Howell.

José Angel Gutiérrez at a La Raza Unida Party rally in 1970. Gutiérrez, like other Chicano and Chicana activists, gained political experience as a War on Poverty worker for SANYO. San Antonio Express-News Collection, Institute of Texan Cultures, University of Texas at San Antonio, #E-0019-085-20. Courtesy of the Hearst Corporation.

Mario Compean, pictured here at the La Raza Unida Party rally in 1970, gave credit to VISTA for providing funding and other resources for the organization of MAYO in the late 1960s. San Antonio Express-News Collection, Institute of Texan Cultures, University of Texas at San Antonio, #E-0019-085-f11. Courtesy of the Hearst Corporation.

Job Corps enrollees from the Dallas area arrive in San Marcos to attend the Camp Gary Job Corps center for men in 1965. The multiracial makeup of this group would change within three years, when the majority of Job Corpsmen would be African American. San Antonio Express-News Collection, Institute of Texan Cultures, University of Texas at San Antonio, #E-0011-087. Courtesy of the Hearst Corporation.

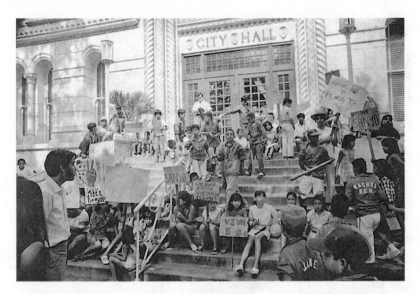

SANYO supporters, mostly children, gather on the steps of city hall in San Antonio to protest proposed reductions in funding for SANYO in 1970. Supporters picketed city hall on several occasions to protest cuts or changes in the agency's role in the community. San Antonio Express-News Collection, Institute of Texan Cultures, University of Texas at San Antonio, #L-6482-A-7. Courtesy of the Hearst Corporation.

Ernesto Cortés, the founder of COPS, is seen here in 1975. Cortés, a protégé of Saul Alinsky, renewed and invigorated community organizing in Texas in the 1970s with the Industrial Areas Foundation. The IAF, though independent of federal administration, has secured millions of federal, state, and private dollars for impoverished areas across Texas for infrastructure and economic improvements. San Antonio Express-News Collection, Institute of Texan Cultures, University of Texas at San Antonio, #E-0038-001-31. Courtesy of the Hearst Corporation.

Beatrice Cortez, the president of COPS, is shown here in 1981. Except for COPS founder Ernesto Cortés, all of the presidents of the organization were women. OEO programs, in contrast, failed to recognize the leadership skills of women activists and neglected women's poverty in general. San Antonio Express-News Collection, Institute of Texan Cultures, University of Texas at San Antonio, #E-0075-010-21A. Courtesy of the Hearst Corporation.

Students gather at Texas Southern University to protest police brutality in Houston prior to the 1967 riot and gun battle on the campus. Published with the permission of the Robert J. Terry Library, Special Collections, Texas Southern University.

TSU students are quarantined prior to being searched for firearms after the police raid on the campus in May 1967. Police fired nearly 2,000 rounds into Lanier Hall, a dormitory from which an unknown shooter fired about two dozen shots at police. Published with the permission of the Robert J. Terry Library, Special Collections, Texas Southern University.

President Johnson visited with Senator Ralph Yarborough in Austin on a campaign stop in 1964. Yarborough, who was in a heated reelection race with Congressman George H. W. Bush, strongly defended War on Poverty programs in Texas against attacks from conservative Democratic Governor John Connally and Republican Senator John Tower. Center for American History, UT-Austin. Photograph by Russell Lee.

The conditions captured in this 1949 photo by Russell Lee had not improved much when the War on Poverty came to El Paso in 1965. Improving living conditions in tenement buildings on the city's south side became one of the primary goals of MACHOS. Center for American History, UT-Austin.

Congressman Henry B. Gonzalez was a titan in Texas politics in the 1960s. Although a strong supporter of civil rights, Lyndon Johnson, and the War on Poverty, Chicano activists criticized Gonzalez for his unwillingness to share power or embrace the values of the Chicano movement. Center for American History, UT-Austin.

Making Maximum
Participation Feasible

FIVE   *Community Action in Urban Texas*

Recent scholarship on the War on Poverty focuses on the significance of community action and other OEO programs to the political mobilization of marginalized groups at the grassroots level. African Americans, Latinos, Native Americans, and women in general, already activated politically for the civil rights revolution, saw the OEO as a means to include and advance the cause of economic justice on their agendas. Civil rights activists took the OEO's principle of maximum feasible participation seriously—for them it was feasible for the poor to participate by running the programs in their communities.[1] This represents a departure from the earliest scholarship on the War on Poverty, which tended to depict confrontations over OEO funds between local civil rights groups and city hall, often controlled by local Democratic machines, as a liability for LBJ and the overall Great Society agenda. There was little or no acknowledgment that in many cases community action was working according to its design.

Just about everyone in OEO assumed that local governments would run the poverty programs and recruit the poor to work in them to achieve maximum feasible participation.[2] Shriver and his team never seemed to grasp that empowering the poor was the whole point of community action theory. Chicago organizer Saul Alinsky and other social activists had designed community action to politically organize the poor to give them a louder, more unified voice in their battles with intransigent mayors and city councils.[3] The young academics who introduced the concept experimentally in the Kennedy administration's juvenile delinquency programs hoped that community action had the potential to forge "the disinherited into a political instrument capable of compelling the reconstruction of communities."[4] LBJ liked the idea of the poor participating in their own betterment. The president probably envisioned noble unemployed men rolling up their sleeves and swinging pick axes like something out of the New Deal. He certainly did not anticipate that men and women from poor neighborhoods, people whom Johnson considered friendly constituents, would march into planning meetings demanding federal money from city governments controlled by the Democratic Party.[5]

As CAP developed, advocates of the poor embraced this original concept of community action and maximum feasible participation, much to the surprise of the administration and often to the annoyance of local politicians. Chicago Mayor Richard Daley likened maximum feasible participation to "telling the fellow who cleans up to be the city editor of a newspaper."[6] In a 1965 letter to Bill Moyers, Daley angrily asked, "What the hell are you people doing? Does the President know he's giving money to subversives? To poor people that aren't a part of the organization?"[7] In June of that year the U.S. Conference of Mayors sent a resolution to LBJ condemning CAP for "fostering class struggle" in American cities.[8]

To put an end to such criticism, Congress eliminated the troubling maximum feasible participation guideline from the renewal legislation for the EOA for 1966. The amended act fixed the amount of poor participation at one-third of the membership of local CAA policy-making boards.[9] This retreat from maximum feasible participation stoked the anger of local leadership in low-income communities. In April 1966 Shriver was booed off the stage of the first annual convention of the Citizens Crusade Against Poverty, an activist group led by former Kennedy antipoverty warrior Richard Boone, for abandoning maximum feasible participation.[10] Under attack by the poor and by the mayors, Shriver attempted to resign as OEO director in order to salvage his own political future.[11] Johnson refused the resignation but privately scolded the director for allowing so many "kooks and sociologists" to infiltrate his program.[12]

The new scholarship on the War on Poverty makes it clear that Shriver and local party kingpins like Daley were not simply dealing with the handiwork of "kooks and sociologists." Instead, historians on the local level have illustrated the extent to which those representing the poor embraced the concept. By retreating from maximum feasible participation, the OEO began the gradual dismantling of the Community Action Program because it was functioning the way it was supposed to.

In cities across Texas, CAP increased local activism on behalf of the poor.

Black and Mexican American civil rights activists, church leaders, and white progressives worked together to stand up for the ideal of maximum feasible participation of the poor. San Antonio, El Paso, and Houston developed the most extensive programs in the state and exemplified the potential that federally funded community action groups had to mobilize low-income communities.

From the earliest beginnings of local CAPs in Texas through early 1967, conflicts over War on Poverty programs in the state were never as simple as liberal versus conservative. While CAPs contended with ideological opposition from conservatives, a basic difference of opinion also emerged about what the OEO should provide to the poor and what poor participation should entail. Local establishment figures, even those with a genuine concern for the poor, clearly wanted to maintain control of OEO funding and set the terms for the involvement of the poor. The poor and their advocates from the civil rights movement clearly saw things differently. They increasingly came to demand that the indigenous leadership of low-income Mexican American or African American communities should control programs and federal funding independently from city hall.

SAN ANTONIO

In San Antonio, a conservative, predominantly Anglo, and business-oriented clique dominated city politics and stymied efforts at social reform in the city's vast low-income neighborhoods throughout the 1960s. This clique acted through a nonpartisan political organization called the Good Government League (GGL). The GGL, which had nearly three thousand members by 1965, worked behind the scenes to field candidates who served the interests of "the socially prominent and the economically powerful."[13]

An anonymous GGL nominating committee controlled city government through the selection of candidates for city council and the mayor's office. The nominating committee included prominent local businessmen who were, according to later San Antonio Mayor Nelson Wolff, "the real decision makers on the big issues that affected San Antonio."[14] In secret meetings reminiscent of some smoke-filled bygone Tammany Hall, the nominating committee selected candidates who displayed a commitment to the political and economic values of the city's business leadership.[15] Nearly 80 percent of GGL members were Anglo, but the league did not outwardly work to maintain Anglo dominance in the city. This became the virtual effect of the league's control of city politics, as political scientist Rodolfo Rosales has explained, because the GGL "was able to define political inclusion in terms of their class interests," and the vast majority of San Antonio's affluent citizens were Anglo.[16] The GGL emphasized the inclusion of a few upper-class blacks and Mexican Americans for, as one member put it, "visibility and ego input."[17] Most of the nonwhites who were admitted to membership in the GGL, like 65 percent of GGL candidates, came from the more affluent north side of the city.[18] Between 1955 and 1971, GGL candidates won seventy-seven of eighty-one city council seats.[19]

The GGL backed candidates from both parties in order to divide the constituency of its only opposition in local politics—the Bexar County Democratic Coalition.[20] Founded in 1959, the coalition consisted primarily of Mexican Americans from the west side, African Americans from the east side, organized labor, and Anglo liberals. The dominant Mexican American leader of the coalition, Bexar County Commissioner Albert Peña, also led PASSO.[21] Peña became the most vocal opponent of the GGL in city politics. In its greatest victory, the coalition elected Henry B. Gonzalez to the House of Representatives in 1961. Although Gonzalez, an integral figure in city and state politics since the 1940s, was not involved in building the coalition, Peña organized an "intensive get out the vote" campaign that ensured Gonzalez the victory.[22] The GGL still controlled city politics when the War on Poverty began, but the drive to secure OEO dollars mobilized Peña's coalition. As discussed earlier, Peña made headlines statewide when he attacked Governor John Connally for "declaring war on the War on Poverty."[23]

In the winter of 1964–1965, Mayor Walter McAllister formed a board of directors for the Economic Opportunities Development Corporation (EODC), which the OEO recognized as the city's official CAA. The OEO granted the board $30,523 in March 1965 to formulate a strategy.[24] Although a public meeting was held to discuss the EODC's mission, the agency developed according to the priorities of the mayor's office and the GGL.[25] Nearly a year passed before the EODC began to function.[26]

Despite the GGL, San Antonio provided fertile ground for community action. The city's Mexican American community had a long tradition of community activism. Organizations like LULAC and the American GI Forum had used confrontational methods and political organizing throughout the postwar period to improve the status of San Antonio's Mexican American community. A notable example, the Student Improvement League, a LULAC-backed organization led by Eleuterio Escobar, fought a prolonged struggle against the San Antonio school board for improvement of schools on the west side. Although educational facilities for Mexican American students remained far from equal to those of whites, by the 1960s Escobar's organization had made substantive gains in new school construction and increased enrollment.[27] San Antonio's Mexican American community, already attuned to political activism when CAP began, moved quicker than city hall to take advantage of the War on Poverty.

The Roman Catholic archdiocese tapped into the activism of the city's Mexican American community when it established the San Antonio Neighborhood Youth Organization (SANYO) in spring 1965. SANYO originated as a local division of the Neighborhood Youth Corps.[28] Father John Yanta, a dynamic young priest who directed the Archdiocesan Catholic Youth Organization, became the prime mover behind SANYO after reading about the NYC in a Catholic magazine. Yanta decided to take advantage of the NYC to create a comprehensive "recreational, cultural, and civic improvement program" for San Antonio's poor families.[29] While the EODC board stumbled to get started through 1965, SANYO developed a variety of programs for children and their families. SANYO received its first NYC grant of $440,460 in May 1965, nearly a year before the OEO certified EODC as San Antonio's CAA.[30]

Through thirty neighborhood centers established primarily in church buildings on the city's west side, SANYO provided recreational and civic activities for low-income youth. SANYO offered teenage enrollees pay for community service projects such as park or roadside cleanups and assistance in local schools, libraries, hospitals, or church facilities.[31] The experience of Irma Mireles, who would later become the director of San Antonio's Mexican American Cultural Center, provides a good example of the type of work SANYO enrollees performed. Mireles enrolled in SANYO in 1965. Like many SANYO enrollees, Mireles, the oldest of six children, went to work in order to supplement her family's income. Along with two of her brothers, she worked a few hours after school during the academic year and all day during the summer. Because she had clerical skills, Mireles worked as a typist and file clerk for various SANYO offices. She also worked as a reading tutor for her fellow enrollees because it was common for bilingual Mexican American children to be illiterate in both English and Spanish. The SANYO administrative office hired Mireles on a full-time basis to perform clerical work in 1967.[32]

Each neighborhood center employed youth counselors, usually male college students, to provide young role models for adolescents. One SANYO counselor remembered that his job primarily involved counseling his enrollees about basic job skills such as "punctuality, work ethic, appearance, hygiene, skills, the whole gamut."[33] This emphasis on presentability became central to SANYO's work with teens. Enrollees wore uniforms—a blue skirt or pants and a white shirt. As an enrollee Mireles "detested" the uniform because she "didn't like being singled out as poor."[34] Counselors provided advice to youths about urban dangers such as gangs, drugs, and sex and offered an outlet for troubled adolescents to discuss personal and family problems.

While the agency's various youth programs reached nearly twelve thousand kids and employed 962 youth counselors in its first year alone, Yanta expanded SANYO's role to provide assistance to adults as well. The neighborhood centers offered adults job referrals, night schooling, and access to a credit union.[35] Adults became involved in the administration of SANYO through various committees that were formed as new demands arose.[36] Before the EODC began to function as the city's CAA, SANYO became an effective multipurpose antipoverty agency that functioned well beyond its capacity as an NYC program.[37] As such, SANYO earned praise around the state and throughout the OEO as "one of the most effective and highly popular programs in the country."[38] The organization's early success drew enough attention to compel OEO director Sargent Shriver and LBJ to visit SANYO and speak to Yanta in 1966.[39]

In part, SANYO thrived because of the support and influence of Archbishop Robert E. Lucey and Congressman Gonzalez. Because the archbishop had a personal friendship with Lyndon Johnson, Lucey had as much influence in the antipoverty effort as any man in the city. He had delivered the invocation at the 1965 inauguration, and LBJ appointed him to the ten-member National Advisory Council on the War on Poverty. Because Lucey had influence within the community and important connections in Washington, SANYO received special attention from the OEO. The archbishop's connections, according to his biographer, made "SANYO the biggest and most active poverty agency in the Southwest."[40] Gonzalez had a close political relationship with LBJ as well. He served as a strong congressional advocate of most of the president's domestic initiatives, including the War on Poverty.[41] Yanta later recalled that if SANYO "needed anything, all I had to do was call Henry, it was that simple."[42] The influence of both Lucey and Gonzalez became integral to bringing SANYO about $9 million in federal funds within its first three years—more than one-third of all War on Poverty funds spent in San Antonio.[43]

Father Yanta's leadership also proved central to the success of SANYO. Yanta, a native Texan who later became the first Polish American bishop in the state, was described by an Austin reporter as "a dreamer whose ideas worked" for his leadership of SANYO.[44] OEO field inspectors reported that SANYO's success was "largely due to the courage and organizational ability of Father John Yanta" and that the priest and his staff enjoyed their reputation as "the shock troops of the poor and disheartened."[45]

As executive director of SANYO, Yanta adhered to the spirit of maximum feasible participation. From its inception SANYO developed a reputation, according to a CAP inspection report, as an agency that "basically serves the Mexican-American community."[46] Some 80 percent of the SANYO board of directors came out of the city's poorest Mexican American neighborhoods. The inclusion of women in the organization emerged as one remarkable indication of SANYO's adherence to the principle of maximum feasible participation. Although few women received salaried administrative jobs above the level of secretary, SANYO had a more equitable gender balance than most government-sponsored agencies. Women formed 25 percent of SANYO board members and youth counselors.[47] Julian Rodriguez, SANYO's personnel director, said women's roles in SANYO were "not about affirmative action."[48] The agency depended upon outspoken, active women as rank-and-file volunteer leaders on the board of directors and in the neighborhood centers. The inclusion of women in SANYO mirrored their activities in local politics. Rosales has argued that westside Chicanas formed the "backbone" of the Bexar County Democratic Coalition.[49]

To complement its adherence to the principle of maximum feasible participation, SANYO became a forum for grassroots political organizing. Yanta encouraged political activism. He recognized the War on Poverty as an opportunity to organize poor neighborhoods in the city against "the Good Government League and other institutions [that] kept these areas disorganized and under oppression."[50] SANYO sponsored "Civic Action workshops" to encourage political activism in neighborhood centers to sow the "kernels of leadership" among the poor. The workshops taught participants how community action could work to pressure local government to address the needs of impoverished areas. A SANYO bulletin explained that the workshops "awakened" the "community action sleeping giants" of San Antonio's poorest neighborhoods.[51] Each neighborhood center created a neighborhood council that became, in Yanta's words, "community action groups which develop grassroots leadership to deal with grassroots problems."[52]

The active, involved membership of SANYO's neighborhood councils increased the political influence of the west side. In 1967 SANYO neighborhood councils united under the Greater San Antonio Federation of Neighborhood Councils, an independent agency that served as a political pressure group for the city's low-income neighborhoods. The federation pressured local government to address specific needs, such as street lights, drainage, and school funding, and to lobby for War on Poverty funds.[53] A cadre of volunteer activists, led by westside resident Joe Freire, made the federation into what a local journalist described as "a vibrant, if unwieldy, political force."[54] The federation established councils in census tracts that represented 250,000 people—more than a third of the city's population.[55] One SANYO board member suggested that because the federation was such a "huge operation . . . the politicians in our city were looking at us as a giant that was going to ripple the water a bit."[56] As the federation became larger and more politically active, city officials categorized SANYO, along with other Chicano-led organizations such as the Committee for Barrio Betterment, as a "pressure block" that could manipulate the electorate.[57] Yanta later explained that because of SANYO's growing political influence there were "parts of the establishment, such as business and the GGL, that we made very nervous."[58] One reporter foresaw a "revolutionary political reshuffling . . . a whole new political structure in the community, and it's going to emerge in part out of SANYO— through the neighborhood centers and through its ability to control as many jobs and as much money as it controls."[59]

SANYO had built a strong, politically active organization well before the EODC, the city's official CAA, prepared an organizational proposal acceptable to the OEO. Beyond the planning grant it received in March 1965, the OEO allocated no other funds to the EODC for that year, as administrative changes and quarreling board members created continuous delays. The OEO regional office in Austin rejected the EODC's first two proposals because the policy-making board they would create failed to include, in accordance with the maximum feasible participation doctrine of CAP, sufficient low-income representation. The first proposal, which OEO rejected in October 1965, included no poor representatives in policy-making functions.[60]

A planning committee chaired by the Reverend Gerald McAllister, a canon of the Episcopal Diocese of San Antonio and the son of the mayor, prepared the second proposal.[61] An OEO official described Gerald McAllister as "inconsistent and fuzzy in his thinking" and someone who "thinks of himself as acceptable to both sides but really classified as spokesman for his father and the Good Government League."[62] The second proposal specified that low-income representation on the policy-making board would be fixed at about one in four (eighteen of sixty-six) board members. The criteria for selecting representatives for the poor, however, focused on race rather than income. The plan called for fifteen Mexican American and three black board members from neighborhood councils to be organized under the EODC—including some already established by SANYO.[63]

Archbishop Lucey attacked the EODC plan as "totally unacceptable, vulnerable and impossible" and predicted that the EODC board would collapse before the OEO's January 31 deadline for 1966 CAP applications. Lucey declared that the persons selected to represent the poor could not serve impartially because "their own jobs and livelihood are subject to the power structure."[64] At least twelve of the eighteen proposed board members, Lucey said, depended in one way or another on city government for their paychecks. Some had jobs in the housing authority or in school districts that made them "vulnerable, and this is no way to handle $3 Million (the amount requested by the EODC application)."[65] The archbishop further criticized the proposal because those selected to represent the poor were not poor themselves. Lucey concluded that the city's "power structure," which he specified as the GGL, had a tendency to "go to the poor and decide 'we're telling you what you need.' What arrogance!"[66] Lucey assailed the use of racial quotas as selection criteria for board members: "No Irish . . . no Italians, no others at all? Why, this is a violation of the Civil Rights Act."[67]

The new proposal and the archbishop's response to it created uproar throughout the OEO. Regional community action manager Don Mathis explained in a telegram to OEO chief Shriver that the archbishop's involvement "considerably complicated the situation and dimmed the hopes for a resolution."[68] Mathis informed the EODC board that the application was unacceptable, but, in a statement that reveals an essential ambiguity in CAP policy, he indicated that the OEO could not dictate any specific way to revise the proposal:

> Mr. Shriver has consistently refused to define maximum feasible participation of the poor in such a way as to limit their partnership in programs for their benefit. Therefore . . . it has never been the policy or practice of the OEO to draw up detailed plans for a community's attack on poverty. The Southwest Regional Office has repeatedly offered its assistance . . . But we have not dictated, and cannot dictate solutions.[69]

While the Economic Opportunity Act included no specific requirement for the inclusion of minority representatives, the regional office of the OEO required "minority group representatives *at least* in proportion to popula-

tion" as a "special condition" to be fulfilled before the EODC board's application could be approved.[70] The EODC's plan to include eighteen members
of ethnic minorities on its sixty-six-member board violated this condition
because Mexican Americans comprised nearly half the population of San
Antonio. The plan also precluded, in Mathis' words, "the possibility of low
income Anglo-American participation."[71] The proposal further attenuated
the intent of maximum feasible participation because minority board members would fulfill a "double representation role," meaning they were to serve
as representatives of the poor and of minority populations.[72]

Mathis explained to the EODC board that the primary problem was that
the board abused the flexibility of community action. He said the EODC's
proposal "treated minimum requirements as maximum limits."[73] By placing
racial quotas as criteria for board membership, EODC had violated the intent of maximum feasible participation: "in general . . . the word *maximum*
suggests that a community should ask 'what is the most we can do?'—never—
'what is the least that we must do?'"[74]

Mathis informed Shriver that McAllister was willing to "let the program
die before adhering to the (OEO's) guidelines."[75] Mathis also indicated that
behind McAllister in the GGL there were "four or five rock-ribbed, ideological conservatives fanning the flames, personally hoping the program will
fail."[76] Mathis did not specify who these "rock-ribbed" conservatives were
but presumed that they would rather have no War on Poverty funds in San
Antonio than satisfy the OEO's maximum feasible participation guidelines.

The EODC would have collapsed had it not been for Henry B. Gonzalez.
The congressman, at McAllister's request, secured from the OEO regional
office in Austin an extension beyond the January 31, 1966, deadline.[77] OEO
Southwest regional director Bill Crook said McAllister and the EODC board
were "showing every sign of capitulation" before Gonzalez' intervention.
The press and television news in San Antonio had "focused a hot light on the
resistance and [were] insisting that [the EODC] put politics aside and give
the poor a legitimate voice on the board."[78] When he secured the deadline,
Gonzalez inadvertently furnished a "gleeful and vengeful victory for Mayor
McAllister and his anti-Great Society forces" because the extension allowed
EODC to deter the negative media attention that city hall had received for
an obvious attempt to limit poor and minority participation on the EODC
board.[79]

Gonzalez' intervention saved the EODC when many of his constituents
wanted it to die. The action especially irked civil rights activists who were
convinced that the EODC would limit Mexican American, black, and poor

participation in the program. Ralph C. Caserez, vice chairman of the state GI Forum, castigated Gonzalez on behalf of his organization after the extension was secured:

> Let's face it, Mr. Gonzalez, City Hall runs the EODC, the same as the Good Government League runs City Hall, and as long as they are given the upper hand "*la raza and los negritos*" are never going to be given the chance to serve on the board unless they belong to the GGL . . . I was hoping you would have stayed out of it . . . but now that you have secured an extension I believe you should also make it plain that it is their last extension and to give the poor a chance to serve on the board, after all not all of the poor are dumb as Rev. [Gerald] McAllister once said.[80]

Two weeks after Gonzalez intervened, the EODC board agreed to a new proposal calling for a thirty-member board that included three members each from the city council and the county commissioners court, six from local educational or welfare organizations, nine from religious or civic organizations, and nine from "areas and groups served"—meaning the poor.[81] OEO officials in both Washington and Austin accepted the new board. Crook telegrammed Shriver that the new "CAP in San Antonio, by maintaining fidelity to principle and guideline, has established a dialog between factions . . . heretofore separated by [a] deep chasm."[82] Crook could not foresee that the War on Poverty would soon be the cause for even wider chasms among unexpected factions.

EL PASO

El Paso and San Antonio shared many social and economic characteristics when the War on Poverty began. El Paso featured segregated residential areas and high unemployment rates among non-Anglos.[83] Although Mexican Americans made up half the population of the city, residential and educational segregation persisted through the late twentieth century.[84] Anglos controlled the economy of El Paso, while Mexican Americans remained trapped in poverty with limited access to high-paying jobs.[85]

An elite clique of Anglo businessmen and professionals, dubbed "Kingmakers" by the local press, dominated El Paso politics through the 1960s. Politically, most of the Kingmakers were conservative Democrats. They generally opposed the type of liberal activism that characterized the national party throughout the 1960s. As long as the Kingmakers held onto power, the city government resisted spending on social welfare measures. El Paso resident José Patino explained the situation best in a letter to the *El Paso Herald-Post*: "We all know that Kingmakers will keep on favoring the areas where only people of high social and economic position live. They will keep neglecting areas of the city where there has never been sewer service, bus service, and other things."[86]

Anglo dominance of city politics in El Paso had begun to wane as the activism of El Paso's Mexican American middle class led to substantive gains. Most notably, activist groups orchestrated the election in 1957 of Raymond L. Telles as the first Mexican American mayor of a major American city. While John Kennedy cut short the Telles administration when he appointed the mayor U.S. ambassador to Costa Rica in 1961, the Telles victory required the Kingmakers, as Mario Garcia has argued, to "respect the political influence that Mexican Americans could wield if they chose to do so."[87]

Grassroots organizers working from the city's barrios began taking advantage of federal antipoverty programs before the Johnson administration. Local Mexican American activists received funding from Kennedy's juvenile delinquency program to establish the Mexican American Youth Administration (MAYA). MAYA worked from within the barrios to organize youth, targeting the leadership of local street gangs who were "eager to engage in direct confrontation with city officials."[88] MAYA focused almost solely on local politics. As Chicano youth activism expanded in the later sixties, MAYA emerged as the primary organizational base for the movement in El Paso.

The El Paso County Commission bypassed MAYA to create a service-oriented agency called Project BRAVO (Building Resources and Vocational Opportunities), which became the city's main CAA, directed by local accountant Fred Smith.[89] As happened in many cities, the organizers of Project BRAVO billed the program as an effort to lower school dropout and youth crime rates, but in working toward this goal BRAVO focused on providing services to families and eschewing the political focus of MAYA. By June 1965 the OEO approved a $237,911 grant to Project BRAVO for administrative costs, a Barrio Program, a Head Start preschool, and adult training and remedial literacy courses.[90] By 1966 Project BRAVO administered approximately $1.5 million in projects and by 1968 more than $2 million.[91] El Paso received more funding per poor person than other large cities in the state. The OEO spent only about $10 per poor person in Dallas, while El Paso received nearly $41 per poor person. El Paso received more OEO funding per capita than any city in the state except for Laredo.[92]

The wretched housing conditions of the city's south side induced a conflict within the local antipoverty effort between those who advocated using CAP as a means of political organizing and those who favored the service approach of BRAVO. Unsafe tenement buildings continued to line the streets of south El Paso through the 1960s. Tenement occupants rented their homes from absentee landlords who paid little attention to sanitary conditions, heating and cooling, or fire safety. A report from the HEW explained that the conditions "tax the endurance of residents."[93] Few tenements had indoor plumbing, heating, or air conditioning. Rats and roaches prevailed. As many as twenty families shared a single toilet. Simple maintenance and basic repairs went unattended.[94] The city government neglected to enforce building codes. The city had, according to one local civil rights activist, "been negligent in providing laws and ordinances to control the spread of slum areas."[95]

The housing situation became tragic in July 1967 when a fire swept through a tenement building in El Segundo Barrio, El Paso's poorest neighborhood, and killed three children—Ismael, Orlando, and Leticia Rosales (eight, seven, and four years old, respectively). As the children slept, bedding too close to an unventilated gas heater caught fire. The fire swept through the old building, which had no fire escape, and burned the children alive.[96]

In the days following the fire, the American GI Forum and several church groups organized mass demonstrations to protest housing conditions in El Segundo Barrio. The protests began at Sacred Heart Catholic Church, where mourners held a mass in the children's honor, and continued on to city hall, where an estimated three hundred marchers lambasted the city and county governments for failing to enforce building codes. The marchers blamed the Kingmakers and the city government for the deaths of the three children. "Mayor [Bert] Williams and the city council have persistently refused to enforce the inadequate inspection code," one marcher announced. "They have allowed hundreds of unsafe fire traps, housing thousands of people, to remain in South El Paso . . . They are directly responsible for the death of these innocent children." Pickets at the protests read, "Don't Let Our Children Die" and "Fire Traps Should Burn Empty."[97]

Local officials became nervous over protests in the wake of the fire. The mayor blamed the protests on "very few politically motivated individuals [who] see fit to use this tragic event as a sounding board for their own purposes, whatever they are."[98] The University of Texas at El Paso hosted a conference after the fire to study the social, economic, and political conditions of south El Paso. Sociologist Clark Knowlton, who attended the conference, concluded in reference to the rioting of the 1960s that the living conditions in

El Segundo Barrio might spark a "holocaust" of violence in El Paso.[99] Like its counterparts elsewhere in the state, El Paso's civil rights community looked toward the OEO as an advocate in the continuing struggle to improve slum conditions in areas like south El Paso.[100]

While all agreed that OEO dollars could help, wide disagreement emerged on what approach should be used. Project BRAVO assistant director Joe Rubio explained to the local press that the purpose of the War on Poverty was not to organize politically but to "encourage people to break the links of ignorance, disease, fear and apathy that keep them chained to poverty [with] educational programs . . . job training and counseling, health education, vocational rehabilitation, [and] home management."[101] Through its Barrio Program, Project BRAVO also opened neighborhood centers where the poor could attain information on federal and state welfare benefits and employment opportunities.[102] Rubio's approach to the War on Poverty was consistent with the vision of LBJ and Shriver as he elaborated to a reporter that CAP offered "remedial programs, not welfare ones which subsidize the poor with doles and handouts."[103]

Yet, for many within El Paso's barrios the service orientation of Project BRAVO compromised political empowerment for modest benefits. In 1967 the leadership of MAYA organized a competing program called the Mexican-American Committee on Honor, Opportunity, and Service (MACHOS). Led by activist José Aguilar, MACHOS became more active in the barrios than Project BRAVO. Aguilar required MACHOS workers to live in El Segundo Barrio. He and his staff encouraged residents to organize politically to pressure local government for services, not to wait for the OEO or traditional welfare programs to do it for them. MACHOS organized food and utilities cooperatives and demonstrations to pressure local landlords to improve living conditions in the tenements.

Although OEO had retreated from the maximum feasible participation emphasis by 1967, MACHOS exemplified it. MACHOS community workers went into the tenements to encourage residents to get involved. As attendance in the meetings expanded, MACHOS workers turned leadership over to the residents themselves. The neighborhood groups promoted their own managers and organized independently. Neighborhood groups met in homes, church buildings, and schools. They planned for and organized the types of services being offered from the top down by BRAVO—citizenship and English classes for new immigrants, tutoring for students, employment counseling, and health education. MACHOS exemplified the type of grassroots participation that was the original purpose of community action as envisioned by those who designed it.[104]

In terms of political activity, MACHOS focused on the housing problems of south El Paso. In May 1968 MACHOS organized a picket at the home of M. D. Springer, a landlord who owned several tenements in El Segundo Barrio. Springer had removed doors and windows from buildings when tenants were late with rent. MACHOS, in turn, sued him for failing to maintain healthy living conditions. Such pressure became a common MACHOS tactic as the agency, historian Benjamin Marquez notes, moved to the "forefront of the Southside's push for housing improvement."[105]

Aguilar steered MACHOS toward less confrontational solutions as well, to show that the agency was not just looking for a fight. MACHOS offered to provide labor if landlords agreed to pay for home improvements. MACHOS convinced one landlord to pay for concrete to cover the dirt courtyard of a tenement building where rainwater stagnated. MACHOS supplied volunteer labor, the landlord purchased the concrete, and the OEO regional office provided funds for tools.[106]

Aguilar drew praise from the OEO. Field representative Frank Curtis applauded MACHOS for its proactive attempts to include the poor, while BRAVO seemed to avoid organizing altogether. Curtis concluded that "the only successful organizing in El Paso is done by MACHOS . . . they are efficient, they do their homework, and pick their fights carefully. BRAVO could learn a lot from them."[107]

Curtis blamed the "timid and cautious" approach of BRAVO director Fred Smith for the agency's failures. Smith resisted political action. As an accountant by profession, Smith appeared "much more concerned with the Auditors rapping his knuckles than with getting things moving." Smith displayed little concern for "reaching to the poor to give them a voice." Instead he focused on maintaining a "respectable 'accountability,' i.e., not in financial trouble and pleasing to the public." Curtis saw MACHOS as motivated and BRAVO as lacking "any sense of purpose." Without effective management, he said, BRAVO became a "chaotic mess of programs which have little relationship with each other."[108]

To support MACHOS and oppose BRAVO, southside resident Eugenio Montelongo created Amigos de MACHOS. As a member of the MACHOS board of directors and a target-area reprehensive, Montelongo exemplified the spirit of participation by the poor. In a public hearing Montelongo attacked BRAVO when Fred Smith attempted to exclude MACHOS from a

$2 million increase in funding in 1968: "Project BRAVO can keep all its two million dollars, we don't want anything from Project BRAVO, we are through with Project BRAVO and its programs."[109] The audience at the meeting, including members of Smith's own staff, burst into applause. Smith notified the OEO regional office in Austin that Montelongo's attack "was a put up job" by Aguilar and the MACHOS staff, who clearly wanted "MACHOS to become the CAA for El Paso."[110] Considering the enthusiastic response to the attack, it was also clear that many involved in El Paso's War on Poverty agreed with Montelongo.

HOUSTON

As the sixth largest city in the nation and having a large population of poor blacks, Houston conformed to the type of urban complex the War on Poverty seemed best suited to serve. The record of the OEO in Houston, as in San Antonio and El Paso, featured a struggle between local government and civil rights organizations demanding that community action serve to enhance the political ascension of disadvantaged groups.

After two rejected proposals, the city received its first grant for program development and administration in fall 1965.[111] The city and county governments named their original CAP the Houston–Harris County Economic Opportunity Office (HHCEOO). To direct the program, the HHCEOO board of directors hired Charles R. Kelly, a minister and the head of a local civil rights organization called the Houston Council on Human Relations.[112] The HHCEOO opened its doors near the end of December 1965.[113] At the same time the city developed a second agency, Job Opportunities for Youth (JOY), to serve as the city's NYC delegate.[114] While JOY remained independent of the HHCEOO through its first full year, to cut administrative costs these two agencies fused in May 1967 to form the Houston–Harris County CAA (HCCAA). JOY then became Houston Action for Youth (HAY), a delegate agency of the HCCAA.[115]

Whatever the acronym, Houston developed the most expensive CAA in the state, spending nearly $4 million in fiscal year 1966 and more than $8 million in 1968. Once the HHCCAA was fully developed, the NYC and Head Start became by far its most expensive programs, taking up three-fifths of all costs. Other than administrative expenses, HAY, as the NYC delegate, remained the costliest HCCAA program.[116]

When the CAA finally began operation, advocates for Houston's black community had high hopes for the effort. The *Houston Informer* celebrated the beginning of the local War on Poverty as a sign of hope for the "poor and jobless."[117] The city government, especially Mayor Louis Welch, had relatively warm relations with black residents. As a city councilman, Welch endeared himself to the local African American community when he participated in a sit-in at the segregated cafeteria in city hall.[118] The mayor's reputation bolstered optimism within the black community that city hall could create an effective local War on Poverty effort.

Within a little more than a year of the CAA's opening, however, African Americans in Houston generally lost confidence in the local War on Poverty. The *Texas Observer* reported in 1967 that "it seems apparent that the Negroes in the poorest parts of town are feeling almost no impact of the effort; many of them say they haven't even heard of a poverty war."[119] Most black leaders in the city did not fault the OEO for the failures of community action in Houston. They placed blame squarely on the shoulders of the city's political leadership. The HCCAA focused its energies on providing temporary services to needy individuals rather than attacking the root causes of poverty. City hall apparently made the War on Poverty another cumbersome welfare bureaucracy that refused to acknowledge the need for institutional change. "The War on Poverty could be a way to channel the energies of Negroes," one HCCAA employee said, "but it would annoy the mayor and the city councilmen and eventually they'd have to admit that things have not been right here."[120] City hall, in other words, had no interest in using the War on Poverty to promote real social change.

The HCCAA did not, however, retreat from proactive involvement in the community merely because of some hidden agenda of the mayor and city council. The agency turned to a service orientation also because of conflicts with established civic organizations in the community. In 1967, for example, HCCAA workers sought to mobilize the low-income citizens of the Settegast neighborhood of Houston to protest alleged police brutality. The leaders of an extant organization in Settegast demanded that the HCCAA remove community action workers for attempting to organize the poor. As in many other cities, community action in Houston often failed when the antipoverty warriors sought to impose an agenda on low-income communities.[121]

Influential leaders within the black community in Houston expressed frustration with Welch and city government for the limitations of the War on Poverty. The Reverend William Lawson, a Baptist minister, explained to the *Texas Observer* that "part of [the problem] stems from the War on Poverty.

We say 'community action,' then they run up against city hall." Many within the black community in Houston, Lawson explained, considered the War on Poverty a "smokescreen" that camouflaged the unwillingness of the white establishment to promote any real social change.[122]

At the same time, Welch wrote Shriver to voice his "deep concerns" over the operation of CAP in Houston. The mayor accused OEO workers of deliberately trying to instigate violence and confrontation with local authorities. From Welch's point of view the OEO hired people who sought to change HAY into a program to train militant revolutionaries. To substantiate the claim the mayor quoted a criticism of the HCCAA staff from a HAY employee: "They are not intent on rapid social change and do not employ the concept of power in their social theory. Given the political structures of the day, their approach is of little significance in forming a larger power base for the poor." Extrapolating the HAY employee's comment to its highest possible extreme, the mayor said, "The most rapid social change is revolution." He asked Shriver, "Is revolution the goal of OEO?"[123]

In 1967 the HCCAA board fired another local minister, the Reverend Earl Allen, who had served as the agency's director of community development. According to the *Forward Times*, a competitor of the *Houston Informer* that tended to take a more militant stance on local issues, Allen and several other employees were dismissed because of their outspoken views and opposition to what they termed the "ineffectiveness" of the local War on Poverty program.[124] Allen then organized HOPE (Human, Organizational, Political, Economic) Development Inc., a biracial, independent antipoverty agency supported by local churches and contributors.[125] Only an independent agency like HOPE, Allen argued, "could effectively do the kind of job they were not allowed to do while employed for HCCAA."[126]

Allen sought to obtain federal funding for HOPE. The target population was "too poor to support their own families," and he argued that those who managed the HCCAA only obstructed the antipoverty effort in Houston's black community:

> The so-called white liberals and do-gooders . . . for the most part
> have continued to exploit the black man, economically, intellectually,
> and otherwise, while pretending to be working for his best interest.
> No organization, except one that is operated and supported by black
> people and completely free from outside pressures can be expected
> to work uncompromisingly toward the improvement of the black
> community.[127]

Allen argued that the only way to fight an effective War on Poverty was for liberal whites to "surrender control" of War on Poverty programs.

HOPE never gained federal funding, but Allen's call for an independent antipoverty campaign run by black people illustrates a trend that became the primary source of conflict over the War on Poverty in Texas. After the initial burst of optimism and enthusiasm, community leaders grew impatient with the War on Poverty. Local antipoverty activists increasingly came to demand that OEO-funded agencies be controlled from within low-income urban communities, not through local governments. The development of the Federation of Neighborhood Councils in San Antonio, of the Amigos de MACHOS in El Paso, and of HOPE in Houston all demonstrate that Mexican Americans and African Americans in Texas embraced the War on Poverty at the grassroots even as the OEO began to distance itself from the goal of maximum feasible participation.

Race Conflict and the
War on Poverty in Texas

SIX

On September 12, 1968, more than two thousand angry protesters marched through the narrow streets of downtown San Antonio to stage a demonstration at city hall. SANYO supporters staged the protest to compel the EODC to place control of funds for the Concentrated Employment Program (CEP), a new effort introduced by the OEO to bring jobs into low-income areas. Police and reporters stood by as speakers provoked "a super-charged emotional upheaval" of shaking fists and chants from the crowd.[1] The protesters, mostly Mexican American, endured the late-summer heat because they had grown impatient with the lack of nonwhite involvement in the administration of the local War on Poverty. Albert Peña brought the protest to a climax when he declared, "The city and the county should stay out of the poverty program and let the poor people run it . . . San Antonio will never be the same again. The people of the barrios and the ghettos have organized!"[2]

The local news emphasized the racially charged atmosphere of the demonstration, which featured Mexican American and black speakers "blasting the 'administration,' the Good Government League, and the white man in general for conducting a poverty program 'not aimed at helping poor folks.'"[3] Among those who addressed the crowd, local NAACP chapter president S. L. Deckard echoed Albert Peña's statement and added that "the Anglo built the ghetto and the Anglo maintains it . . . the black man and the Mexican have listened long enough to the white man telling them what to do. Tonight we are going to tell the white man what to do."[4]

The demonstration showed the new direction of the civil rights movement. Deckard's vow that blacks and Latinos would "tell the white man what to do" contrasted with the integrationist vision of Martin Luther King Jr., whose assassination five months earlier served to solidify what many already had decided—that minority groups needed power more than integration. The San Antonio demonstration in 1968 made clear another crucial factor—civil rights activists did not accept the colorblind conception of the War on Poverty that was a guiding principle of the OEO since 1964.

Peña's declaration that the "barrios and ghettos" had organized also disguised the tension that lay beneath the surface of black-Latino unity in American politics. In the late 1960s, an increasing proportion of the Latino population recognized that the values and the practical needs of their communities did not always mesh with those of blacks and indeed sometimes conflicted. Latino leaders took exception to the assumption that they had merely followed the lead of blacks in civil rights struggles. After all, *Delgado v. Bastrop* came before *Brown v. Board of Education*. Similarly, as the Latino population stood poised to surpass African Americans as the nation's largest minority, many black leaders came to view Latinos as a threat to their political agendas.

Historian Nicolas Vaca refers to the sixties as a time when Latino-black relations were viewed with "rose-colored lenses." The "Latinos and Blacks united against the 'white oppressor' perspective," Vaca concludes, "expressly swept any differences between the minorities under the rug."[5] The notion of unity between the nation's two largest minority groups continues to characterize the historical memory of the decade, yet tensions between the two groups even then were not far below the surface and occasionally came into the open. In Houston, electoral coalitions that brought Mexican Americans and African Americans into a unified coalition could have won citywide elections, but Mexican Americans tended to back white candidates. Curtis Graves, a black member of the state legislature, lost a 1969 mayoral election to incumbent Louis Welch largely because he won less than 27 percent of the Mexican American vote.[6]

As militant racial movements shifted the ideological bent of the civil rights movement away from the emphasis on integration toward one of self-determination and cultural identity, both black and Latino groups criticized the OEO's effort to portray the War on Poverty as a colorblind effort. Black and Latino leaders demanded control of local OEO programs within their own communities without interference from even well-intentioned outsiders.

Competition for OEO funding, in short, pitted groups within the liberal coalition against one another, injuring the spirit of consensus that ushered Johnson into the White House with such a spectacular margin in 1964.[7]

Indeed, race became a primary focus within the War on Poverty. For many Texans of all races, the term "poor" became almost synonymous with black or Mexican American. As OEO programs expanded in Texas, Mexican American leaders complained that the chronic poverty of the barrios was all but ignored due to the Johnson administration's overarching concern with black poverty. Although the OEO made special efforts to include Mexican Americans, such feelings of neglect remained and continued to inform attitudes toward the War on Poverty long after the OEO faded away. In major cities in the state, a similar pattern emerged in which the smaller minority, be it African Americans in San Antonio or Mexican Americans in Houston, complained of neglect from local CAPs that seemed focused on the concerns of the larger group.[8]

Meanwhile, low-income Anglo Texans did not engage in the War on Poverty for the most part. Whites stayed away from CAP and the Job Corps due to the association these programs had with minority groups. It was evident that local white political leaders in Texas refused to take advantage of the OEO despite the millions of available dollars. In VISTA, in contrast, the extent of white participation became a problem. The idealism and naïveté of the volunteers, mostly college-educated, middle-class whites, handicapped the program. With only a year to serve, the volunteers came into poor neighborhoods wanting to get things done fast but were largely ignorant of how life in the state's barrios and ghettos worked.

THE RETREAT FROM THE COLORBLIND AGENDA

OEO director Sargent Shriver and his staff continued their effort to disassociate the War on Poverty and the black civil rights movement. Despite the OEO's best efforts to present the War on Poverty as colorblind, both opponents and supporters continued to view it as a "help the blacks" program.[9] Indeed, many liberals came to consider an emphasis on black poverty necessary to shift the movement from civil rights to economic justice. Following the 1965 Watts riot in Los Angeles, Martin Luther King Jr. became convinced of the connections between joblessness, poverty, police brutality, and violence. The OEO stood as more or less the only agency with the resources to bankroll a national economic rights movement.[10] As economist Ben Seligman pointed out in 1968, "It would not be far off the mark to say that it was neces-sary to convert a civil rights movement into a War on Poverty."[11]

OEO policy cemented the association between the War on Poverty and black civil rights. To address complaints of discrimination in local programs, Shriver created an Office of Civil Rights, directed by Samuel Yette, a former *Ebony* magazine editor. Yette's appointment came, Shriver said, in response to "questions that have been raised in the press and elsewhere concerning equal employment in the OEO."[12] A year later Shriver appointed seven "civil rights coordinators" for each of the OEO regions. Gregorio Coronado, an attorney who served as the Equal Employment Opportunity Commission (EEOC) compliance officer in Lubbock, became the OEO civil rights coordinator for the Southwest regional office in Austin.[13] After Shriver appointed the regional coordinators, civil rights issues became central to OEO policy. Compliance with the Civil Rights Act and the inclusion of representatives of minority groups in proportion to each community's population had been a guideline for CAP development from the beginning. By 1966, however, the regional civil rights coordinators, who were responsible only to Shriver and Yette, could deny the approval or continuation of CAP grants if local organizations failed a "civil rights clearance."[14] With such policies in place, OEO assistant director Yarmolinsky later recalled, "by '65, '66, OEO was, if not a black, a very dark gray agency, and when we were putting it together it hadn't the faintest touch of gray tinge to it."[15]

Another reason the OEO was often considered a help-the-blacks program involved the agency's focus on urban poverty.[16] Although the Economic Opportunity Act was drafted before the Watts riot, a common assumption among contemporaries was that the OEO was targeted at urban blacks to prevent riots. Jerome Vacek of Navarro County Community Action com-plained to Senator Yarborough that his county's program and other rural programs in South Texas had been cast aside because of the fear of riots. Vacek informed Yarborough that rural War on Poverty activists "resent the use of [OEO funds] to cool demonstration in the hot cities . . . The big cities hog far more than their share of OEO funds."[17] In fairness to the OEO, the urban bias of War on Poverty funding had more to do with the limitations of Shriver's budget than with riot concerns. Big cities received more OEO funding because they had larger concentrations of poor citizens and because urban governments and organizations had the staff and expertise to develop CAAs.[18] Contemporaries, however, tended to blame the alleged black bias of the OEO for its urban emphasis.

The OEO staff continued to fight the perception of black bias throughout the decade. To further compensate for perceived racial bias, the OEO Office of Civil Rights required each regional office to submit a monthly "minority gap report" to the agency's headquarters in Washington. The report detailed how many members of minority groups worked for each regional office. By November 1968 the Southwest region employed 56 members of minority groups out of a total of 217 employees—23 African Americans, 28 Mexican Americans, 4 American Indians, and 1 "Oriental-American."[19] Bill Crook, the head of the OEO's Southwest regional office in Austin, recognized the political importance of including minorities in high-profile positions. In 1965 Crook hired minorities for his top two assistants. Crook hired an African American, Herbert Tyson, as deputy director and a Mexican American, Tom Robles, as regional CAP manager. Crook said hiring these two men "would fill our top three spots with an Anglo, Negro, and Mexican American . . . while this wouldn't be the most popular thing [in Texas], it is something that I would like to do."[20]

Job Corps administrators strove to overcome its image as a program geared only at blacks as well. On the OEO's 1967 newsletter list of "the ten biggest myths" about its work was the assumption that the "Job Corps serves only Negroes"; in fact 54 percent of participants were African American.[21] Because Americans in the 1960s associated the term "civil rights," as in the Office of Civil Rights, with blacks, Yette's assistant Harvey Friedman suggested changing the name of the Office of Civil Rights to dilute the association between the movement and the War on Poverty: "Due to the extreme hostility manifested in many southern communities by the words 'civil rights,' we [should] change the name of our office from civil rights to something less antagonistic, such as Division of Equal Opportunity."[22] Friedman's efforts notwithstanding, a bias toward African Americans remained a basic misconception of the OEO throughout its history.

MEXICAN AMERICANS AND THE "INSULT BY OMISSION"

Mexican Americans complained throughout the Johnson years of neglect from the Great Society in general and blamed much of this neglect on the administration's preoccupation with black poverty. When in the wake of riots in 1965 Johnson held a White House conference called "To Fulfill These Rights," the president extended no invitation to Mexican American groups. This "insult by omission" enraged Mexican American leaders.[23] In

March 1966 Mexican American leaders walked out of the EEOC meeting in Albuquerque, New Mexico, to protest this neglect. EEOC chairman Franklin Roosevelt Jr. organized the meeting specifically to discuss the commission's focus on job discrimination on blacks at the expense of Mexican Americans. When Roosevelt failed to attend, Bexar County Commissioner Albert Peña called for a boycott of the meeting. It came to an abrupt end because almost all of the invited delegates answered Peña's call.[24] The leaders of the walkout, in turn, sent a letter of protest to President Johnson. The letter accused the EEOC of "a total lack of interest and understanding of the problems facing six million Mexican Americans."[25]

The War on Poverty stood out as the facet of the Great Society that offered the least to Mexican Americans. Rudy Ramos, an attorney for the American GI Forum—an organization that had strongly supported Johnson—accused Shriver and the OEO staff of excluding Mexican Americans from administrative positions and of neglecting Mexican Americans in local programs. Ramos condemned the OEO for employing "only one Mexican American in OEO D.C. headquarters; no Mexican Americans in policy making functions, no Mexican Americans in Migrant branch, no Mexican Americans in Shriver's office."[26]

Hector García, a strong Johnson ally and a cofounder of the American GI Forum, complained to Shriver personally of a lack of Mexican American involvement in the CAP in Corpus Christi, García's hometown. García spoke for the Community Committee on Youth Education and Job Opportunities, which was formed to protest the lack of Mexican American representation on the Corpus Christi CAP board and staff. García complained to Shriver that while Mexican Americans comprised the vast majority of the poor population in Corpus Christi, Anglos heavily outnumbered Mexican Americans in CAP administrative positions and on the board of directors. Although "90 percent of people living in the target areas are Mexican Americans, most of whom don't speak English," he said, none of the administrative staff spoke Spanish. García asked the director, "Is this right in your opinion?"[27]

In response, CAP director Cecil Burney reported to Shriver that the board had difficulty finding Mexican American applicants with the experience and qualifications he sought. While Burney did not specify the qualifications he was seeking, he agreed that "preference should be given to residents of target areas which are predominately Mexican Americans."[28] He informed the OEO that he "violently" disagreed, however, with the practice of hiring "less qualified persons based on the color of their skin."[29] Shriver apparently agreed with García, forwarding his letter to the regional office with a handwritten note that said, "Garcia does make sense here. Can't we get more Mexican Americans in jobs of high visibility and power in [the Corpus Christi] CAP?"[30] García and other officials of the GI Forum continued throughout the decade to advocate more Mexican American employment in the OEO.[31]

To compensate for such neglect, OEO staff made an extra effort to include Mexican American civil rights organizations, especially the American GI Forum and LULAC, both of which traditionally allied with the Democratic Party. In the wake of the EEOC walkout in 1966, LULAC and the GI Forum became the only civil rights organizations in Texas to receive a direct grant from the OEO to run an antipoverty program. Project SER (Service, Employment, Redevelopment) began that summer with an OEO grant for $362,450 as a demonstration program under Jobs for Progress Inc., a nonprofit corporation run jointly in five states by LULAC and the GI Forum. Project SER offered job training, remedial education, English-language classes, and a "skills bank," a list of skilled Hispanic workers for employers.[32] LULAC and the American GI Forum billed SER as a program "for those in the Southwest who face unique problems largely because of cultural differences."[33] In Texas, SER opened job centers in Houston, Corpus Christi, El Paso, and San Antonio. The design of SER drew widespread applause. Labor Secretary Willard Wirtz praised SER as a "unique" program that blazed "new trails to full employment and higher earning power."[34] Ultimately, budget constraints disappointed SER supporters in LULAC and the GI Forum. The GI Forum passed a resolution in 1967 to withdraw support from SER because few "tangible efforts" had been made to implement the program.[35]

OEO officials made further efforts to compensate for the neglect of Mexican Americans. In response to the GI Forum's criticism of the OEO, for example, Shriver informed Rudy Ramos that six Mexican Americans worked in the Washington office and thirty-four worked in the regional office, including the Western regional director, Dan Luevano.[36] Bob Allen, the director of the Texas OEO, proclaimed in 1967 that Texas Mexican Americans had "not been neglected in the over-all effort to fight poverty."[37] To support this statement, Allen listed nearly $12 million in programs that specifically benefited Mexican Americans in Texas alone. Yet, considering the prevalence of poverty among Mexican Americans in the state and the $140 million the OEO spent in Texas by 1967,[38] only $12 million might have qualified as neglect.

The OEO's efforts failed to convince Mexican American leaders, many of whom continued to argue that their communities' needs were not being addressed adequately. More and more voices argued that the primary cause of this neglect was the OEO's focus on black poverty. Young activists coming out of the Chicano youth movement stood among the first to cite the OEO's inordinate emphasis on African Americans as the cause of the neglect. "Chicanos had high hopes," Rodolfo Acuña explains in *Occupied America*. "In the end they fared badly: [OEO] planners knew little about Chicanos, fitting most programs to preconceived needs of blacks."[39] José Angel Gutiérrez recalls in his autobiography, *The Making of a Chicano Militant*, that "the War on Poverty . . . was basically aimed at and geared toward blacks . . . [while] the rhetoric from Washington was that the war was for all people."[40] Gutiérrez recognized the irony of the War on Poverty's neglect of Mexican Americans in that LBJ had firsthand experience with Chicano poverty in South Texas. Despite this experience, Gutiérrez notes, Johnson "did little to incorporate our national community into his domestic policies."[41]

"MEXICAN VERSUS NEGRO APPROACHES" IN THE CAP

In CAPs on the local level, accusations of bias seemed to depend on which group had the larger low-income population. Just as the national Mexican American community accused the OEO of bias toward African Americans, in cities where Mexican Americans formed the largest proportion of the poor, African Americans accused the local CAA of bias toward Mexican Americans. Shirley Anderson, an anthropologist who lived in a low-income Mexican American neighborhood in Dallas in the early 1970s, recognized "Black and Chicano competition for power" as a basic handicap of the War on Poverty. Such competition, Anderson explained, created "conflict and factionalism within several agencies" that perpetuated a perception of OEO programs as "wasteful, inefficient, and 'dangerous.'"[42]

San Antonio, the first city in the state to get into the War on Poverty, illustrates this dynamic best. Despite the black-Latino unity displayed in the 1968 city hall protest, the conflict between the EODC and SANYO was primarily between Mexican Americans from the Federation of Neighborhood Councils and the city's Anglo establishment. Many within the city's African American community felt left out of the War on Poverty altogether.[43]

In early 1967 leaders from San Antonio's African American community successfully lobbied the EODC for the establishment of Project FREE (Family, Rehabilitation, Education, Employment), a delegate family-service agency for San Antonio's predominantly black east side. FREE functioned in a similar way to SANYO, but FREE activities placed greater emphasis on African American culture and specific needs of blacks. Although SANYO had operated on the east side of the city, African American leaders deemed a separate organization necessary because they sought to control antipoverty funding for their own neighborhood and SANYO was headquartered on the opposite side of town.[44] Project FREE director Charles W. Black, the pastor of Mount Zion Baptist Church, contended that blacks needed a separate agency to serve as "a protector of the Negro community in a city where the Mexican-American population was, by many standards, poorer but better organized and closer to the power structure."[45]

The Reverend Black accused Father Yanta of neglecting the needs of the east side.[46] Yanta, who had organized SANYO neighborhood centers on the east side and cooperated with other black leaders, criticized the EODC chairman, Pepe Lucero, for "[throwing] in his lot with Rev. Black and his black brothers" because FREE cost SANYO about $150,000 a year in funding from the OEO.[47] Although FREE never developed the political pull that characterized SANYO, an OEO inspection report indicated that competing "Mexican versus Negro approaches" to poverty debilitated the War on Poverty in San Antonio.[48] The rivalry over funding came to an end in 1969 when the OEO discontinued funding for Project FREE. Julian Rodriguez recalled that some tension remained between SANYO and African American leaders, but SANYO "worked well on the East Side."[49]

A similar pattern emerged in El Paso. That city's main CAA, Project BRAVO, focused on lowering dropout rates and youth crime in the barrios of the city's south end.[50] Through its Barrio Program, Project BRAVO ran a Head Start preschool, job training, and remedial literacy courses. Like the struggle between the EODC and SANYO, competition emerged between Project BRAVO, a service-oriented agency, and the more politically motivated community action group MACHOS.[51] As in San Antonio, El Paso's small black minority protested the neglect of their concerns by both agencies.

In March 1968 three African Americans who were either fired or refused employment in Project BRAVO's Barrio Program accused the CAA staff of discrimination. Executive director Fred Smith reported the case to the OEO in Austin. The regional office sent CAP inspectors to El Paso to investigate the accusations. While the inspectors found no hard evidence of discrimination, they reported to OEO that "there is *at least* covert discrimination against Negro employees."[52]

Black El Paso residents involved in the program argued that discrimination in Project BRAVO was obvious. One African American who worked for Project BRAVO as a barrio worker reported to the inspectors that "wherever possible, Negroes are excluded from employment and only enough Negroes

[are] employed to keep the Negro community mouth closed."[53] Robin Robin-son, a black retired Army officer, accused the Project BRAVO staff of "sys-tematic exclusion" of African Americans not only in employment but in CAP services.[54] Robinson argued that Project BRAVO only began to involve Afri-can Americans in the program either as employees or as clients when black leaders confronted the CAA in the local media. In all, ten African Americans who had been involved with Project BRAVO agreed that the CAA discrimi-nated against the black community.

Most agreed that the CAA had not "taken the initiative" to involve Afri-can Americans in the program.[55] The Reverend Albert Pitts, a prominent black community leader in El Paso, concluded that Project BRAVO was "de-signed to deal with Latin-Americans, with their special cultural differences and language barriers, who comprise most of the El Paso poor."[56] While the task would be more difficult because the African American population was scattered throughout the city, Pitts urged the agency to employ more black "barrio" leaders to reach out to African Americans.[57]

The patterns that emerged in San Antonio and El Paso also emerged in Houston with, as might be expected, the roles reversed between the city's mi-nority residents. Activists challenged the Harris County Community Action Agency for its failures to include black leaders in the distribution of OEO funds.[58] While conflicts between the city's black community and whites hin-dered the HCCAA's programs, Mexican American leaders in Houston ac-cused the HCCAA of neglect due to the agency's emphasis on black poverty. Although they represented a smaller minority with less political pull, Mexican American leaders demanded separate control of War on Poverty funds for their community.

Among civil rights organizations in Houston, none strove more diligently to gain a fair share of War on Poverty resources for Mexican Americans than the United Organizations Information Center (UOIC). The UOIC was formed to provide a "united front" for thirty-seven Mexican American organizations in Houston. The War on Poverty ranked among the highest priorities of the UOIC. Arnoldo De León notes that the organization led drives to improve employment and education but "most importantly" strove "to secure a share of the poverty program funds for the Mexican American neighborhoods."[59] UOIC leaders accused the HCCAA specifically of ignor-ing the needs of the barrios. A. D. Azios, a UOIC spokesperson, complained in 1968 to OEO regional director Walter Richter that the HCCAA developed "no tangible program" in Mexican American neighborhoods with high rates of unemployment. Azios concluded that Mexican Americans received only a "token program which is totally inadequate, unequal in its application, and completely discriminatory."[60]

Hector del Castillo, president of the Sembradores de Amistad (Sowers of Friendship), also accused the HCCAA of unfair transfers of funds from programs benefiting Mexican Americans.[61] The Sembradores de Amistad focused on providing educational financial aid to poor Mexican Americans in Houston.[62] Like many other such organizations in the state, the Sembradores considered the OEO a vital ally in struggles with local power structures. "We know that you have the interest of the Mexican American at heart," del Castillo reported to Richter, "[but] we also know that your wishes are not being carried out in Harris County."[63] He informed Richter that the HCCAA made an "arbitrary and capricious" transfer of $305,000 from a program for an impoverished barrio for "programs not related to the Mexican American community."[64]

The competition for OEO resources between black and Mexican Texans occurred elsewhere on the local level. In Los Angeles the two groups also competed for funds. Los Angeles–based organizations like the Mexican American Political Association (MAPA) complained to the OEO of bias because of all of the attention devoted to the black community following the Watts riot. Congressman Ed Roybal of East Los Angeles complained to the OEO that it seemed as if Mexican Americans would "have to riot to get attention" from the OEO.[65]

"NOT REACHING THE POOR WHITE"

Texans, like most southerners, had shown strong support for federal social programs since the New Deal.[66] Yet when the War on Poverty emerged, white Texans showed little interest although most poor Texans were white. OEO Southwest regional director Crook concluded that whites stayed away because of the association between federal welfare programs and minority groups. "WE ARE NOT REACHING THE POOR WHITE," Crook explained to Shriver in a 1966 report. "Many local communities are working on the assumption that once the program achieves a degree of success, the poor white will come in. This is, I think a false assumption [due to] the inability of the poor white to overcome his racial bias."[67]

Crook's statement reveals much about the deep association that had developed between race and federal antipoverty initiatives by the 1960s. Texans had ranked among the strongest supporters of the New Deal because millions of dollars came into the state while little money went out in taxes. Less than

1 percent of Texans paid federal income tax in the 1930s.[68] As the economy of the state improved dramatically after World War II, however, poverty became proportionately less common among whites, and tax rates rose along with incomes. Unlike those of the Depression era, federal programs now seemed to offer little to white Texans except higher taxes. Fewer whites needed assistance, but even those the War on Poverty might have helped proved reluctant because, as evident from Crook's assessment, poor whites did not want to associate themselves with programs that seemed targeted at minorities.

Some poor whites complained of neglect because of the OEO's presumed emphasis on black poverty. One Houston woman, Mrs. C. O. Wade, complained in a letter to Senator Yarborough and Congressman Bush that "the poverty programs—especially the HCCAA—discriminates against needy white people."[69] Wade, a disabled widow who lived on $71 per month from Social Security, had heard about projects in which volunteers helped poor people make home improvements. Her roof was falling in, but the HCCAA apparently ignored her requests for help. Bush informed her that the HCCAA had the materials and should repair her house, but she still did not receive any help. From her perspective, she was being discriminated against. "So far as I can find out," she explained to Yarborough, "none of L. B. Johnson's poverty programs, nor any of the Federal Welfare programs, includes help for needy white people."[70]

RACE ISSUES IN THE JOB CORPS AND VISTA

As with the CAP, race issues also led to controversy in the Job Corps and VISTA. White Texans who might have benefited from the Job Corps shied away from enrolling at Camp Gary, seemingly because the program had a reputation as a program for blacks. VISTA suffered from a similar problem, but instead of whites avoiding the program because it seemed designed for minorities, African Americans and Mexican Americans complained that VISTA was filled with white idealists who were ignorant of black or Latino culture.

For the OEO, the unpopularity of the Job Corps among whites was a product of the widespread perception that the "Job Corps serves only Negroes." To dispel the myth, OEO publicist Deborah Wagner explained that "approximately 50 percent of the Job Corps enrollees are white. This figure necessarily varies from day to day, as shown by the exact count in January [1967] which registered 54 percent of enrollees as Negro."[71] Another of the ten myths was that "young people in the Job Corps come from the criminal element of society. They have fights, they riot; they cause trouble in the community."[72]

While the majority of Job Corps enrollees had no criminal record, more than one in four had been arrested for "minor anti-social behavior," and 10 percent had at least one conviction.[73] The image of the Job Corps as a haven for "ghetto-hardened blacks," in Paul Conkin's words, made it a hard sell for many Texans regardless of the program's results.[74]

OEO marketing efforts emphasized racial integration in Job Corps centers as a benefit of the program. In 1965 Shriver touted the Job Corps as an example of how integrated educational facilities could work. "In the Job Corps," the director explained, "the experts said, 'you can't mix white boys from the rural south with Negroes from the northern city slums. Race riots will take place.' Well, once again the experts have been wrong. We've mixed [them] and we've not had one single incident of racial tension."[75] A pamphlet advertising the New Waverly center indicated that life in an integrated "group living" environment with "men of different ethnic groups" helped a corpsman become a more "well rounded citizen."[76]

As with other War on Poverty programs, a simple lack of white involvement perpetuated the perception of the Job Corps as a program for African Americans. Black corpsmen predominated because white youths showed less interest. When the Job Corps began to recruit enrollees, recruiters expressed dismay in their inability to attract whites. Approximately three hundred blacks attended the first Job Corps "recruitment experiment," held in December 1964 in Washington, D.C. Because of the demographics of Washington, the recruiters anticipated that African Americans would attend the meeting in far greater numbers but "did feel, however, that through mass media . . . we would be able to hit at least some white youth. Apparently our efforts were to no avail because there were no white adolescents in attendance."[77] Job Corps officials concluded that no whites attended because "it seems clear that white youths, unless under the guidance of some adult, will not attend a program in what is clearly perceived as someone else's 'turf.'"[78]

Ironically, although more than half of Job Corps enrollees were African American and it was viewed as a program targeted at blacks, white graduates gained more economic benefit from the program than black graduates because of continued discrimination in hiring practices. White Job Corps graduates received an average increase in annual earnings of more than 86 percent, compared to 71 percent for blacks. The unemployment rate among white Job Corps graduates stood at 5 percent less than among blacks who completed the program.[79]

OEO officials confronted a lack of white enrollment as a public relations problem for the Job Corps. In response to the preponderance of black applicants, in late 1964 Job Corps director Otis Singletary worried that "minorities becoming majorities in some (or all) of the Centers" would reinforce the unwanted public image of the program. Singletary determined to impose a racial quota because "the 'ghettoization' of centers will handicap recruiting of 'majorities,' and generally diminish the acceptance of our centers."[80]

To overcome "an environment which continues some ghetto racial patterns" in Job Corps centers, Singletary devised a plan to "keep racial balances in selection and assignments, and maintain proportions which approximate the racial proportions of the universe of potential Corpsmen." He intended to maintain racial balances in secret. He concluded that fixed racial ratios would draw criticism from civil rights groups, so he planned to use race information on application forms to divide black applicants among Job Corps centers. This "judicious use of existing, nondiscriminatory, geographic criteria," he argued, could "avoid many of the effects we fear." Singletary understood that "the plan won't stay secret [and] minority hostility toward it will grow with time." He sympathized with African Americans for the problems of discrimination but said the Job Corps would attract too much unfavorable attention from less sympathetic elements if blacks formed majorities in the centers.[81]

When Camp Gary first opened, its population very closely replicated, in Singletary's words, "the racial proportions of the universe of potential corpsmen." In 1965 whites formed 56 percent of enrollees at Gary. African Americans and Mexican Americans comprised 34 percent and 10 percent, respectively. As Gary enrollment grew, white enrollment decreased sharply. The proportion of blacks rose to 65 percent by 1968, and Mexican American participation rose to 18 percent of all enrollees. White enrollment in the same period declined to 14 percent.[82]

The development of the New Waverly Conservation Center provided an instructive example of how apprehensions about the target population of the War on Poverty informed opposition to the Job Corps in Texas. New Waverly, a small town north of Houston on the fringe of the Sam Houston National Forest, had a depressed economy because of shifts in the lumber industry and farming. Yet developers had high hopes for the future of the community as a suburban refuge for Houstonians weary of the troubles of urban life. When the OEO proposed opening a center in New Waverly, investors and community leaders worried that the presence of Job Corps trainees would hinder development. Luther E. Hall, a New Waverly resident who served as a spokesman for local developers, contacted every elected and appointed official involved with the OEO, including the governor and Shriver, to protest the New Waverly camp. Hall explained that his "potential customers are families moving out of Houston to escape congestion and life in close proximity to mal-adjusted people . . . WITHOUT THE INFLUX OF THESE FAMILIES, THAT AREA HAS NO ECONOMIC FUTURE. The establishment of this camp will infest the community with that very element of society from which the moving families are trying to escape."[83] Hall indicated that the mayor of New Waverly and the county judge were both "violently opposed to having the camp in the county."[84]

VISTA did not have the public relations problems that plagued the Job Corps, but the racial divide in VISTA was reversed. Most volunteers came from white, middle-class backgrounds but were tasked in low-income minority communities.[85] Armed for the most part with little more than liberal arts degrees, the young volunteers had nothing practical to offer the poor other than mounds of idealism and enthusiasm rooted in the New Left activist spirit of the 1960s.[86] Such volunteers often came into the program with lofty goals of making radical changes in low-income communities through direct action and grassroots organization. They hoped, it seemed, to replicate the hard-fought triumphs of the civil rights movement in a single year. As one observer noted, "Many VISTAs are naive dreamers who enter the program because they think they can accomplish something. Many picture themselves as a kind of knight in shining armor on a white horse going out to save the world."[87]

A stint in VISTA began with a six- to eight-week training regime designed to subdue the idealism and naïveté with which many volunteers entered the program. One volunteer recalled that "whatever grandiose expectations one might have had upon entering VISTA were dulled in training sessions."[88] Essentially the trainers informed the new recruits not to expect to create any dramatic changes as they faced intransigent local establishments and the entanglements of bureaucracy. Trainers prepared the volunteers for the likelihood that the poor themselves would present the greatest obstacle to their efforts. A VISTA trainer explained that his job "was to prepare them emotionally and mentally for their assignments" by diminishing any romantic notions the volunteers might have about low-income culture. The volunteers learned to expect "attempted sexual relations, sob stories, guilt trips, appeals for money, things which had little or no relation to their projects."[89] The training often proved impractical for volunteers' day-to-day tasks once they entered local projects, but most volunteers agreed that they needed the training to gain "confidence in your actual ability to live and work in poverty."[90]

VISTA established most of its projects in Texas in African American or Mexican American neighborhoods where residents were unaccustomed to seeing any whites on a regular basis, much less young white men and women going from door to door asking people to attend meetings. With only a year to accomplish something, the volunteers often sought to elicit action from people before they understood local conditions. Ed Idar of the American GI Forum from San Angelo recognized that the outsider status of volunteers fundamentally handicapped the program. Idar watched with dismay as the volunteers would "come to a neighborhood, hold a few meetings, and then want to march on city hall."[91]

Soon, the assistance of idealistic young whites would be less welcome as a militant phase of the civil rights movement engendered a new sense of independence among Mexican Americans and African Americans in Texas. While only a minority demanded Black Power or embraced Chicanismo, the impact of these movements on the War on Poverty illustrates the profound and long-lasting effects of racial nationalism on the culture and politics of the state. Minorities came to demand financial assistance from government and increasingly sought to control antipoverty funding for their own communities on their own terms.

The War on Poverty
and the Militants

SEVEN   *The OEO and the Chicano Movement*

The events of 1965 cast doubt on the substance of the liberal legislative accomplishments of 1964. The passage of the Civil Rights Act and the Economic Opportunity Act and Lyndon Johnson's electoral victory all seemed less substantive as Watts burned and Alabama state troopers beat young marchers at Selma. For those civil rights activists who would lead the militant phase of the civil rights movement after 1965, Selma and Watts were unsurprising evidence of the failure of the liberal agenda. That mounted police beat peaceful marchers in Selma proved that the Civil Rights Act had failed to vanquish racist violence. Similarly, the riot in Watts proved that the Economic Opportunity Act and the War on Poverty had done little to alleviate chronic urban poverty. For the militants, Lyndon Johnson was just another white politician, big on promises but unwilling to share power and unable to bring about any real change.

The perceived failures and limitations of Lyndon Johnson's liberalism created the conditions for the militants to move to the forefront of the civil rights movement. When Martin Luther King Jr. referred to a "marvelous new militancy" at the 1963 March on Washington, terms like "Chicano" and "Black Power" remained outside the national discourse on race and civil rights. Dynamic figures like Malcolm X and Reies López Tijerina were sources of inspiration, but the activists who would lead the Chicano and Black Power movements did not assert these labels into the national consciousness until 1966. That spring, Rodolfo "Corky" Gonzales, the founder of Denver's Crusade for Justice, began to use the term "Chicano" to describe the emerging militant ethos of the Mexican American civil rights movement.[1] It was in June 1966 that Stokely Carmichael emerged from the Greenwood, Mississippi, jail to make "Black Power" a national slogan.[2]

Even after the vocabulary of Chicanismo and Black Power became common, the specifics of the militant agenda remained unclear and continued to evolve into the 1970s. Some militant civil rights activists, influenced by New Left antiwar and anti-establishment activists coming off college campuses, came to admire and see socialism as a potential goal. In the later sixties, the Black Panthers began to embrace some aspects of Marxist ideology. Members of La Raza Unida Party, the political outgrowth of the Chicano youth movement, would visit Cuba for an audience with Fidel Castro in the early seventies. Yet few had the time to sit down and read Marx or Mao, and neither Chicanos nor the Black Power movement developed independent or fully articulated leftist programs.

Cultural pride was the most salient aspect of the militant ethos. The militants were the first to use the accoutrements of culture, in terms of language, art, dress, and music, to identify themselves. Pride in culture is significant because it led the militants to reject integration and assimilation as civil rights goals. The idea that ethnic minorities should eschew their own cultures to assimilate into the American mainstream required them to forgive and forget centuries of racial discrimination and abuse. Anger over this history and the chronic poverty it created motivated racial militancy in the sixties more than anything else.

As they matured and ideas gelled, Chicano and black militants moved beyond anger to develop more coherent sets of goals. Self-determination emerged as the fundamental aspect of the militant agenda. The time had come for them to take what they deserved without the acquiescence or even the help of whites, rejecting Dr. King's warning that civil rights activists could not "walk alone." Demands for self-determination were coupled, however, with demands for economic justice. This led the militants to view the War on Poverty as long-overdue recompense for centuries of racism and discrimination. As the militant ethos expanded in influence, Chicano and Black Power activists in cities across Texas laid claim to the OEO programs in their communities.

While most historical narratives about the civil rights movement suggest that Mexican Americans followed the lead of African Americans in civil rights activism, this was not the case in Texas. Mexican American leaders of the postwar era led the way in desegregation and political involvement. The same was the case among the militants, as Chicano nationalism emerged in Texas before the Black Power movement had a significant influence in the state.

As "poor" and "low-income" became almost synonymous with racial minorities in discussions about the War on Poverty in Texas, lower-income whites in the state were reluctant to identify themselves as poor or to become involved with OEO programs because of that association. But nonwhites also defined the OEO's maximum feasible participation mandate on racial terms. A suspicion of white paternalism and covert racism emerged among Mexican Americans in relation to government antipoverty schemes. This deep mistrust informed the relationship between Mexican Americans and white liberals before anyone used the term "Chicano" as a label for a movement. Some concluded that whites, no matter how genuine their intentions, could not comprehend the unique social and political values of the barrio. Moreover, because Mexican Americans had no way to distinguish friendly Anglos from unfriendly, racist *gringos*, whites could not be trusted with the administration of federal antipoverty dollars in Mexican American communities.

Yet the story is more complex than just mistrust between races or suspicions of white paternalism in the War on Poverty. The history of the relationship between the OEO in Texas and the Chicano youth movement demonstrates that the emergence of the militant ethos created a divide between the Chicanos and their predecessors in the Mexican American generation. Mexican American activists of the postwar era embraced integration and patriotism as the most prudent paths toward economic and political empowerment for Mexican Americans. For Chicanos integration meant forgetting the discrimination, abuse, and theft that had defined life for Mexicans in the United States, most of whom lived in territories seized from Mexico by military conquest. Furthermore, assimilation into the American mainstream meant abandoning Mexican culture. According to the view of history Chicanos developed, their ancestors had not voluntarily chosen to become Americans in the first place. Conflicts over OEO programs between Chicano activists and Mexican American liberals illustrate that the militant ethos was not simply racial but also ideological.

State politicians, both conservatives and liberals, worked to extricate the influence of Chicano militancy from the War on Poverty. Governor Preston Smith, who took over from Connally in 1969, shut down VISTA projects at the request of local officials concerned with militant involvement in the War on Poverty. Newly appointed OEO director Bertrand Harding—who served as director until March 1969, when he was replaced by Nixon appointee

Donald Rumsfeld—did not override the governor's veto, which suggests that the OEO had little interest in defending Chicanos, either.

CONFRONTING "GRINGO PSEUDOLIBERALS"

Central features of the militant ethos in regard to governmental antipoverty efforts included suspicions of white paternalism and a recognition of Anglo cultural insensitivity. No matter what whites' intentions, Chicanos concluded that Anglos could not overcome their inherent ethnocentrism. Native Texan Armando Rendon explained this sentiment well in *Chicano Manifesto*, singling out the OEO to exemplify the insult of white paternalism. From Rendon's perspective, the "gringo pseudoliberals and guilt ridden do-gooders" of the OEO attempted to solve the problems of the barrios with a complete disregard for the values of the culture. As an example Rendon described an encounter between OEO consultants and a Mexican American community group in an unnamed South Texas town. Such staff reviews of locally designed programs were common, but in this instance the OEO staffers insulted the local people because "only a handful of the audience understood the gringos [who were] so presumptive as to belittle their program but not even being able to do so in their own language." Rendon viewed the efforts of Anglo antipoverty workers as ultimately self-serving. "Chicanos will no longer permit their barrios to be used as laboratories," Rendon declared, "at least not by Anglo cientificos . . . at least not for free."[3] Rendon wrote *Chicano Manifesto* as the *movimiento* reached its crescendo in the early 1970s, but the evolution of this suspicion toward white welfare paternalism was evident in the OEO bureaucracy during the formative months of the Chicano movement.

In 1966 the OEO appointed Gregorio Coronado, a GI Forum representative from Lubbock, as the civil rights coordinator for the agency's Southwest regional office. Within a few weeks of his appointment, regional director Bill Crook accused Coronado of deliberately creating a "backlog" of CAP applications. Coronado seemed convinced that CAP applicants and the regional staff deliberately excluded Mexican Americans. Crook informed Yette that Coronado acted "with suspicion towards the office and everyone in it [as if] he is the only one standing between the minorities and a raw deal by OEO."[4] "Frankly," Crook complained to Shriver himself, "I resent the hell out of the suspicion that seems to be the basic premise for the operation of civil rights here."[5]

Other OEO officials confirmed Crook's assessment of Coronado. Aster Kirk, the deputy regional director, reported an attempt he made to discuss civil rights issues with the coordinator. Coronado refused to discuss it with

Anglo officials who "just don't understand the civil rights problems in Texas." Kirk said Coronado had "reservations regarding the commitment of the Southwest Region Staff . . . to the centrality of civil rights in our work [and] seems inclined to 'find' civil rights issues in policy."[6] Fred Baldwin from the OEO Office of Inspection was sent to Austin to investigate the matter. Baldwin explained in his report that Coronado assumed that the regional staff lacked concern for civil rights issues "when, in fact, the backgrounds of our people show the opposite."[7]

While Coronado created friction at the regional office, no individual in Texas protested the underrepresentation of Mexican Americans in War on Poverty programs more than his wife, Dominga. She proposed to solve the problem of white paternalism by placing Mexican Americans in positions of responsibility. In 1966 she served as chairperson of the War on Poverty Committee of the GI Forum in Lubbock. When the Lubbock County Community Action Board applied for a grant in late 1965, Mrs. Coronado politely asked Bill Crook to encourage the city board to include members of minority groups on the CAP board of directors.[8] By April 1966, her patience exhausted, Mrs. Coronado threatened to stage a major protest in Lubbock over the "UN-DEMOCRATIC" manner in which CAP developed its board of directors. She warned that a public demonstration remained the only weapon available to minority groups "as long as local groups are controlled by RACIST power structures, as is the regional office [of the OEO]." If the OEO took no action, she continued, then it would be up to "the politicians and power structures [to] explain to the Mexican-American boys fighting in Viet Nam why we are still discriminated against."[9]

Dominga Coronado requested that the Texas OEO hire a Mexican American person to run a regional office rumored to be opening in Lubbock. She complained to Governor Connally that "if a Mexican American is not placed in this office, then only the Power Structures will be advised again and again, and the poor Mexican American people will not be advised and consequently will not benefit."[10] Walter Richter, who at the time directed the state OEO, informed her that the governor had no plans to open a regional office but did name Joe Meador to act as a consultant for the Panhandle-Plains region. Richter said that while nine of twenty-one people in the state office were Mexican American, the Texas OEO had

not selected any staff people on the basis of race, but on qualifications, which must include a deep concern and compassion for the poor, whatever their race. I cannot believe that you subscribe, as your letter clearly suggests, that members of only one race are capable of carrying out the spirit and the letter of the Economic Opportunity Act.[11]

According to a report from CAP in Lubbock, the situation became "sticky" when both Coronados got involved. At a meeting of the Lubbock County Community Action Board, Mrs. Coronado stood up to harangue the board "when who should appear on the floor but Mr. Coronado from the Office of Economic Opportunity." Due to his position as an administrator with the OEO, the local officials in Lubbock felt that he "was attempting to destroy the confidence of the people . . . the implication being that we were misleading the people when we said that we were attempting to follow the instructions of the OEO." Dominga Coronado ended the rebuke with a comment that would have threatened local officials even in remote Lubbock: "You remember Watts, don't you?"[12]

OEO headquarters stepped in and silenced the Coronados. Bill Crook pleaded with Yette about the situation: "It seems that Mrs. Coronado WANTS a demonstration in Lubbock . . . I see no way for this office to escape involvement and embarrassment. Perhaps you are better at handling wives than I am. What do you suggest?"[13] Shriver ordered Yette to quiet the Coronados, especially Dominga: "Your man, Coronado, has got to keep his wife out of activities which impede our whole program state-wide. If he wants to continue this work, maybe he should leave us and do something else."[14] Yette had Mr. Coronado transferred to become the civil rights coordinator at the San Francisco Regional Office.[15] Dominga Coronado later became the national chairwoman of the American GI Forum Ladies Auxiliary and served as an adviser for the Job Corps women's program.[16]

While OEO officials managed to silence the Coronados, the language the couple used to protest the operation of the War on Poverty in Texas reveals the values of the Chicano movement as it began to take shape. Suspicions of white paternalism were obvious in the Coronados' complaints. The Coronados clearly believed that whites, regardless of their capabilities or sympathies for the poor, could not understand or effectively cope with the unique problems of Mexican American culture. They seemed convinced that whites systematically excluded Mexican Americans from OEO programs. Such suspicions would soon grow into explicit demands for control of War on Poverty programs in barrios and ghettos across the state. While only a minority of Mexican Americans in Texas identified themselves as "militant," the Chicano movement would shape the War on Poverty in Texas as the militants took the lead in civil rights activism across the state. At the same time, the War on Poverty helped shape the Chicano movement.

THE WAR ON POVERTY AND THE ORIGINS OF THE CHICANO MOVEMENT

Chicano militancy emerged in cities across the Southwest, but the primary centers of the movement included Denver, Los Angeles, and San Antonio. Small groups coalesced under the influence of the Black Power movement, the New Left coming out of the universities, and Marxist revolutionaries from Latin America. Some of the founders of the Chicano movement had been active in the leading student organizations of the decade—including Students for a Democratic Society (SDS) and the Student Non-violent Co-ordinating Committee. In Los Angeles budding Chicano activists formed the United Mexican American Students. Denver Chicanos formed the Crusade for Justice under Corky Gonzales. In Texas the Mexican American Youth Organization was formed by José Angel Gutiérrez, Mario Compean, and other college students in San Antonio.

The Chicano movement grew out of a long tradition of political activism among Mexican Americans. The cadre of leaders that preceded the Chicano movement, the Mexican American generation, made significant legal and po-litical strides. They had been active since the early twentieth century and accelerated their efforts in the postwar period through organizations such as the American GI Forum and LULAC. Before *Brown v. Board of Education*, the GI Forum and LULAC used the legal system to challenge the systematic dis-crimination and segregation Mexican Americans faced. Unlike black leaders, however, the Mexican American generation viewed the struggle as that of an immigrant group striving to integrate into the American mainstream. They encouraged their children to speak English and get college educations.[17] They were intensely patriotic and viewed military service as a masculine rite of pas-sage and a guarantor of inclusion in politics. The Mexican American genera-tion produced political figures of national significance, among them key allies of Lyndon Johnson like San Antonio Congressman Henry B. Gonzalez and Dr. Hector García of Corpus Christi, the leader of the American GI Forum. Johnson appointed García as an alternate ambassador to the United Nations, where he became the first American to address the General Assembly in a language other than English.

Yet the Mexican American experience differed from that of either immigrant groups or African Americans. Many had not descended from immigrants at all but from families with roots in Texas and the Southwest that predated the United States and even the arrival of Europeans. Gus García and other attorneys from the GI Forum and LULAC argued as much in the *Hernandez v. Texas* case before the U.S. Supreme Court in January 1954. Pedro Hernandez, a farm laborer from Edna in Jackson County, murdered his employer. The jury that tried him was all white. In his defense García argued that the systematic exclusion of persons of Spanish surname from juries throughout Texas violated the Fourteenth Amendment. García convinced the justices that Mexican Americans were "a class apart" from the biracial definition of the Fourteenth Amendment confirmed by the *Plessy v. Ferguson* case. Still unfamiliar to most Americans, the *Hernandez* case was a landmark decision that predated *Brown v. Board of Education*.[18]

Defining Mexican Americans as a "class apart" informed the development of Chicano identity in the sixties, but the militants stepped away from the Mexican American generation to redefine the Chicano relationship with the United States. Chicanos concluded that they had become Americans not by choice but through military conquest. Through generations they were denied civil rights, swindled or squeezed out of property, and brutalized by armed militias like the Texas Rangers. Furthermore, the war in Vietnam lacked the clear sense of "good versus evil" that defined historical memory of World War II. As more Mexican American boys came home in flag-draped coffins, the Chicanos could see no value in the sacrifice. An unwillingness to forgive injustices past and present and a deep sense of cultural pride motivated the young Chicanos in the sixties to abandon the integrationist ideals and American patriotism of the Mexican American generation.

Chicanos were inspired by what Ignacio García has called a "slightly new breed" of Mexican American political activist that came to the forefront of the movement in the early sixties.[19] Foremost among this new breed in Texas was Albert Peña, a Bexar County commissioner (1956–1972) who had served as a leader in the Viva Kennedy clubs that contributed decisively to the Democratic victory in the state in 1960. These political clubs in Texas organized into PASSO in 1961, with Peña as president. He had a confrontational, clamorous style that diverged from that of most public figures of the Mexican American generation. Along with PASSO executive secretary Albert Fuentes and the support of the Teamsters Union, Peña orchestrated the 1963 electoral takeover of Crystal City, presaging the political victories La Raza Unida would achieve in the early 1970s. As in many towns and cities in the border region of the state, impoverished Mexican Americans comprised the majority of the population, yet wealthy Anglos controlled the municipal government and the economy of Crystal City. PASSO put five Mexican Americans on the election slate for city council. When *los cinco candidatos* won the election it sent a "shockwave" through the state.[20]

Peña was a transitional figure in Texas politics. He remained loyal to the national Democratic Party of Lyndon Johnson even as Chicanos rejected LBJ and the liberals in the later 1960s. But Peña accused the state Democratic Party run by Governor Connally of racism and obstructionism. Peña was a leading figure in the insurgent liberal coalition of the state party, and the War on Poverty ranked among the coalition's highest priorities through the sixties.

As the War on Poverty assumed top priority for Mexican American political activists, civic-minded youth from across the state took advantage of employment offered by various OEO programs, especially the local CAPs. The OEO agencies that employed Mexican American young people showed a preference for college students as the most capable, most motivated, and most idealistic people available. While these qualities were a natural fit for the War on Poverty, these same young people often were drawn to militancy in the racial politics of the sixties. In his book on the Chicano movement, Carlos Muñoz explains that War on Poverty programs provided a "training ground" for future Chicano activists across the nation.[21] Prominent figures of the Chicano movement worked for OEO programs. Corky Gonzales directed the CAP in Denver and served on a national committee appointed by LBJ to develop War on Poverty programs for the special needs of the Southwest. Gonzales, who authored "Yo Soy Joaquin," a poem considered a manifesto of the Chicano movement, left the OEO in protest to create the independent Chicano group Crusade for Justice in 1966.[22]

In Texas several prominent figures in MAYO, among the most influential organizations of the Chicano movement, worked within War on Poverty programs. José Angel Gutiérrez, the most vocal and controversial member of MAYO, worked as a youth counselor in SANYO. Mario Compean, another founding member of MAYO, worked in VISTA. Ramsey Muñiz worked for the Model Cities Program in Waco. Muñiz became the first Mexican American to appear on the ballot for governor in Texas when he ran on the Raza Unida Party ticket in 1972. The party grew out of MAYO and became the most influential political product of the Chicano movement in Texas. The 6 percent of the vote that Muñiz took away from conservative Democrat Dolph Briscoe made Briscoe the first governor in the state's history to take office without an electoral majority.[23]

Working within CAP organizations gave young people valuable lessons in political organization and confrontation. CAPs developed methods for reaching out into neighborhoods to organize and get people involved. They often conflicted with local and state government over funding or strategy. For young assistants working within CAPs, even those not in leadership roles, the experience proved invaluable for future confrontations. Irma Mireles, who later became the director of the Mexican American Cultural Center in San Antonio, recalled that her experience with SANYO "opened my eyes . . . [to] how the politics worked . . . and gave me a sense of how people working together as a community can do something. It was the first time that I saw the Mexican Americans speaking out."[24]

Along with employment and lessons in political confrontation, OEO programs provided access to people. Gutiérrez recalled that many NYC enrollees "wanted to get involved [and] expressed frustration about political issues in school or the neighborhood and MAYO offered an outlet for that."[25] In his autobiography Gutiérrez explains that MAYO followed the example of other militant groups that had "infiltrated" War on Poverty programs and "used those structures and resources to expand their organizing." Gutiérrez recalled that "many future organizers for MAYO came from these NYC programs."[26]

MAYO leaders used VISTA to expand their organizing. When the OEO included VISTA in the War on Poverty, its resemblance to the Peace Corps faded as volunteers became involved in community political organizing.[27] While VISTA volunteers worked on infrastructure projects or taught basic literacy classes, they also emerged as "a dedicated cadre of antipoverty shock troops [and] a twenty-four-hour-a-day resource for community action efforts."[28]

Historian Ignacio García describes VISTA as crucial to the expansion of MAYO. VISTA provided MAYO with "a larger financial base," which assisted the organization's growth "from one chapter in San Antonio to more than thirty" by the end of the sixties. Mario Compean used his position as a recruiter and trainer for VISTA to expand MAYO. Thanks to VISTA, Compean explained, "MAYO had 200 people loose . . . We had a budget. We had salaries for people. We had transportation. We had telephones. We had travel monies. So consequently that really allowed MAYO to expand."[29]

MAYO was not the only Chicano organization to benefit from the OEO. In Wisconsin the OEO provided funding to United Migrant Opportunity Services Inc. (UMOS) to provide services to migrant families working near Milwaukee. UMOS was led by Genevieve Medina, a native of Crystal

City, Texas. Medina used the vehicle to organize and provide employment to Tejanos who had migrated to Wisconsin with their families. "The strong presence of Cristaleños and Texas Mexican youth activists," Marc Rodriguez explained, "primed the pump for Chicano control of UMOS as the Chicano Movement took hold."[30] In Los Angeles the OEO funded The East Los Angeles Community Union (TELACU). This agency emphasized economic development with a focus on services for women through the Chicana Action Services Center.[31] The OEO, in short, was crucial to the development of Chicano activism as it broadened into a national movement.

THE CHICANOS TAKE ON THE LIBERALS

War on Poverty programs facilitated Chicano organizations as the movement expanded through the later sixties, but the Chicanos nevertheless were dissatisfied with the OEO's efforts in the barrios, especially as most of the programs continued to be managed by whites. In San Antonio few questioned Father Yanta's importance to SANYO, but it was evident in the late 1960s that Chicano activists would no longer accept Yanta or anyone who was not Chicano as a leader on the west side. A charter member of the SANYO board of directors described this sentiment in an anonymous interview: "Father Yanta, with all due respect, was a *gringo*. At that time [we] couldn't see a *gringo* trying to be the great white pope of the Mexicanos. It wasn't said publicly. But privately, among some of us, there were those kind of remarks."[32]

As early as December 1966, however, an agency called the Inter Mexican American Association for Gainful Enterprise (IMAGE) publicly challenged SANYO's lack of Mexican American leadership. IMAGE leaders criticized Yanta for allegedly requiring his enrollees to speak English while participating in SANYO activities. When an IMAGE spokesperson informed the local media of the rule, Yanta countered that the rule had been approved by SANYO's founding board, which was 62 percent Mexican American. The same board eliminated the rule as impractical in August 1966.[33] Nevertheless, an IMAGE spokesperson declared that communications problems in SANYO were the result of a lack of Mexican American leadership:

> I think SANYO is sick because of its leadership—it lacks minority representation . . . We thought the War on Poverty was supposed to help the poor and the decisions would be left to the poor. But the big three of SANYO are all non-Mexican-American. We make a demand that ethnic and minority groups be placed on the policy making levels

of SANYO. None of the present leaders are identified with the people they serve.[34]

The IMAGE criticism angered Yanta. In a memorandum he titled "Enemies From Within," he complained to the archbishop that "the hypocrisy of this IMAGE gang is beyond me . . . this is the same crowd that calumniated Your Excellency both verbally and in print . . . and dispel hate for our great Congressman [Henry B. Gonzalez] . . . It's pretty difficult to defend liberal causes with jerks like these around!"[35]

Yanta sought to isolate SANYO from militant Chicano activists or "the people Henry B. [Gonzalez] calls 'professional Mexicans' [who] have been at odds with us because we've remained aloof and tried to get along with all groups."[36] In March 1970 Yanta fired nine counselors from SANYO who, according to an unnamed source in the *San Antonio Express*, had conspired to have all Anglo and black SANYO workers discharged. The source alleged that Yanta fired these nine "militant Chicano types" because they had staged a "sick-in" by refusing to come to work until their grievances were addressed.[37] The dismissed workers reported their problem to state Senator Joe Bernal, who addressed them to Monsignor Martin, the chancellor of the archdiocese. Bernal informed the chancellor that the counselors had been loyal to Yanta but felt that "counseling given to drop outs was not relevant or sensitive to the culture or situation of the youth involved."[38] Bernal indicated that while SANYO had "developed many admirable programs," it was "evident that some people within SANYO are not sensitive to and understanding of the cultural diversity within this community."[39] Bernal accused Yanta of allowing "little difference of opinion [while he ran] SANYO like a 'political machine' with very tight control from the top."[40] In the end Rodriguez invited the fired counselors to have a hearing with Yanta and the archbishop, but the group refused further negotiations.[41]

The Chicanos sought to exclude not only whites but also Mexican Americans who did not embrace the racial ideology of the movement. Mexican American officials who seemed like puppets for Anglos became targets of criticism as the Chicano movement grew in influence. In San Antonio the local community action board appointed José "Pepe" Lucero as the executive director of the EODC, the city's primary CAP. Although Lucero tangled with Father Yanta of SANYO over funding, residents of the city's barrios widely considered him a "Tío Tomás" for his attempts to subdue SANYO's political influence in the city, seemingly at the behest of the city's Anglo-dominated political establishment.[42] In El Paso the local CAP, Project BRAVO, appointed a Mexican American director named Saul Paredes as chairman of the CAP board of directors. Local Chicano leaders likewise considered Paredes a "Tom."[43] At one point Paredes forbade Project BRAVO staff from wearing pin-on buttons that read "Mexican Liberation."[44] The regional office of the OEO informed Paredes that he could not force employees to remove the buttons, but his aversion to the message illustrates a divide that the ideology of the Chicano movement created within the Mexican American community.

The Chicanos also accused the OEO of tokenism or cronyism in reference to those Mexican Americans the OEO employed. Gutiérrez described Mexican Americans employed by the OEO as "token Mexicans" who were for the most part close allies of the Johnson administration.[45]

The clash between the Chicanos and the liberals climaxed in October 1967 when Chicano leaders staged a series of protests in El Paso during a summit of Lyndon Johnson, Mexican President Gustavo Díaz Ordaz, and Texas Governor John Connally. The purpose of the visit was to return to Mexico a six-hundred-acre strip of land along the Rio Grande called the Chamizal Territory. Mexico had disputed the American claim to the land since the late nineteenth century, when the Chamizal shifted away from the Mexican side of the border with the currents of the river. The protests that coincided with the Chamizal summit illustrate the Chicanos' outrage and disappointment at the failures of Johnson's agenda. Gutiérrez explains in his autobiography that "the virtual exclusion of Chicanos in the developing of War on Poverty programs" stood out as a primary complaint voiced by the activists who had gathered in El Paso.[46]

Johnson was reluctant to attend the summit because of the bad press that would accompany the protests, but his Mexican American allies convinced him to attend to shore up his political relationship with the Mexican American community. At the urging of his Mexican American allies, Johnson created the cabinet-level Interagency Committee on Mexican American Affairs. To head the committee the president appointed Vicente Ximenes, a pioneering civil rights activist from the American GI Forum and a longtime ally of Johnson who was already working with the White House as a member of the EEOC. Ximenes organized a series of cabinet committee hearings on Mexican American affairs to coincide with the Díaz Ordaz visit.[47]

The emerging leadership of the *movimiento* organized a protest and a rump conference in El Paso through the same weekend. Chicanos and Chicanas lined the streets of the city to shout at the presidents' motorcade. They shook picket signs with angry slogans in English and Spanish like "TODAY WE PROTEST, TOMORROW, REVOLUTION!" and "Don't Ask Rich Mexicans to Talk for the Poor."[48] It must have been difficult for LBJ to maintain his composure. The Mexican president probably sympathized with Johnson. After all, Díaz Ordaz had radicals of his own to deal with in Mexico. Governor Connally would have been accustomed to angry shouts in Spanish by late 1967. Johnson, on the other hand, considered himself a friend to Mexican Americans. Yet there he was, riding in a limousine with the president of Mexico, on his way to a conference on Mexican American affairs planned by his Mexican American friend, while scores of angry young Chicanos jeered at his motorcade as it passed through El Paso.

Ximenes actually invited many of those among the protesters to attend the conference. Movement leaders considered Ximenes one of the administration's token Mexicans who seemed to be the "Chicano destined for all appointments" due to his ties to LBJ.[49] Most of the Chicano activists refused the invitation, believing that a boycott of the conference would send the clearest message to Johnson. MAYO leader Gutiérrez convinced Chicano leaders to hold the rump conference. They enlisted local Catholic clergy who opened the doors of the Sacred Heart Church in El Segundo Barrio for the protesters. It was in the dim light of the old church that the leadership of the Chicano movement first agreed on the term "La Raza Unida" to label the political and cultural objectives of their movement.[50]

THE MILITANT MESSAGE AND OPPOSITION TO THE WAR ON POVERTY

Chicano leaders, like Black Power activists, recognized that the fear of violence was a source of strength for their movement. MAYO leader Gutiérrez came under attack from the press in April 1969 when he delivered his notorious "eliminate the gringo" speech. What Gutiérrez said remains controversial, but he explained his statement in an interview with *San Antonio Express* reporter Kemper Diehl:

> You can eliminate an individual in various ways. You can certainly kill him, but that is not our intent at the moment. You can remove the basis of support that he operates from, be it economic, political, or social. That is what we intend to do.[51]

The exchange between Gutiérrez and the reporter is instructive. Diehl pressed Gutiérrez to clarify the statement: "If nothing else works, you are going to kill all the gringos?" Gutiérrez replied, "We will have to find out if nothing else will work." Diehl asked again, "And then you are going to kill us all?" Gutiérrez repeated, "If it doesn't work, I would like to add to you that if you label yourself a gringo then you are one of the enemy."[52]

Gutiérrez' responses to Diehl's questions were purposeful. Regardless of how Gutiérrez qualified his statement, Ignacio García contends that "for Anglo-Americans the words 'eliminate the gringo' would be all that they remembered, and so would most of the more angry Chicanos in the barrio. For Gutiérrez, the ambiguity and individual interpretations served the cause well."[53] Although Gutiérrez was careful to explain that any violence by Chicanos "would be self defense," he understood that removing the possibility of violence from the discussion weakened their position. The threat of physical violence captured attention and provoked demands for an immediate response to a greater extent than the nonviolent tactics of the early civil rights movement did. The implicit violence in the militant message, however, created a problem for the OEO in Texas because some of these militant organizations were connected to the War on Poverty.

Indeed, OEO administrators made some effort to include the militant movements in individual programs. In Texas one of the most controversial agencies the OEO funded was the VISTA Minority Mobilization Program (MMP). The MMP was the brainchild of Mexican American activists Gonzalo Barrientos and José Urriegas.[54] The two proposed MMP to VISTA because they "watched well-intentioned volunteers from outside Texas spend their whole VISTA stint trying to learn the barrio culture while, at the same time, people in those neighborhoods searched desperately for employment."[55] To avoid this paradox, Urriegas and Barrientos suggested that VISTA recruit local residents, give them a short course in VISTA tactics, and put them to work in community organizing.[56] To get the program off the ground, the two lobbied the Texas OEO through state Senator Bernal.[57] With Bernal's support the MMP enrolled fifty-five ten-week volunteers and eighteen one-year volunteers by the end of 1968.[58]

MAYO depended heavily on VISTA for financial support, and at the same time, MAYO's agenda had a fundamental influence over the activities of the MMP volunteers. Along with teaching volunteers the basics of VISTA community organizing, MMP trainers like Compean placed special emphasis on building an appreciation for Chicano heritage.[59] Compean stressed confrontational political tactics similar to those employed in the earlier black civil rights movement but "foregoing the use of nice language."[60] As VISTA volunteers, MAYO members targeted the youth of the barrios especially, emphasizing the need for young activists to polarize communities over issues between Anglos and Chicanos.[61]

To this end, VISTA/MMP volunteers became involved in one of the primary tactics of Chicano activists—the school walkout. Through the late 1960s and early 1970s Chicano groups staged school walkouts, often called "blowouts," throughout the state.[62] In cities across South Texas, Mexican Americans students in public schools boycotted classes to protest the Anglo cultural bias of the curriculum. The blowouts focused attention on the idea that high Mexican American dropout rates resulted from curricula that assumed English proficiency and placed no value on understanding Chicano culture.

While MAYO and other Chicano organizations led numerous school boycotts across the nation in the 1960s and early 1970s, MMP volunteers led by Urriegas backed a school walkout of the Edcouch-Elsa Independent School District in Hidalgo County. Urged by the MMP and MAYO activists, student leaders demanded that the district add Spanish-language instruction and other Chicano-related material to the curriculum. They sued the district for $50,000 in miscellaneous damages. The district administration simply expelled the students who organized the walkout. Federal Judge Reynaldo Garza, a Kennedy appointee and longtime ally of Lyndon Johnson, rejected the students' suit. Garza called the whole walkout concept "ridiculous" but ordered the district to readmit the expelled students.[63] Students reported that VISTA volunteers offered to finance the school strike and attorneys' fees through the OEO's legal services branch. VISTA helped students prepare a list of demands and facilitated the printing of flyers and petitions.[64]

In San Antonio, the SANYO-backed Federation of Neighborhood Councils sponsored a thirty-person VISTA project using MMP and regular VISTA volunteers. The regular VISTA volunteers, who came to San Antonio from all over the country, evidently approved of the MMP effort. Jeff Stromer, a volunteer from New York, said, "MM's have a great awareness of poverty and can work more easily with the people" than non-Chicanos could.[65] The MMP influence over the San Antonio VISTA project involved placing a greater emphasis on teaching barrio children about Mexican art and culture. MMP volunteers spent more time in the neighborhoods informing residents about the availability of services or trying to get them involved in community activities.

The MMP program in San Antonio generated controversy when volunteers became "deeply involved in organizing neighborhood residents to win decision-making power in agencies and programs that directly affect them."[66]

VISTA volunteers mobilized residents to oppose an amendment to the Texas Constitution that would place a cap on individual welfare assistance.[67] The cultural message of volunteers influenced by the Chicano movement drew the most vociferous opposition to the MMP in San Antonio. Local politicians accused MMP volunteers of distributing "hate gringo" literature in the barrios.

Such accusations and the implied threat of violence created opposition to VISTA programs associated with the Chicano movement. In March 1969 newly elected Governor Preston Smith, a conservative Democrat, closed the VISTA project in Val Verde County because county commissioners blamed the volunteers for initiating a protest rally over police brutality and for "fomenting racial tension."[68] The governor went further, ordering the VISTA volunteers to leave Val Verde County and mobilizing state troopers armed with machine guns to squelch the protests.[69] Smith ordered the cancellation of the VISTA program despite objections from the Del Rio CAA and the OEO regional office in Austin. He declared that "the abdication of respect for law and order, disruption of democratic processes, and provocation of disunity among our citizens will not be tolerated."[70]

With the cancellation of the VISTA project in Val Verde County, Governor Smith unwittingly provided the inspiration for one of the major protest events of the Chicano movement. More than two thousand activists from all over the Southwest descended on Del Rio with the hope of instigating a "Chicano Selma" to reveal Anglo racism against Mexican Americans to the rest of the country.[71] Although Governor Smith avoided a violent confrontation, the protests generated one of the fundamental statements of principle to emerge from the Chicano Movement—the Del Rio Manifesto. It accused the county commissioners and the governor of shutting down the VISTA program because "nervous power-wielders [saw] the growing assertiveness of the poor served by VISTA Mexican Americans as a threat to their traditional supremacy."[72] The manifesto condemned the entire "Anglo-controlled establishment" for waging a war of cultural genocide on the Chicano people:

> There must be something invincible in our people that has kept alive our humanity in spite of a system bent on suppressing our difference and rewarding our conformity . . . in a color mad society, the sin of our coloration can be expiated only by exceptional achievement and successful imitation of the white man who controls every institution of society. La Raza condemns such a system as racist, pagan, and ultimately self destructive. We can neither tolerate it nor be part of it.[73]

The Del Rio Manifesto further expressed the racial "magnificence of La Raza" as a "spiritual and biological miracle" and the centrality of Spanish language to the survival of Chicano culture. Few public statements provide a better summation of the spirit of militant Chicano nationalism. The manifesto concluded with a warning to the governor and the county commissioners that they were "inviting serious social unrest if they do not immediately rescind their VISTA cancellation." After reading the manifesto to a crowd of protesters, MAYO leader Gutiérrez symbolically nailed it to the courthouse door.[74]

The Del Rio Manifesto indicates that Chicano activists had embraced the War on Poverty but understood that local and state officials provided the greatest obstacle to the realization of maximum feasible participation. The manifesto concluded that the power of "arbitrary termination by local and state officials" offended the "VISTA principle of self-determination."[75] It called for legislation to protect the VISTA/MMP program because "unless the ideal of self-determination is upheld with our poor at home, the entire world will judge us as hypocritical in our attempt to assist the poor abroad."[76] Despite the protests and the manifesto, however, the OEO regional office did not reestablish the Val Verde County MMP program.[77]

OEO director Bertrand Harding, who replaced Shriver in 1968, could have overridden Smith's veto and continued the project. The fact that he stood aside while the governor shut down VISTA in Val Verde County suggests either a change in policy at OEO headquarters or an unwillingness to defend a program run by militant civil rights activists. Harding's inaction foreshadowed the direction the agency would take during the Nixon administration.

Governor Smith's closing of the VISTA program in Val Verde County was in keeping with the attitude of the conservative Democratic establishment in the state toward antipoverty policy and civil rights protests. Chicano involvement with VISTA came under attack from Representative Henry B. Gonzalez, a central figure in the state's liberal coalition. An aide to Gonzalez considered the MMP "a special headache because lots of kids who later became Hispanic radicals in the late sixties were involved in those programs."[78] The conflict between Gonzalez and MAYO over VISTA illustrates the broader tension between the younger generation of Chicano militants and the Mexican American generation that came of age during the Depression and World War II.[79] It is also possible that the congressman viewed the Chicano leadership as a threat to the liberal coalition upon which he depended in the San Antonio area. Gutiérrez said Gonzalez ran the Democratic Party in San Antonio like a machine politician who had little patience with "the indigenous leadership" of the rising Chicano youth movement.[80] Gonzalez, in turn, referred to MAYO. leaders as "brown thugs" who styled their organization "as the embodiment of good and the Anglo-American as the incarnation of evil. That is not merely racist, it is drawing fire from the deepest wellsprings of hate."[81] Gonzalez contended that MAYO leaders were "really advocating violence" because occasional statements by group members called on Chicanos to "eliminate the gringo."[82] When Gonzalez complained about the connections between the VISTA/MMP program and MAYO, a "fierce hassle" ensued that ended in the dismissal of two MMP volunteers in San Antonio.[83]

The strong reaction of Gonzalez toward the MMP suggests that the issue was not simply racial. Gonzalez was a Mexican American politician with a track record as a forceful proponent of civil rights. He quit his first job out of law school as a probation officer in Bexar County because the judge for whom he worked refused to pay black staff members the same as whites.[84] Gonzalez said he was accused of being a "Communist" and a "nigger lover" for his civil rights stance. But the Chicanos considered Gonzalez one of the liberal establishment's token Mexicans. José Angel Gutiérrez condemned Gonzalez:

> Henry B. had made it a lifetime goal to nip incipient Mexican American leadership in the bud. He was against PASSO and against lowering the voting age to 18. Later in the decade he would be against the formation of the Mexican American Legal Defense and Education Fund, against the extension of the Voting Rights Act to cover Texas, against MAYO, against our school walkouts, against everything that was to empower us during the Chicano movement. Henry B. made it safe for the gringo racist to be against us. He was their couch to sit on.[85]

Gutiérrez argued that Gonzalez was simply protecting his turf, that he did not want any political competition coming from the "indigenous leadership" of the Mexican American community.[86]

It is clear, however, that Gonzalez also rejected the racial nationalism that was the foundation of the Chicano movement. Gonzalez minced no words in denouncing MAYO's *malo gringo* stance as "reverse racism":

> This new dogma is just as fantastic as the old cries about "Wall Street imperialists" of years back, and as xenophobic as the know-nothings of a century gone by. It is as evil as the deadly hatred of the NAZI's, and as terrible in its implications as the rantings of demagogues warning against the "mongrelization of the races" by white supremacists.[87]

Gonzalez continued to embrace the patriotic ideals of the Mexican American generation. "I cannot find evidence that there is any country in the world that matches the progress of this one," the congressman argued. "For all our inequity, all our admitted failings, for all the urgent unmet needs, this country is the living embodiment of a revolution that the so-called militants only play at."[88]

Gonzalez overreacted to the Chicanos who were, after all, angry young people in a time of angry young people. The leaders of MAYO had neither the capabilities nor any real intention to eliminate the gringo through violence. Chicano organizations even had a record of working with sympathetic whites who embraced the militant message and employed militant tactics. Marc Rodriguez found in his study of the migrant communities in Texas and Wisconsin that the

> Chicano movement was in fact a movement made of Mexican Americans and other citizens who sought to improve the lives of poor people, workers, and minorities. In contrast to much of the literature on the Chicano Movement of the 1960s, the movement brought together like-minded Anglos, African Americans, and others with the great variety of *meztizo*, or mixed ancestry people, that made up the Mexican American population.[89]

In Laredo two white VISTA volunteers named Neil Birnbaum and Doug Ruhe employed the language and the tactics of the Chicano movement in forming Volunteers in Direct Action (VIDA) in 1967. VIDA organized pickets of local businesses that refused to raise wages to the $1.25 minimum demanded during the 1966 Labor Day march in Laredo. Rumors spread that VIDA intended to "turn the march into a bloody riot and they were going to burn cars." VISTA regional director James Cox fired both volunteers when Governor Connally threatened to close all VISTA programs in Texas if volunteers continued to "rock the boat."[90] Cox fired Birnbaum and Ruhe for their "irresponsibility and immaturity," but Ruhe argued that they were fired for "doing their jobs to effectively and overtly" after Cox urged them to "stay in the background." Ruhe accused officials at the regional office of greenlighting the development of VIDA as a "clandestine operation [but] suggested a covert strategy to protect themselves and their precious jobs." Despite being fired, Ruhe and Birnbaum vowed to stay in Laredo; they declared, "We will not be frightened away by Laredo politicians, bureaucrats, slave wage employers, or any other *patrones. Viva la justicia! Viva la causa!*"[91]

Representative Gonzalez' attacks on the Chicanos and the firing of Ruhe and Birnbaum suggest that the growing influence of the militant ethos generated a reaction that went beyond the defense of white supremacy. Ruhe and Birnbaum were fired by fellow whites for imitating Chicano militants. Gonzalez attacked fellow Mexican Americans for their militant rhetoric. Conflicts over militant involvement in War on Poverty programs were rifts over racial ideology, not just a continuation of the drive to overcome white supremacy. Neither conservatives like Connally nor liberals like Gonzalez had patience for militants using federal money to fuel protests, especially when the militants' angry talk reflected a basic disdain for American values. While only a few programs in the state had any association with Chicano radicals, these few examples provided ample ammunition for OEO opponents to challenge the agency. The OEO would be further handicapped by its association with militant groups as rioting became routine in American cities every summer through the latter half of the 1960s.

A "Preventative Force"?

E I G H T　　　　*Urban Violence, Black Power, and the OEO*

The Black Power movement did not develop as extensive an organizational base in Texas as did the Chicanos with MAYO. Black Power nevertheless paralleled the Chicano movement in the state. Young people came under the influence of national leaders like Stokely Carmichael, who rejected integration as a goal when he assumed leadership of the Student Non-violent Coordinating Committee in 1966. The only black Texan to gain national recognition within the movement was Bobby Seale, who grew up in various Texas cities as his father, a single parent of three children, moved frequently to look for work. Seale came of age in Oakland, California, where he helped create the Black Panther Party (BPP). Carl Hampton, a Black Panther organizer originally from Houston, returned to his hometown from Oakland to open a Houston chapter of the Panthers. Unable to get an endorsement from the national Black Panthers, in 1969 Hampton instead formed the largest militant organization in the state, the People's Party II (the first people's party being the BPP). Like the Panthers, the People's Party II focused on teaching self-defense, confronting police brutality, and providing services to the poor such as food and clothing. The Houston Police killed Hampton in a 1970 shootout in the city's Third Ward.[1]

The incendiary rhetoric of Black Power leaders linked the movement to the rioting that Americans came to expect during summers in the late sixties. In turn, opposition to War on Poverty programs in cities with large African American populations became entwined with the fear of urban violence that hung heavily over American cities through the 1960s. In Houston, as in many other cities nationwide, critics of the War on Poverty accused the OEO of condoning or creating the conditions for rioting.

As he had with the Chicanos, Governor Preston Smith used his veto authority to extricate the influence of the Black Power movement from the War on Poverty. In Marshall, Smith shut down a VISTA program in the summer of 1969 for printing a newsletter that featured Black Power slogans and messages. Donald Rumsfeld, as OEO director, took no action to override the governor's veto or reinstate the VISTA project in Marshall. Following the Del Rio protests and the Marshall incident, VISTA officials hesitated to begin new projects in Texas during Smith's tenure as governor for fear he would shut them down too.

Fears and threats of violence plagued the Job Corps, which had ranked among the most popular OEO programs from its inception. The OEO seemingly created a prisonlike atmosphere at the Camp Gary Job Corps center in San Marcos. Official reports from Camp Gary featured accounts of violence and gang activity. Because so few whites showed interest in the program, African Americans formed a majority of Job Corpsmen at the camp. Camp Gary thereby received criticism from whites in San Marcos who viewed the corpsmen with suspicion and African Americans who came to view the Job Corps as more or less a device to get young black men off the streets.

Unable to shake the association between the War on Poverty and the violence that plagued black communities, OEO officials attempted to use fears of urban violence to justify the antipoverty effort. Under attack by local officials who considered the War on Poverty the cause of urban unrest, OEO officials in Washington and at the regional office in Austin defended and promoted CAP and the Job Corps as riot-prevention measures. This effort triggered reactions from the black community that antipoverty programs should not be targeted at rioting but at poverty. It also upset rural Texans involved in the antipoverty fight who accused the OEO of an urban bias in its effort to end the rioting. Critics discovered that a small number of OEO employees actually participated in the rioting, providing more ammunition to those looking for reasons to blame the War on Poverty for the violence.

BLACK POWER AND THE FEAR OF URBAN VIOLENCE IN HOUSTON

Tension between police and minority groups remained high in Texas cities throughout the sixties, but open violence erupted only in Houston. The threat of rioting was a central concern in Houston throughout the 1960s. Following the Watts riot, Houston Mayor Louis Welch refused to admit that violent outbursts like the Watts riot posed a threat in Houston until local sociologist Blair Justice informed him that the underlying causes of urban violence in other American cities pervaded Houston.[2] Justice, whom the mayor hired as an adviser, spent the summer of 1965 discussing the issue with residents of the city's ghettos and "had come face to face with people in Houston who felt that rioting was the only way to stimulate action." By 1966 Mayor Welch had come around to Justice's point of view that it seemed "clear that the biggest issue in the minds of people, both black and white, was violence."[3]

OEO officials recognized the potential for rioting in Texas. Houston stood on the top of the regional office's list of worries. "I am especially concerned about Houston," Bill Crook explained to Sargent Shriver in 1966. "I am told there will be no [NYC] money available for that city. I consider it extremely important that special attention be given to Houston and that as many kids be tied down by employment as possible."[4] As Southwest regional director of the OEO, Crook conducted a "study of potential 'summer tensions'" in the major cities within the region.[5] To help pacify potential rioters, Crook organized an agreement between CAA directors "in case trouble erupts."[6] Each director agreed to send resources and personnel to help cool tensions if any violence occurred.

The epicenter of urban violence in Houston was the Third Ward, home to Texas Southern University. TSU was established in 1947 by the state legislature in an attempt to obstruct the integration required by the Supreme Court's decision in the *Sweatt v. Painter* case.[7] Few institutions in the state benefited from the War on Poverty as much as TSU. Among Texas universities TSU ranked behind only Prairie View A&M, another historically black college, in total OEO funds spent. In 1966 the OEO provided TSU students with $131,622 for a work-study project, $74,420 for high school teacher training classes, and more than $540,000 for pre-college and high school seniors' college preparation programs. In contrast, students at the much larger University of Texas received a bit more than $185,000 for all OEO-sponsored programs.[8] TSU had long been a center for civil rights activism in the city. As the focus of the civil rights movement changed after 1966, TSU students got swept up in the Black Power fervor.

In April 1967 the Friends of SNCC, a local affiliate of the national body, attempted to gain recognition from the TSU administration as a student organization. The popularity of the Black Power message among young blacks transformed SNCC from a focus on nonviolence to a militant stance. In public statements SNCC leaders proclaimed violence as the only message that might break the complacency of white society. SNCC leader Stokely Carmichael warned, "If we don't get justice we're going to tear this country apart."[9] Like the Chicano movement, the Black Power movement influenced many black Texans to abandon integration and legal protest for an emphasis on black political empowerment, cultural pride, and radical social and political change.[10] To limit militant agitation on campus, the TSU administration declined the application and fired the faculty sponsor of the Friends of SNCC. This step prompted the Friends of SNCC, according to the administration, to lead a "series of disruptive incidents involving a small segment" of the TSU student body.[11] The administration blamed the disruptions, including attempts to block off Wheeler Avenue through campus, on "a coterie of professional outside agitators."[12]

Tensions among the police, the TSU administration, and the Friends of SNCC increased on April 15, when Stokely Carmichael arrived in Houston to give a talk as part of a speaking tour of southern colleges and universities.[13] Carmichael spoke to a crowd of 1,680 at the University of Houston, not far from TSU.[14] To limit Carmichael's media exposure, local officials and the press conspired to impose a low profile on the visit. The assistant managing editor of the *Houston Chronicle* arranged to run a one-column, back-page story on the visit, and a local television station's news director refused to air an interview with Carmichael. Further, *Houston Chronicle* editors refused to print an article on Carmichael's speech written by a *New York Times* reporter in Houston.[15] Bill Helmer, a writer for the *Texas Observer*, argued that "fear" of the Black Power message led Houston's white establishment to attempt to mute Carmichael because "white leaders don't know how to cope with the rising Negro revolution, and are unwilling to do so."[16] Carmichael's appearance placed local authorities on high alert because "pre-meeting rumors had it that certain groups were prepared to create trouble at the slightest provocation."[17]

Following Carmichael's visit, tensions between the Houston Police and black student protesters remained high and climaxed in a gun battle at the TSU campus on May 16. Students staged demonstrations on the campus over a variety of issues, but Houston's civil rights community counted police brutality among the greatest problems blacks faced in the city. On May 16 officers passing through the campus of TSU called for backup as a barrage of rocks and bottles struck squad cars. As more police arrived, students blockaded Wheeler Avenue, a source of rancor for TSU activists because it divided the campus in half. Building materials from a nearby construction site littered the street. A barrel of tar was set aflame. Officers took cover as a shot rang out from Lanier Hall, a dormitory on Wheeler Avenue. While about two dozen shots came from the dorm, police unloaded on the building with an estimated two thousand rounds. A stray bullet, almost certainly fired by the police, ricocheted off a wall and killed Houston Police Officer Louis Kuba, a twenty-five-year-old rookie cop with a pregnant wife at home.[18]

After the fatal shooting of Officer Kuba, the police stormed Lanier Hall and arrested 488 students, most of whom did not participate in either the demonstrations or the shooting.[19] The police ransacked the dorm, and several students later accused officers of brutality at the jail.[20] A writer for the *Houston Informer* described the actions of the police as a "nightmare" for students that engendered more distrust for the authorities. "Stokely Carmichael," the *Informer* reporter warned, "gained new adherents when the first group of students were jailed."[21] On the other hand, the grand jury that investigated the incident concluded that the police "acted with restraint" and "in the best interests of the community."[22] The grand jury concluded that "the trouble was caused by a few agitators and trouble-makers," and it indicted five students on murder charges for inciting a riot that led to the death of Kuba. The so-called TSU Five would soon become a problem for the War on Poverty in Houston.[23]

Events through the rest of the summer of 1967 proved that outside agitators do not make trouble in a vacuum. The prevalence of poor housing conditions, inequitable city services, and unemployment in Houston's ghettos, especially the Third Ward, led to further frustrated outbursts. Through July and August, angry black Houstonians, mostly young men, smashed storefront windows, threw Molotov cocktails at police, and hurled bricks at white motorists passing through the Third Ward. In August tensions climaxed when a white service-station attendant shot a black man in the Third Ward. The *Forward Times* reported that the victim was a relatively well-respected local resident who had no intention of robbing the store.[24] Neighborhood youths responded by burning down the gas station, looting white-owned stores, and setting fire to a local supermarket owned by a Chinese American family. Through the next day, twenty white-owned businesses were firebombed. The emerging riot subsided but, Justice wrote, "tensions were high in the community and the fuel for an explosion was just waiting for ignition."[25]

The incidents at TSU and the violence through the summer of 1967 provided ammunition for critics of the OEO. The HCCAA later hired two of the TSU Five for a community outreach program called Project Go. The hiring of two indicted rioters provided a link for critics of the OEO between the War on Poverty and urban violence.[26]

One of the more embarrassing episodes in the history of CAP illustrates the connection between the OEO and heightened fears of violence in Houston during the summer of 1967. The General Services Administration reported to the FBI that HCCAA property control manager George Harris ordered surplus telescopic rifle sights from the Air Force, purportedly to be converted for use as microscopes for a CAP job training program. The OEO canceled the order as soon as the FBI began an investigation into the matter but cooperated in order to avoid any hint of a coverup. The Houston Police, according to OEO director Sargent Shriver, "evidently couldn't resist the temptation of releasing the information to the press."[27] Once the press released the story, Senator John Tower and other War on Poverty opponents jumped on the incident as an example of how the OEO supported subversive activities.[28]

The FBI quickly cleared the HCCAA of any wrongdoing, but the incident proved embarrassing enough for Tower's liberal counterpart, Senator Yarborough, to request a personal report on the issue from Shriver. The director concluded that the Houston Police exaggerated the event to discredit the OEO. To soothe the senator, Shriver explained that George Harris was "a white, sixty-four-year-old former deputy sheriff from Harris County," implying that a man with such attributes had no subversive intentions.[29] The significance of the incident, Shriver said, was that it "illustrate[d] how intemperate and ill advised people can raise doubts and suspicions about perfectly innocent activities. Totally false charges are repeated and repeated and repeated. Hitler called this the technique of 'the big lie.'"[30]

Mayor Welch's office gave credit to the HCCAA for cooling tensions through the summer. Blair Justice convinced the mayor to enlist HCCAA employees to serve as "peacekeepers" in the Third Ward as the violence began to escalate.[31] The HCCAA helped organize a "block watcher corps" of War on Poverty employees, resident volunteers, and members of other neighborhood organizations. With the block watchers standing at street-corner posts throughout the Third Ward, the throwing of Molotov cocktails and other acts of violence by local youths stopped.[32]

The black community tended to blame the shortcomings of the HCCAA for the violence. A complaint from Third Ward resident George Gray indicated a general dissatisfaction with the War on Poverty in the Bayou City. Gray blamed the "POWERS THAT BE," meaning the local political establishment, for compromising the effectiveness of the program.[33] The HCCAA had become so bureaucratic, Gray argued, that "any attempt to try to get to the root of the problem only ends in a DEAD END STREET. Passing the buck and sweeping the rancor UNDERTHE RUG is the ORDER OF THE DAY."[34] Because of the HCCAA's failures, Gray explained in a letter to LBJ, "the poor people in Houston have become so bitter in [the] extreme in their criticism that they may unintentionally add to the atmosphere of violence."[35] Members of the black press found that the public had developed a generally negative attitude toward the HCCAA. In an open letter to the HCCAA staff, editorialist Sonny Wells of the *Forward Times* reported in March 1968 that his editorial desk received "complaints from inside the organization about how lackadaisical you go about taking care of the poor and . . . the slipshod manner in which you handle government money."[36]

Black Power militants blamed the atmosphere of violence on the unwillingness of white officials like the mayor to "surrender control" of War on Poverty programs.[37] Mayor Welch accused "instigators" within OEO programs of contributing to the violence. The mayor claimed that CAP workers substantiated his fears with threats. Following the TSU incident, a group of HAY workers marched into his office and threatened a riot unless the HCCAA turned control of the War on Poverty over to the black community. An assistant paraphrased the statements of the workers:

When is your racist mayor going to wake up to the fact that this town is going to burn if he doesn't do something? The shooting by students at TSU was justified because the white man has been oppressing the Negro for 300 years and now it is the black man's turn. Don't you know this town is going to burn and there are people just waiting to loot the stores?[38]

The mayor claimed that the OEO workers were associates of the Reverend Earl Allen, who was fired from his post as the director of community development for the HCCAA and in 1967 started HOPE Development.[39] HOPE came under fire in the wake of the violence that year. Allen was called to testify before a U.S. Senate committee in 1968 to try to explain the violence. He used his testimony to describe the sensibilities of militant civil rights activists to the committee: "I am a militant. I define militance as the aggressive, positive, assertion of rights of all people, without regard to racial or ethnic background."[40] While this seems a mild statement, Allen threatened local governmental officials when he proclaimed, citing the Declaration of Independence, that it was the "right of the people to alter or abolish" government if it no longer served their interests. Allen said he was "not encouraging—and certainly not threatening—violence," but he implied that violence remained inevitable and understandable given the gross inequalities blacks suffered.[41]

Allen expressed confidence that community action following the War on Poverty model offered a way to prevent urban violence. HOPE apparently proved its ability to prevent violence in 1967. Many in the black community credited HOPE with "cooling tensions that might have led to riot" while HCCAA staffers stood on the sidelines.[42] Allen called for the creation of more "local action agencies" led by "responsible militants" who had the capacity to "avert the violence."[43]

LIKE IT IS IN MARSHALL

As with the VISTA/MMP program in Val Verde County, militant messages led Governor Smith to shut down a VISTA project in East Texas at the behest of local officials. The project sponsored by the Harris-Panola Community Action Agency (HPCAA) facilitated the printing of a newsletter for the African American community in Marshall. The newsletter, *Like It Is*, featured Black Power messages that alarmed local white officials. *Like It Is* emphasized self-reliance and responsibility, black pride, and the unity of blacks against "white oppressors."[44] The newsletter threatened whites because it provided candid information on the priorities of local government officials and called for boycotts of stores that did not hire blacks. "There is no better time," a writer for *Like It Is* declared, "for Black men to bring Whitey to his knees."[45]

Like It Is also explained the role of VISTA volunteers to residents of Marshall's African American neighborhoods. In a story titled "VISTA: To Be Used, Not Abused" the author wrote that VISTA volunteers "are usually college students who have volunteered one year of service to the War on Poverty. Most of them are white and they almost always come from middle class. In other words: all they know about poverty is what they read."[46] Nevertheless, *Like It Is* encouraged African Americans in Marshall to take advantage of the VISTA volunteers: "It is the community's decision how to use the VISTA. The government has never gave something for nothing before, so don't let the government give you a VISTA for nothing now—USE THEM!"[47]

Local officials requested the governor's intervention in early August when vandals painted Black Power slogans and obscenities on the Confederate monument in the city's courthouse square. While the authorities did not capture the culprits, white residents quickly connected the Black Power message in *Like It Is* to the incident. Local leaders accused VISTA of organizing a black boycott of a Marshall store. Franklin Jones, the HPCAA president, wrote Governor Smith to defend the VISTA volunteers. As soon as the vandalism was discovered, Jones explained, "the red necks started the hue and cry that the publication of *Like It Is* was responsible for the vandalism."[48] Jones suggested that War on Poverty opponents vandalized the memorial knowing that the VISTA volunteers would be blamed. "After all," Jones conjectured, "Hitler did burn the Reichstag and laid it on the communists."[49]

Jones also wrote an editorial letter to the *Marshall News Messenger* defending the work of the VISTA program. He criticized the local officials who requested the cancellation of the program from Governor Smith for stereotyping the volunteers as "outside agitators."[50] The "racial frictions" that emerged because of the vandalism revealed problems that "will fester and become worse if ignored."[51] Jones called on the white community to "discard the conception that, 'we treat our niggers good,' and if the outside agitators would leave them alone we would not have any trouble."[52]

Although no evidence emerged connecting VISTA to the vandalism, county officials in Marshall demanded that the governor cancel the HPCAA VISTA project for "fermenting [*sic*] racial disturbance."[53] The governor complied with the request and required the VISTA project to shut its doors.[54] Smith's actions made it almost impossible for VISTA to begin other projects in East Texas. In Texarkana, the Texas-side city council voted not to endorse the development of a VISTA project on their end of town. VISTA officials in Arkansas backed down from starting a project on the Texas side of Texarkana, though the city council's rejection did not legally prevent them from initiating the project, because they feared Smith would stifle the effort at the behest of local officials as he had in Marshall.[55]

RACE AND VIOLENCE IN THE JOB CORPS CENTERS

The atmosphere of violence created a poor public image for the Job Corps. Acts of violence, gang organization, or crime in Job Corps centers and host communities received much more media attention than Job Corps graduates getting jobs. Job Corps opponents fed off the bad press generated by the centers.[56]

In 1966 a special Republican Planning and Research Committee on the OEO found a questionnaire in the press from a Job Corps camp application packet for camp directors. The Job Corps designed the questionnaire to gauge how an applicant might respond to a series of hypothetical situations in which corpsmen became involved in violence, theft, homosexual activities, and racial tension. Questions regarding two situations in particular alarmed the committee members: "Assume that one of the boys has reported a superficial knife wound . . . You know that once knifings begin, they tend to become more prevalent"; and "Assume that you receive a call at 3 a.m. from the police chief [that a corpsman] has been accused of rape and assault with a local teenager as his victim."[57] Because the application packet included the questionnaire, members of Congress assumed that it included "situations to which, presumably, the director would have to react."[58] Such evidence damaged the reputation of the Job Corps among legislators.

In Texas the Job Corps appointed a public relations official, former Connally speechwriter Julian Reed, to encourage more positive publicity. The hiring of Reed became a controversy in itself as critics called his $12,000 annual salary "extravagant waste."[59] Evidently, however, Reed performed his job well. An analysis of publicity from Camp Gary after his hiring suggests that unfavorable news decreased to about 13 percent of all news items on the center during his tenure.[60]

Even with a public relations professional on the payroll, incidents of violence and criminal activity at the Gary center buoyed the unsavory reputation of the Job Corps in Texas. Rumors and reports came out of Camp Gary of routine fights, gang organization in barracks, and occasional knife wounds.[61] Otis Singletary received an anonymous report that portrayed Gary like a maximum-security prison. The report described food riots, brutal fighting, rampant drunkenness, intimidation of staff, and harassment of local girls. The anonymous informant, who received his information from a Camp Gary dropout, described the scene for Singletary:

> Some Negroes have taken over. Every barrack is one group or gang
> and a big Negro is the barracks leader who tells them what to do . . .
> There are all sorts of vulgar words on the walls . . . The boys get
> rough on weekends and pull out the plumbing. [Three] boys from
> camp Gary were bound over to the federal grand jury in Austin for
> badly beating up another Job Corps trainee . . . San Marcos was a
> quiet religious town [but now it] is rumored that many mothers will
> not send their daughters to the local college because of the behavior
> of some of the Camp Gary trainees.[62]

Riots erupted at Gary in 1967 and 1970. Enrollees fought among themselves, set fire to automobiles, and ransacked facilities. When the smoke cleared, police confiscated Molotov cocktails and firearms from the barracks.[63]

With consent from the Johnson administration, Congress began to scale back the Job Corps as early as 1967. Along with capping the program at 42,000 enrollees, appropriations for the Job Corps declined from a peak of $304 million in 1966 to $278 million when Johnson left office. The number of centers declined from 123 in 1967 to 53 in 1969. In part, the rising cost of the Vietnam War caused Johnson to cut appropriations for the Job Corps because of his reluctance to raise income taxes. The Job Corps stood out as an easy target for cutbacks because of its high expense and growing unpopularity.[64] The Job Corps lost momentum as the showcase program of the War on Poverty well before Richard Nixon entered the White House.

THE OEO AS A RIOT-PREVENTION PROGRAM

In the wake of the Watts riot, Sargent Shriver and his staff avoided connecting poverty and urban violence to evade criticisms that the OEO primarily sought to pacify black rioters. In a letter to Houston Congressman George Bush, Shriver answered such criticisms by stating that he and his staff had "since the inception of the poverty program, tried to make it abundantly clear that ours is not an anti-riot agency."[65] As the director of the OEO Office of Civil Rights, Samuel Yette sought to exclude riot prevention from the OEO's mission. Since most major civil disturbances in the 1960s occurred during the summer, many African Americans concluded that the OEO devised NYC and CAP summer programs to subdue rioters. Yette told Shriver that there was "great skepticism among Negroes that all the government is concerned with is avoiding riots and that they want to temporarily bribe people into submission."[66] Yette advised that "special pains must be taken" to include "elements of a continuing program in anything that is done" during the summer.[67]

Behind the scenes, however, Shriver and other antipoverty warriors alluded to the potential for riots to justify War on Poverty costs. Before Watts, Shriver reported that "it will not be a long hot summer" for the more than a million children enrolled in Head Start and other OEO summer programs in 1965.[68] In a memo to Lyndon Johnson, in response to a *New York Herald Tribune* article in July 1965, Shriver argued that the prevention of riots was one possible role the OEO could help play. The article "indicates that the most significant single thing combating potential riots this summer is your war against poverty. We may be 'over the hill' in our continuing struggle to have this program properly understood by the newspapers."[69] In a letter to budget director Charles Schultze, Shriver made the case that the OEO might help prevent civil disorder: "The ferment occurring in poverty areas, although it is troublesome, is nonetheless an indication that the poor are being excited about the creation of a new chance . . . a program stand still at this time would [cause] a reversal and an alienation . . . or a search in entirely new and perhaps dangerous directions."[70] Among the talking points in notes for his 1966 budget appeal Shriver wrote that a cutback in OEO spending might lead to "spontaneous riots" or "political exploitations" in urban ghettos.[71]

As the OEO's reputation slipped in the wake of urban violence, the antipoverty warriors became much more vocal about the utility of the War on Poverty as a riot-prevention program. The OEO's change of tune on its riot-prevention capabilities was in response to accusations that the War on Poverty was the root of the problem. Critics blamed the riots on the OEO either because the agency educated the poor about their oppression or because CAP workers instigated the violence directly. Sam Yorty of Los Angeles argued that civil rights activists and the OEO caused the 1965 Watts riot. Officials in Newark contended that the "inflammatory remarks" of CAP staff caused a "tremendous upheaval" that led to the devastating riot in that city in 1967.[72]

In response, OEO officials launched an intensive effort to convince opponents that the War on Poverty did not organize protest rallies and that it instead represented the best interests of communities. At a meeting in El Paso sponsored by the Chamber of Commerce and LULAC, Sargent Shriver addressed those who accused the OEO of inciting demonstrations or riots. Shriver said the OEO's reputation as "the program that causes all of the trouble" was unfounded.[73] OEO programs were designed primarily to build employment and educational opportunity or to reduce obstacles to individual opportunity such as inadequate health care. Shriver explained further that the OEO "does not condone rioters" and that the antipoverty warriors were "squarely on the side of law and order."[74] The OEO's job training and educational programs, Shriver concluded, "reduce the number of revolutionaries."[75]

Yette agreed that a substantive War on Poverty had the potential to limit rioting, but he remained committed to the idea that programs "must be of real benefit and not appear as merely riot preventive."[76] He opposed recreational programs and "make-work jobs" but made several specific suggestions for summer programs such as work for OEO clients to run voter education and registration drives. Yette said such a plan would be "so basically American and democratic that it could not be opposed openly by even the most outspoken politician."[77] He also concluded that a voter program might "enlist the spirit of idealism and optimism that is the best of America [and] would as a by-product consume the otherwise potential rioter."[78] Interestingly, Yette even proposed as an alternative a "patriotic effort to support the Vietnam War," though he admitted such an effort might "not be well received by minority groups."[79]

Theodore Berry, national director of CAP, reported that "mayors and police chiefs felt OEO summer programs helped prevent violence" in cities where no riots occurred.[80] The OEO conducted a survey of thirty-two cities across the country where no rioting occurred and found that in half of these cities the CAAs "calmed down bad situations."[81] Berry argued that "far from being a contributing factor, Community Action is a preventative force."[82] He reported specifically that "in 14 cities municipal police and CAA's had joint programs to prevent riots."[83] The OEO created a report, titled "Southern Peacekeeping Activities," that measured the success or failure of CAAs in the South according to the "acid test" of riot prevention. A New Orleans CAA official "shut up" a group of white community leaders by reporting, "Look the only reason we haven't had a riot is because of what [the CAA organizers] are doing out there."[84]

In Texas, Berry included Dallas, San Antonio, and Corpus Christi on the list of thirty-two cities where Community Action Agencies served as a "preventative force" against rioting. OEO officials claimed that decreased crime rates in these cities were "related to increased summer jobs" provided by the OEO.[85] Specifically, the Corpus Christi Police credited a summer jobs program with a decrease in juvenile delinquency; Sergeant C. B. Mauricio informed OEO inspectors that "criminal activity is at a standstill in those neighborhoods where the program is operating . . . the results were nothing short of fantastic . . . I would say that juvenile crime in general has been cut in half by the OEO."[86] OEO officials credited lower summer crime rates in San Antonio to a Big Brothers project sponsored by the CAA that featured San Antonio Police officers who volunteered as mentors for youths from disadvantaged areas.[87]

The OEO did briefly advertise the Job Corps as a way to prevent urban violence. *Job Corps Reports*, the annual review of the Job Corps for 1968, had a two-page spread titled "Riot Prevention: Job Corps Program." It presented a chart that compared the "profile" of a "Job Corpsmember" and a "Typical Rioter." Based on the Johnson administration's 1967 *Report of the Commission on Civil Disorders*, the chart indicated that rioters and Job Corps members came from the same age groups, completed similar levels of education, and had comparable employment opportunities. The chart showed that among Job Corps enrollees, 60 percent came from a "broken home," 68 percent came from a household headed by an unemployed person, 60 percent lived in substandard housing, 39 percent came from a "family on relief," and 49 percent came from a family in which "both parents had less than 8th grade education."[88] The report did not offer specific percentages for rioters but concluded that they shared profiles similar to those of Job Corpsmen in the various categories.

Along with CAP and the Job Corps, some antipoverty warriors argued that shifting the OEO's attention from the cities to rural areas might help prevent rioting in states with large rural populations. Not long after assuming his position, Yette launched an effort to bring the War on Poverty to the rural South that he called "Operation Dixie." Yette explained in a memo to his staff that

> over one-third of the residents of Watts have arrived from the South during the last few years; approximately 1,000 continue to arrive each month . . . they are poorly educated, often functionally illiterate. They lack training for skilled jobs and they lack the educational competence to acquire the necessary skills.[89]

Yette said the riots occurred because "urban slums have been glutted with Negro refugees from the rural South."[90] One-third of the residents of Watts at the time of the riot were "exrural southern Negroes." The fact that the "rate of Negro unemployment nationally had been reduced to 'only' about double that of whites" offered little consolation to the estimated 30 to 60 percent of young urban black men who remained unemployed.[91]

Antipoverty activists in Texas recognized the problem rural migrants faced as they moved into the cities. A charitable group called the Crescent Foundation proposed to the OEO regional office in Austin and the Labor Department a "family strengthening plan" to assist rural blacks in sixteen counties between Austin and Houston.[92] The plan, presented as an "economic equalizer," called for a "combination of rural, industrial, and intellectual forces" to create jobs for some 3,500 families to "achieve the purposes stated by the president in regard to civil rights."[93] The idea received favorable attention from Assistant Secretary of Labor Stanley Ruttenberg as a pacifying influence in "an area that had the potential for riots."[94] The economic strengthening of families, a Crescent Foundation spokesperson said, "is the main thing [needed] to stave off a holocaust."[95]

Along with rural officials like Jerome Vacek of the Navarro County CAA, some black leaders in Texas strongly disapproved of the OEO advertising the War on Poverty as a riot-control measure. Sonny Wells of the Houston *Forward Times* received "all these negative letters" complaining that the "poverty fighters" of the HCCAA wasted time in their efforts to "pacify all the hard-core poor folks in Harris County and trying to find a way to spend those fat salaries you are making."[96] Wells blasted the HCCAA because its staff continued to "ignore the complaints [and for] refusals to return our calls at this newspaper."[97] Advertising the Job Corps as a riot-prevention program drew criticism from African American leaders because it implied that the way to solve the problem was to get young black men off the street and away from neighborhoods prone to urban violence. The advertising also suggests a partial retreat from the OEO's emphasis on integration in the centers.

The OEO came under fire when critics discovered that a handful of OEO employees participated in the riots. In Houston and thirty-one other cities where urban uprisings occurred, police departments arrested sixteen CAP employees for participation in the riots. Considering that more than thirty thousand people worked for local CAAs across the nation, Berry touted the sixteen arrests as a remarkably low figure.[98] The concern that CAP contributed to the rioting, however, led Congress to include specific anti-riot measures in the 1967 amendments to the Economic Opportunity Act.[99] The measure required Berry to issue a directive that no OEO employee "plan, initiate, participate in, or otherwise aid or assist in the conduct of any unlawful demonstration, rioting, or civil disturbance."[100] In drafting the directive, Berry's staff felt it necessary to specify that "rioting and similar violence are wholly inconsistent with the goals of community action."[101] The directive advised CAA human resources personnel to "exercise reasonable care in not selecting staff in cases where there is clear evidence of intent to engage in or incite unlawful rioting or civil disturbances."[102]

Before LBJ left office the OEO went from the highest possible ambition, solving poverty in America, to devoting its limited resources to preventing riots. The unfortunate result for the War on Poverty, however, was not less violence but its increased association with rioting and disorder. When the Nixon administration took office, the idea that community action agents caused riots became a basic policy-making principle. Nixon's antipoverty czar, a young Donald Rumsfeld, would in turn use this association to begin dismantling the OEO and redirecting its diminished resources toward apolitical service-oriented projects.

After LBJ

NINE

Republican Ascendance and
Grassroots Antipoverty Activism

In 1968 Ralph Abernathy, the new chair of the Southern Christian Leadership Conference (SCLC), chose to go ahead with a march on Washington that Martin Luther King Jr. had been planning when he was murdered. King called it the Poor People's Campaign. He hoped the event would be a show of unity as people of all races gathered in the capital to dramatize the plight of the poor. King wanted to make clear to the nation that the demands of economic injustice compelled the civil rights movement to continue. In the summer after King's death, some seven thousand protesters gathered on the national mall in Washington and built a camp of tents they called Resurrection City. The march drew very little attention at the time and had no impact on national economic policies. There was just too much going on in 1968 for the Poor People's Campaign to capture public attention.[1] King's assassination and the riots that followed, Bobby Kennedy's assassination, the Tet offensive, and Lyndon Johnson's abdication combined to make Americans weary. Even people sympathetic to King when he came to Washington in 1963 had grown tired of marches. Bertrand Harding, who took over the OEO when Shriver left, wondered whether the Poor People's Campaign accomplished anything:

> I just don't know, and it may be decades before we're really able to judge whether on balance it was a very intelligent thing to do or a very stupid thing to do. I'm very ambivalent about it. I can see it in one perspective where it did dramatize. I can see it in another where

it sickened people who were otherwise supportive, and threw people across the line who were sort of in a middle-of-the-road position.[2]

Harding's ambivalence about the Poor People's Campaign reflects the national disposition toward turning the civil rights movement into a campaign for economic justice for the poor.

Few Texans viewed "the poor" as a group needing a campaign. In terms of group identification, race trumped class. White Texans declined to participate in Johnson's War on Poverty. Even if they recognized their poverty, low-income white Texans showed little interest in taking advantage of OEO programs because they associated the Great Society with the demands of nonwhites. The growing electorate of affluent or middle-class whites in the state, even those Harding described as "supportive" or "middle-of-the-road" in relation to civil rights or the War on Poverty, opposed the OEO due to its association with racial militancy and urban violence. Many African American and Mexican American Texans, under the influence of militant nationalist movements, determined that racial solidarity offered the best way out of poverty. The groups competed with each other over OEO funds and sought to exclude whites from programs. With scant support among white Texans and often bitter competition among nonwhite groups, politicians had little reason to defend the OEO. Indeed, attacking the OEO promised more political benefit.

During the 1968 campaign Richard Nixon attacked the OEO as a prime example of the failure of the Great Society. Once in office, however, Nixon did not abolish the OEO. The new president appointed Rumsfeld, then a young congressman, to oversee a gradual "de-escalation" of the War on Poverty. Rumsfeld worked to both weaken the OEO and make it more consistent with the political philosophy of the Nixon administration. The new director transformed the OEO from an "activist agency" to an "initiating agency," meaning Rumsfeld abandoned the ideal of participation of the poor in creating programs.[3] In Texas, Rumsfeld's transformation limited the political activism of OEO programs. CAAs and VISTA projects became providers of services designed in Washington with little input from the poor themselves. Rumsfeld also streamlined the Job Corps, closing centers in Texas and opening less expensive, nonresident local training programs. Nixon's cutbacks and general opposition to Great Society initiatives compelled administrators to keep OEO programs at a low profile in the state as the 1970s began.

Opposition to the OEO also illustrates the growth of conservatism in the state. The economy of Texas, like the rest of the Southwest, was integrating

into the Sunbelt in the sixties. As the state's population grew and the segregated suburbs began to sprawl, white Texans had less and less immediate
contact with poverty or with nonwhites. With the exception of the Reconstruction era, Texas had been solidly Democratic since it entered the Union.
Working-class Texans supported the New Deal, but whites moved increasingly into the Republican Party through the postwar economic boom and
demographic shift to the suburbs due to the association of Lyndon Johnson's
party with the civil rights movement and urban unrest. Republican candidates in Texas lumped the OEO with the batch of "welfare" programs the
white electorate associated with blacks. Affluent white Texans, no longer in
need of progressive federal programs, had little reason to maintain loyalties
to the Democratic Party. The Republicans also began an effort to woo Mexican American voters in the state to abandon their historical allegiance to the
Democrats by pointing to the OEO's perceived African American bias.

The story of the War on Poverty in Texas did not end with the slow demise
of the OEO. With dwindling support from the federal government, local
people struck out on their own in cities and towns across the state to form
independent grassroots organizations that continued what the OEO started.
This is the real success story of the War on Poverty in Texas. With help from
national groups like the Industrial Areas Foundation (IAF) and the National
Welfare Rights Organization (NWRO), local people learned to build interracial coalitions and to avoid harsh political confrontations. With a clear focus
on fundamental issues like job training, infrastructure improvement, health,
and education, grassroots agencies across Texas made genuine progress long
after the federal government surrendered in the War on Poverty. Bertrand
Harding, trying to find some ray of hope from the decline of the OEO, said
that in the end the agency "awakened this nation to a very real problem that
many, many did not even understand existed four or five years ago. And it's
only through that awakening that we're going to be able to make progress."[4]

THE BACKLASH AGAINST THE OEO

The OEO could not seem to please anybody. The agency was held account-
able for the militant revolt among minority groups, blamed for causing urban
violence or not doing enough to prevent it, and accused of racial bias from
all sides. Harding seemed exasperated by the agency's predicament when he
admitted, "We've been picketed by everybody." Harding lamented that even
advocates of the poor found the OEO liable in "some perverted sense" for the
continuation of poverty itself.[5]

Opponents of the OEO blamed the spread of militancy and urban violence on the War on Poverty. If the War on Poverty did not exist, the logic went, the militants would not have the resources to organize. If the militants were not stirring up discontent in the barrios and ghettos, riots would subside. Los Angeles Police Chief William Parker captured the logic of the opposition when he claimed that the Watts uprising happened because liberals "keep telling people they are unfairly treated."[6] Ray Pearson, a lawyer from El Paso and political ally of Governor Connally, expressed a similar point of view about Mexican American protests in Texas. In 1966 United Farm Workers organizer Magdaleno Dimas called on El Pasoans to "band together" against the Anglo power structure using CAP as a means of organization. Dimas' name became well known in Texas political circles in 1967 for the suit filed on his behalf alleging brutality by the Texas Rangers in breaking up a farmworker strike in the Rio Grande Valley. In response to Dimas' presence in the city and his call for Mexican Americans to use CAP, Pearson blamed the protests on the War on Poverty. Pearson complained to Connally that "this, in a way, indicates that OEO is responsible for certain of our problems."[7]

The idea that the OEO was responsible for racial agitation became a common theme among critics. Nothing reveals this train of thought better than testimony in the Senate Permanent Investigations Subcommittee, headed by Arkansas Democrat John McLellan. The McLellan committee convened in a joint investigation with the House Un-American Activities Committee to determine, according to McLellan's opening statement, "whether the outbreaks were spontaneous or if they were instigated and precipitated by the calculated design of agitators, militant activists, and lawless elements." The committee focused specifically on Houston and the 1967 shooting at Texas Southern University. McLellan called Houston Mayor Louis Welch and HCCAA deputy director Samuel Price to testify specifically about Project Go. Following the TSU incident and facing a potential riot in Houston in the summer of 1967, Price created Project Go to "actively involve the dissenters, the agitators, and the militants in constructive activities."[8]

Given that the TSU incident was minor compared to the open warfare in Watts, Detroit, and Newark, it is evident that McLellan deliberately calculated the focus on Houston to connect the violence with War on Poverty programs. John Herbers, a reporter for the *New York Times*, reported that McLellan had the committee "turn its spotlight first [on Houston] . . . and on the role of federally paid antipoverty workers in that city's turbulence" to create an association between the violence and War on Poverty programs.[9] Less ideologically driven members from both parties sought to steer the committee away from McLellan's strategy. Democratic Senator Abraham Ribicoff of Connecticut sought to blame the riots on slum conditions in the inner cities rather than on the War on Poverty. Republican Jacob Javits of New York said the "slandering of government agencies" might "turn into a witchhunt" to find the guilty party.[10]

Along with the argument that the War on Poverty caused the riots, the OEO came under attack because of CAP's focus on political organizing. Tim Parker, an employee at an HCCAA neighborhood center, tendered his resignation to HCCAA director Francis Williams in June 1968 because he "definitely [felt] that this program has taken a major turn for the worse—we have changed from a 'service to the poor agency' to an out and out 'political machine organizing agency.'"[11] While he criticized the political tactics of the HCCAA, Parker defended the War on Poverty. In a pronouncement that mimicked the public statements of Lyndon Johnson and Sargent Shriver, Parker declared that he "believe[d] strongly in helping the needy, and records will reflect that I have helped to break the poverty cycle of many dozens of people in poverty by making taxpayers out of them."[12] He feared, however, that the politicization of the HCCAA provoked "unrest, protest, [and] marches on our local government offices."[13] The political organizing of the HCCAA left Parker confused as to "what party we will be organizing for [and] just how much of our capitalistic government we are about to try to change."[14]

Militant political organization in CAP, though it occurred in few CAAs, generated much opposition to the program. When black and Chicano militants came to wield influence in local CAAs, the program became a political liability that antipoverty officials and politicians strove to subdue. In San Antonio the EODC sought to quiet SANYO political organizing with reductions in funding. Project BRAVO officials in El Paso discouraged the "pressure tactics" of MACHOS. The regional OEO office forced the shutdown of Project Go in Houston when the agency hired militant activists. Along with CAAs, local governments, and the OEO regional office, state government officials sought to close War on Poverty programs that came under militant influence. Governor Connally vetoed NYC projects in 1966 because activists, including some in PASSO and the United Farm Workers, demanded a living wage for Mexican American farmworkers in the Rio Grande Valley. Governor Preston Smith ordered VISTA projects in Del Rio and Marshall to be closed because local elites wanted to quiet militants in their communities.

The amendments to the EOA passed during the Johnson administration grew out of local reactions against political organizing by civil rights groups.

The Green Amendment of 1967 eliminated maximum feasible participation from the legislation in order to place more control over OEO funds into the hands of local governments.[15] Johnson himself acquiesced to these changes, and though he said a complete retreat from community action would destroy the credibility of the War on Poverty, he required the OEO to limit confrontations with local governments.[16]

Moreover, the OEO became so caught up in competition among various groups that the effort worked against the consensus building Johnson promoted as an organizing focus during his presidency. The competition between blacks and Latinos in Texas reveals how the War on Poverty became more about acquiring as much cash as possible for various social groups than about fighting the underlying causes of poverty. This competition was not only interracial but also intraracial and ideological. In the words of one New Orleans activist, the War on Poverty became a competition to get "the most you can from whoever you can."[17]

When Richard Nixon campaigned for the presidency in 1968, he singled out the OEO as the worst example of the Great Society's misguided liberal activism. Nixon considered the OEO an unnecessary layer of bureaucracy in an already cumbersome welfare system. It is likely that if Nixon had a Republican Congress, he would have dissolved the OEO. Yet he did not seek to completely eliminate federal action against poverty. The Nixon administration actually spent more on welfare measures than the Johnson administration did. Nixon's staff sought to reform the bureaucracy, eliminate programs based on controversial theories like community action, and reduce projects focused on political organizing. In reference to the OEO, Nixon vowed to take "action to clean up this outfit."[18]

NIXON "DE-ESCALATES" THE WAR ON POVERTY

Through his first term, Nixon set out to "de-escalate" the War on Poverty by reorganizing the OEO.[19] He appointed Rumsfeld as OEO director to manage this reorganization. Rumsfeld had served four terms in Congress and later proved to be a controversial secretary of defense under Gerald Ford and George W. Bush. Rumsfeld began by "spinning off matured OEO programs to the line departments."[20] He transferred the Job Corps and NYC into the Labor Department, Head Start to the HEW, and VISTA, with the Peace Corps and the OEO's Foster Grandparents program, into a new agency called Action.[21] By the end of Nixon's first term, CAP and Legal Services, an agency that provided pro bono lawyers for low-income clients, were the only agencies left for the OEO to manage. Strangely, Rumsfeld also deserves some credit for the preservation of the OEO through the Nixon years. Rumsfeld surprised many of his colleagues when he argued that "the agency ought to be kept around if for no other reason than to maintain at least one credible symbol which demonstrates our government's commitment to the poor."[22] His concern may have been preserving his own job, but Joan Hoff concludes that "Rumsfeld succeeded in reorganizing the bureaucracy and realigning the bureaucrats without unnecessarily antagonizing either moderate liberals or conservatives."[23]

Rumsfeld avoided antagonizing local leaders as well, and he used his authority to cut ties between the OEO and militant groups or unfriendly civil rights organizations. He did not exert his authority to override any governor's veto of an individual OEO program. When it came to his attention that a group of attorneys on the payroll of the OEO Legal Services program served on the defense team of Black Panther leaders in New Orleans, Rumsfeld fired the program's top administrators and assumed a higher degree of control over local Legal Services programs.[24]

Rumsfeld's reorganization of the OEO was more than just politicking or bureaucratic reshuffling. As director he realigned the War on Poverty to be more consistent with the attitude of the Nixon administration toward government antipoverty initiatives. Nixon's advisers concluded that poverty had become a source of support and employment for too many people. From Nixon's perspective, the government kept adding new antipoverty schemes that employed bureaucrats and social workers who told people that they were poor and the government had programs to help. This added to the traditional welfare rolls and increased the need for more bureaucrats and social workers. The idea that CAP and the OEO caused the riots of the sixties became established wisdom in the White House once Nixon brought Daniel Patrick Moynihan on as an adviser. In his book on CAP, *Maximum Feasible Misunderstanding*, Moynihan argued that the OEO's failure to follow through on Lyndon Johnson's promises caused the frustrated outbursts of violence in the ghettos. Scholars largely reject Moynihan's basic premise. For one thing, the political conflict that forms the basic storyline of most studies of local CAPs indicates that the program worked because the poor were participating. Perhaps Moynihan was correct in his assessment that the Johnson administration never fully grasped the concept of community action.[25]

Moynihan developed a radical proposal to eliminate the need for welfare called the Family Security System (FSS). He introduced Nixon to the idea of a "negative income tax." In theory, this fundamental reform of the tax system would eliminate the paradox of low-income Americans paying taxes on their meager wages only to get the money back in welfare payments. Instead, the Internal Revenue Service would make cash payments to those below the poverty line to create a minimum income. The negative income tax concept had been proposed by many OEO officials in the 1960s, among them Sargent Shriver, but no one took action on it until Moynihan convinced Nixon of the idea's merits.[26] Other Republicans objected to the proposal, arguing that a negative income tax would add people to the welfare rolls. Moynihan convinced Nixon that the FSS would reduce the costly welfare bureaucracy and help "get rid of social workers."[27] Nixon approved of the FSS because his aides amended Moynihan's original proposal to include a greater emphasis on keeping recipients working while they received assistance. Presumably, the emphasis on economic assistance rather than entitlement led Nixon's staff to change the name of FSS to the Family Assistance Plan (FAP) when they presented it to Congress in 1970.[28]

The FAP passed through the House intact in April by nearly one hundred votes.[29] In the Senate the program came under attack from both sides of the aisle. Conservatives attacked it as a socialistic "guaranteed income" plan. Liberals argued that the $1,600 proposed as a floor on incomes through the FAP would not feed a family of four, much less provide for other needs.[30] The National Welfare Rights Organization considered FAP a "giant step backward" because the income guarantees fell far short of what the poor received through traditional welfare.[31] The FAP died when the Senate Finance Committee rejected the plan in November.[32]

Changes in CAP in Texas demonstrate the impact of the Nixon administration's de-escalation of federal antipoverty efforts. In the 1970s in Texas, OEO programs became oriented toward providing services rather than fostering political organization. SANYO, one of the most politically influential OEO programs in the state, continued to provide various services to high-poverty areas but became entirely apolitical by the mid-1970s.[33] Its new executive director, Julian Rodriguez, de-emphasized SANYO's political role because, he said, the organization was not designed to be an "Anlinsky-style" pressure group. Rodriguez later recalled that he and his staff had "to plan volleyball games and soccer and parties and didn't have time to be political."[34]

SANYO's political activities abated also because the Federation of Neighborhood Councils declined. Without a full-time staff, no one took over the federation's activities when volunteers like Joe Freire went on to pursue other interests.[35] All of the neighborhood councils shut down by the mid-1970s.[36] The depoliticized SANYO experienced warmer relations with the

EODC and GGL members. San Antonio Mayor McAllister became a strong supporter of the organization and often attended SANYO functions. The mayor's granddaughter worked as a volunteer at SANYO in the early 1970s.[37] Rodriguez emphasized working through channels to secure money for youth programs. At this he proved eminently successful. As an organization rooted in the OEO, SANYO showed remarkable resilience. When the Nixon administration closed other NYC agencies around the country in 1973, Rodriguez reaffiliated SANYO under the Labor Department.[38] SANYO continued to serve local youths until 1994. During those two decades SANYO spent nearly $100 million in federal funds and served more than 100,000 kids. The EODC, SANYO's old foe, ceased to exist in 1978.[39]

In El Paso, MACHOS provides a concrete local example of the problems that community action created for liberals in the 1960s. In MACHOS the OEO sponsored an organization that rejected liberal principles of integration and change through voting. MACHOS supporters sought Chicano self-determination, as opposed to integrating into the Anglo-dominated economy, and preferred the use of "pressure tactics" like marches and rent boycotts to using the courts or the ballot box to bring about change. When the Nixon administration cut CAA budgets in 1973, Project BRAVO eliminated funding for MACHOS. Groups of volunteers attempted to continue independently, but without government financing to pay a full-time staff the project collapsed. A lull in barrio organizing accompanied the decline of MACHOS in the early 1970s.[40]

Nixon's retreat from the War on Poverty became apparent in Texas Job Corps programs, too. The Job Corps had come under substantial criticism for costs, limited results, and violence in the centers. At the Camp Gary center in San Marcos, once the flagship center of the Job Corps, enrollment fell well below capacity and staff became apathetic as the Labor Department failed to update facilities. The initial enthusiasm of Gary trainees waned as Job Corps training failed to lead to substantive employment opportunities. The Texas Educational Foundation took little initiative to improve conditions independently. A Nixon administration review of Camp Gary revealed unhealthy living conditions, unsanitary eating facilities, and an abandonment of security and supervision procedures. The Labor Department stripped $100 million from the Job Corps in Nixon's first full year in office.[41]

Some Texans expressed support for Camp Gary despite these problems. When the Job Corps announced the planned closure of Gary in January 1969, associate editor Larry Howell of the *Dallas Morning News* published a testimonial from a Gary graduate that "presents a viewpoint of this federal program seldom heard—from one who benefited from it."[42] The corpsman explained that the Job Corps offered hope that graduates might escape from a "cesspool of slums or a backwoods hill."[43] While problems with the Job Corps, from high costs to "unsavory incidents" at the centers, created "wholesale disgust with the program," Howell argued that the program helped enough graduates to justify continuation of the Job Corps. "What should be," Howell asked, "the going price for transforming a life from hopeless despair to buoyant confidence?"[44]

City officials in New Waverly who had "violently opposed" the opening of a Job Corps center in their area in 1965 came out strongly against the Nixon administration's plans to close the conservation center there in 1969. At committee meetings discussing the closing of centers, Senator Yarborough read testimonials from New Waverly community leaders expressing support for the center. The center benefited the area economically, and the corpsmen provided invaluable labor to improve regional tourist facilities. The mayor of New Waverly argued that closing the center would "not only be detrimental to young men who need educational help to make a living for themselves but will have an economic impact on our community."[45] Charles Wilson, a state senator and the president of the Deep East Texas Development Council, recognized the "New Waverly Civilian Conservation Center" as "vital to the economy of Deep East Texas." Wilson argued that the center was primarily valuable as a source of labor to help "this area capitalize on the recreational potential" of the Sam Houston National Forest.[46]

Despite such support, the Nixon Job Corps closed the Gary, New Waverly, and McKinney centers and opened up Regional Manpower Centers (RMCs) in El Paso and Laredo.[47] The RMC model cut costs and kept the corpsmen—mostly urban blacks outside Texas—out of small towns. Another editorial in the *Dallas Morning News*, in contrast to the piece lamenting the end of Camp Gary four months earlier, commended the president for "moving most of the Job Camps back to the ghettos" by opening the RMCs: "School dropouts and 'hard-core risks' aren't calculated to tone up somebody else's home town any more than they do their native ghettos. That's probably why Nixon will be keeping them home from now on." The author, citing "the mild words of critics," concluded that the Job Corps "didn't 'prepare the trainees to compete for urban jobs.' What it did do isn't certain, but it is certain that the small-town people invaded by this experimental exposure to city toughs . . . weren't prepared for the experience. They complained of drunkenness, violence, and insult." The author held that Nixon failed to dismantle the entire program because of "liberal predictions of new urban violence."[48]

VISTA also shifted away from political activism. Because of controversies like those generated by the Minority Mobilization Program and the Harris-Panola CAA's VISTA project, the Nixon administration distanced the VISTA mission from political involvement. Nixon required VISTA officials carried over from the Johnson administration to limit political activity because, writes historian Zane Reeves, conservatives felt that "at best, the community-organizing approach was naive liberalism; at worst, it was a sinister concoction of activists intent on revolutionizing the masses."[49] VISTA recruiters emphasized skills rather than civil rights idealism or New Left activism.[50] VISTA recruiters especially sought volunteers with skills in education, economics, health, and other fields directly applicable to the work.[51] By the end of 1969 VISTA began to "recruit people with professional backgrounds, rather than general backgrounds."[52] In 1970 the *Texas Front*, the annual report of the Texas OEO, featured a preschool teacher, a "credit union specialist," and an architect as ideal VISTA volunteers.[53] VISTA director Padraic Kennedy explained what the changes meant for potential VISTA volunteers: "Do-goodism is dead, volunteers must bring real skills to the community."[54]

THE GROWTH OF THE TEXAS REPUBLICAN PARTY AND OPPOSITION TO THE GREAT SOCIETY

White Texans, including those who may have benefited from progressive initiatives like the OEO, began to move increasingly into the Republican Party in Texas in the late 1960s. Hubert Humphrey won Texas in 1968 because nearly one in five Texans wanted George Wallace to be the president. In 1972, with less of a third-party challenge, Nixon garnered more than two-thirds of all votes cast in Texas. That same year, La Raza Unida Party gubernatorial candidate Ramsey Muñiz gathered enough votes from Mexican Americans to nearly cost Democrat Dolph Briscoe the election. Jimmy Carter won Texas in 1976 by just three points, primarily because he garnered an estimated 95 percent of the black vote and 83 percent of the Mexican American vote.[55] A Democratic presidential candidate has not won in Texas since 1976, and the governor's mansion in Austin has been occupied by Republicans for twenty-two of the past thirty years.

In part, the growing conservatism of Texas involved the state's integration into the Sunbelt economy of the late twentieth century. New metropolises like Houston, San Antonio, and Dallas seemed to offer an escape from the declining industrial economy in the Northeast. The Sunbelt provided its growing populations with low unemployment, constant construction, freedom from unions, and less regulated and taxed economies. The Sunbelt demanded far less from its citizens for the costs of social welfare programs. Per capita spending in Chicago stood at $9.09 in 1970. The same year Houston spent only $1.16. The Sunbelt shared the racial segregation of other regions in the country.[56] Economic and racial segregation meant that whites who moved into the sprawling suburbs around Texas cities did not have much contact with lower-income Mexican American and African American people. Since the poor were largely out of sight, even whites who did not raise their kids to be racists had compelling reasons to vote Republican. Since poverty was not a problem in their neighborhoods or in their lives, whites naturally supported candidates who promised lower tax bills.

The drift toward the Republican Party began in Texas before issues like abortion and gay rights replaced poverty and racial discrimination as the dominant moral issues of American politics. Republicans understood that millions of white Americans had grown tired of civil rights activism and federal legislation on the behalf of minority groups. Texas Republicans took notice when George Wallace polled well in the Democratic primary in 1964. Tower, the leading Republican in Texas during the 1960s, opposed the Civil Rights Act of 1964 and the Voting Rights Act of 1965.[57] Houston Congressman George H. W. Bush "emphatically opposed [the] civil rights legislation" in his failed 1964 Senate campaign against Ralph Yarborough.[58] "The GOP," Kevin Phillips said, "could form a winning coalition without Negro voters. Indeed, Negro-Democratic mutual identification was a major source of Democratic loss."[59] Richard Nixon employed what Phillips called the "southern strategy" to attract white voters in the South and elsewhere. Many a white concluded, in the words of conservative essayist Peter Schrag, that he had been unfairly "asked to carry the burden of social reform, to integrate his schools and his neighborhood . . . to pay the social debts due the poor and the black."[60]

Opposition to federal civil rights initiatives went hand in hand with opposition to federal welfare measures like the War on Poverty. Phillips argued that Republicans could, without losing elections, simply abandon African Americans and their "poverty concessionaires" in the ghettos.[61] The Republican Party attracted working-class and affluent whites in Texas because it successfully linked the "big government" of the Democratic Party with higher taxes, civil rights, and welfare programs that favored minorities,[62] despite many Texans' support for progressive policies for the poor in previous decades. After all, Lyndon Johnson was a Texan. Even John Connally championed some aspects of the OEO's agenda, especially the Job Corps. Texas conformed to a national pattern described best by Jill Quadango in *The Color of Welfare:* "It was not until the antipoverty programs became linked to the pursuit of civil rights that support waned."[63]

In Texas leading Republicans continued to use these feelings of neglect to gain political favor with Mexican Americans as well as whites. In a 1968 proposal for his congressional platform titled "For the Mexican American Texans—A Future of Fairplay and Progress," Congressman Bush concluded that "at the federal level less attention has been paid to Mexican Americans than to Negroes."[64] The congressman argued that most of his Mexican American constituents felt neglected by the OEO's focus on black poverty: "Because of the demonstrations and threats of violence, Negroes are 'bought off' with federal jobs while the quieter law abiding citizens get nothing but promises."[65] In his appeal to Mexican American voters, Bush specifically cited the HCCAA as an example of a program that benefited "troublemakers" because two Project Go community organizers were indicted for involvement in the 1967 TSU shooting.[66]

Congressman Bush's efforts to lure Mexican American voters by contrasting their concerns with those of blacks reflected a new national trend in Republican strategy. Republican strategists recognized a potential ally in the Latino population due to their patriarchal family values and strong Catholic ties, in contrast to the Democratic Party's association with new liberal causes like feminism and abortion rights. Throughout the Southwest, leading Republicans like Senator Tower, Arizona Senator Barry Goldwater, and California Governor Ronald Reagan gained ground in attracting Latino votes. When Richard Nixon entered the White House, he appealed to Latino votes by supporting bilingual education, an emerging issue in the later 1960s. It is probably not a coincidence that the only Job Corps programs that remained open in Texas were in Laredo and El Paso, cities with Mexican American majorities. It is estimated that Nixon's support from Latinos expanded to one-third by 1972, more than double what he received in 1968.[67]

Republicans did not stand alone in their efforts to lure Mexican Americans away from the Democrats. In 1968 George Wallace's American Party created an organization in Texas to draw Mexican American votes. The so-called Viva Wallace campaign in the 1968 election was meant to tap into the sense among Mexican Americans that the Democratic Party had "too long taken minority groups for granted." Tony Sanchez, co-chair of the Viva Wallace effort, argued that Wallace offered Mexican Americans "a 'choice' while there is little difference between Democrat Hubert Humphrey and Republican Richard Nixon."[68] Although Humphrey carried the state in 1968, thanks primarily to Mexican American voters,[69] the fact that the Wallace campaign went to the trouble of launching an organization to draw Mexican American votes shows that at a minimum the politician who made his career defending "segregation now, segregation forever" recognized the wide disparity of political opinion among Mexican Americans.

THE OEO'S LEGACY AND LESSONS FROM THE GRASSROOTS

Congress discontinued most OEO programs as well as the Model Cities Program when it passed the Housing and Community Development Act of 1974. Federal funding for local projects was organized under the Community Development Block Grant system, which still exists. In 1975 President Ford reorganized the remaining OEO programs under a new agency called the Community Services Administration (CSA). While the CSA functioned through the 1970s, the entire program dissolved when Congress repealed the EOA in 1981.[70] The Job Corps, VISTA, and several individual programs like Head Start continued within other departments.

But the slow dissolution of the OEO did not mean that the War on Poverty ended. It continued long after the federal government surrendered. Perhaps the greatest legacy of the OEO is the mobilization of the antipoverty movement at the grassroots level. While local antipoverty activists worked for decades before the Great Society, the Johnson administration's focus on poverty placed it in the national spotlight. The money funneled to local communities through the OEO, though certainly not enough to achieve its lofty ambitions, provided thousands of civil rights and antipoverty activists with both financial resources and political experience. The OEO's programs educated the residents of lower-income communities on the potential of community action. As government administration of local antipoverty efforts diminished, independent organizers tapped into the roots the OEO planted in the sixties.

Because poor whites remained largely uninterested and disorganized, groups and leaders representing the Mexican American and African American communities seized the War on Poverty as an opportunity to further the freedom movement from civil rights to economic justice. War on Poverty programs facilitated groups and activists representing black and Latino Texans with finances and organizational foundations. The War on Poverty served as a cause around which minority groups rallied. African American and Mexican American leaders conceived of the War on Poverty as an economic extension of Johnson's civil rights legislation and held the OEO to its call for maximum feasible participation of the poor. The programs of key organizations such as SANYO in San Antonio, MACHOS in El Paso, and Project Go in Houston were designed to mobilize the residents of low-income communities as a political force. Each agency contributed to the political mobilization of the poor and made an impact on its respective community. SANYO's Federation of Neighborhood Councils laid the foundation for barrio political organization in the 1970s. The pressure tactics of MACHOS contributed to the creation of new public housing in El Paso. Project Go served as a stabilizing force in the emerging street violence in Houston during the summer of 1967. Further, community action provided a political education to many residents of Texas barrios and ghettos. James Sundquist explained the trend well when he wrote, "Out of the community action milieu are rising political candidates, public office holders, and entrepreneurs as well as agitators and prophets."[71]

Even without federal administration, the spirit of community action politics continued throughout Texas when the Industrial Areas Foundation filled the void left by the demise of the OEO. The IAF is a nationwide network of community organizations founded in 1940 by Saul Alinsky, the Chicago community organizer who pioneered independent community action. IAF activists set out to accomplish many of the goals of CAP. The IAF's "iron rule" that organizers should "never do anything for anybody that they can do for themselves" reflects the basic premise of maximum feasible participation, but the IAF has avoided many of the problems that beset the CAAs and other OEO programs.[72] The IAF began organizing in Texas in the early 1970s and continues to function in cities across the state today through affiliates like the El Paso Interreligious Sponsoring Organization (EPISO), Valley Interfaith in the lower Rio Grande region, Border Interfaith, Dallas Area Interfaith, The Metropolitan Organization (TMO) in Houston, and San Antonio's Communities Organized for Public Service (COPS).

COPS was the first and most successful of these independent community organizations in Texas. The success of COPS through the 1970s and 1980s sheds light on the influence of the War on Poverty on grassroots political organization and the inherent contradictions of governmentally financed community activism. COPS filled a void as SANYO, San Antonio's most active War on Poverty agency, moved away from political activism toward a youth-oriented service program. COPS, like SANYO, used the organization and facilities of the Catholic Church.[73] Many of those involved in SANYO's Federation of Neighborhood Councils worked with COPS. Father Yanta confirmed, "They're using the exact same group of people we had—the parish and its natural community."[74] Church congregations provided the IAF with access to people with shared values, but the appeal to what COPS founder Ernesto Cortés called the "best elements in our religious traditions" strengthened the IAF's efforts. "Unfortunately," Cortés said, religious institutions "are virtually the only institutions in society that are fundamentally concerned with the nature and well-being of families and communities."[75] Using religious institutions and values as a basis for organization proved more effective than government bureaucracy had. It was easy for "rock-ribbed conservatives" to impede development of the EODC in San Antonio as a bureaucratic waste of taxpayer dollars. Challenging a church-based organization was more difficult.

Although COPS has attracted attention from historians, political scientists, and sociologists, scholars have largely neglected the link between SANYO and COPS. Donald Reitzes and Dietrich Reitzes trace the roots of COPS to church organizations in San Antonio:

> [COPS] followed the IAF model of developing an umbrella orga-
> nization of local organizations . . . Local churches were especially
> important in the Mexican American community as meeting places,
> community centers, and educational institutions. The new commu-
> nity organization was designed to be a federation of neighborhood
> organizations.[76]

The SANYO Federation of Neighborhood Councils provided COPS with a foundation for this "new community organization." Father Yanta said part of his original vision for SANYO was to develop leadership from within impoverished communities. SANYO was designed, in keeping with the purposes of community action theory, to be "self-liquidating." Once responsible community leadership developed, SANYO would "cease to exist."[77] COPS in many ways fulfilled Yanta's intentions.

Understanding the connection between SANYO and COPS reveals the influence of the OEO as a catalyst for local community organizing, but understanding the differences between the two agencies explains why COPS continues to succeed while OEO programs failed. In founding COPS, Cortés recognized the paradox of government-sponsored community action through programs like SANYO that could not successfully organize people against local establishments because municipal officials like those who controlled the EODC had too much influence over the way federal money was spent.[78] Yanta observed this paradox in the early 1970s: "I must say, COPS has a great advantage . . . We [in SANYO] always had to keep our funding sources in mind."[79] Even liberal politicians and bureaucrats were unwilling to finance long-term confrontations with local officials, especially when those officials were from the same party. Politicians became uncomfortable with the idea, in the words of one historian, "of government financing a revolution against itself."[80] COPS' independent pressure tactics secured hundreds of millions of dollars from a variety of sources for housing, jobs, and material improvements for San Antonio's barrios. Much of COPS' funding was federal; between 1974 and 1981 alone, COPS secured $86 million in federal Community Development Block Grants, but the money was delivered without a federal bureaucracy, and it bypassed local and state governments.[81] While most community action programs folded once War on Poverty funds dried up, COPS persisted because it remained independent from the federal bureaucracy and the local political establishment.

COPS succeeded also because Cortés avoided race politics and sought to include as many people as possible.[82] The majority of IAF members in Texas were Mexican American, but the IAF did not use race or culture as organizing criteria. Alinsky taught his disciples that race politics limits the development of coalitions and often alienates whites. Race-based organizing was a self-defeating tactic for the obvious reason that racial minorities were just that—minorities who cannot win elections in a democracy. More importantly for the IAF, however, the idea of racial solidarity hinders the solidarity of the poor or working class as a whole. Cortés did not deny or reject Mexican American culture in COPS functions but maintained racial ties in personal and private relationships; he considered the common interests of communities public matters that affect all regardless of race. Getting individuals or groups to understand their common interests was the first step toward building community across racial lines.[83] The IAF and its affiliates have worked to overcome cultural distractions to political unity within the working class. Cortés found that

> there is much misplaced anger, resentment, and fear among working people, who are distracted from their real difficulties by such issues as welfare and immigration. Further dividing different socioeconomic and ethnic groups and polarizing the political system, elected officials and candidates for public office exploit these misplaced sentiments by attacking issues in isolation.[84]

To avoid political distractions, IAF affiliates focus on specific issues most people in a given community will agree are legitimate problems. COPS' first big accomplishment in the seventies, for example, was drainage improvement in San Antonio's westside barrios. Tackling specific issues rather than beginning from a broad-based political or ideological agenda maintains agreement and prevents division. For Cortés, working toward specific, agreed-upon goals would have the effect of building working-class solidarity in an era marked by "the deterioration of the mediating institutions of their communities—families, neighborhoods, congregations, local unions, local political parties, neighborhood schools, and other civic institutions."[85] CAP and other OEO agencies became so caught up in the racial and ideological conflicts of the sixties that Johnson's antipoverty warriors did not understand the simplicity of community action as employed by the IAF: organize people, define common interests, seek solutions, and confront obstacles. IAF organizers understood that political achievements derived from personal relationships. Rather than broadly attacking city hall for poverty and deterioration in the barrios, Cortés taught COPS members to gain input and demand accountability from the specific people responsible for public infrastructure in San Antonio.

Cortés' tactics reflect the IAF focus on "relational power." Personal relationships among individuals across the barriers of race, class, religion, or position build trust and agreement that Alinsky called "social capital." The use of relational power was also evident in the IAF job training programs in Texas: Project QUEST (Quality Employment Through Skills Training) and VIDA (Valley Initiative for Development and Advancement) in the Rio Grande Valley. Rather than beginning with the trainees as the Job Corps had, the IAF first established a relationship with potential employers. IAF workers asked employers what skills they needed in employees, then gained a commitment from those employers to hire people from QUEST and VIDA once they completed the training.[86] Getting input from employers on job training or city officials on infrastructure concerns had the effect of humanizing individuals who had been demonized by activists working through the CAPs in the sixties. IAF groups have turned to political confrontation only when local or state officials have obstructed their goals or refused to listen to their requests.

But local politicians found that cooperating with the IAF served their own interests. Simple numbers made IAF affiliates formidable political organizations. The Metropolitan Organization in Houston registered sixteen thousand new voters in the 1984 election year alone. The TMO was able to reach so many people because it cooked up what one reporter called an *olla podrida* (stew) as a political agenda. In public meetings the TMO gathered input from blacks, Latinos, and working-class whites to build a common agenda that encompassed concerns from neglected parks to flood control to the spread of pornography shops in family neighborhoods. This method compelled candidates to address each issue on the TMO agenda, not to pick and choose issues based upon the demands of isolated race or class groups. The TMO organized according to the principle that the "empowerment of all means the empowerment of each."[87]

The history of the IAF exposes key weaknesses of the OEO model. By maintaining independence from government bureaucracy (but not government financing), developing personal relationships, building coalitions across race and class lines, and building consensus about agendas, the IAF avoided many of the problems that plagued the OEO. The CAPs, VISTA projects, and Job Corps all became mired in bureaucracy, hindered by politics, and torn apart by racial divisions. The IAF avoided these problems and has coordinated concrete improvements in infrastructure, voter participation, school achievement, and job training throughout Texas for more than three decades.

The IAF's record remains significant because it continues to expose poverty as a moral issue. Father Alfonso Guevara of Valley Interfaith in Brownsville has said that part of the IAF mission is to "make private pain public" because "making the pain public build[s] the energy and commitment to bring that pain—and the actions needed to relieve it—to a wider public stage where officials would have to recognize it."[88] In no other place was the IAF more successful at exposing the pain of poverty than in the *colonias*, or settlements, near El Paso and throughout the Rio Grande Valley. The colonias, unincorporated settlements with populations that reach into the thousands, are among the most impoverished places in the country. Poverty in the United States is often derided as merely "relative deprivation," meaning even the poorest Americans would be considered rich in most of the developing world; however, the people of the colonias would be considered poor anywhere on the globe. Today, nearly a half-million colonia residents live without such basic services as clean water and electricity. With no water treatment facilities, residents of the colonias face health concerns like epidemic cholera and dysentery that are unimaginable to most Americans.[89]

In the 1980s EPISO and Valley Interfaith became the first IAF affiliates to organize people in the colonias. With just three paid organizers, EPISO went into the colonias and held meetings, gathering audiences from two hundred to as many as three thousand, as a step toward bringing their problems to the light of public scrutiny and to register voters among the many American citizens there. EPISO workers registered some twenty thousand voters from the colonias in 1987. In EPISO public forums, schoolteachers reported that children in the colonias had high rates of absenteeism due to health issues. When children did come to school, teachers often sent them home because of vomiting, diarrhea, ringworm, or head lice. EPISO arranged bus tours of the colonias to give public officials a personal look at the depth of the problem. By organizing residents and exposing the poverty of the colonias, EPISO compelled city and state officials to approve a bond issue to build a treatment plant to provide clean water for 78,000 colonia residents.[90]

The untold history of grassroots antipoverty activism since the sixties exposes another key weakness of the OEO: the virtual exclusion of women from Johnson's War on Poverty. The IAF includes women in positions of responsibility. Except for Cortés, all of the presidents of COPS were women.[91] Beatrice Cortéz, president of COPS in the early 1980s, explained why women were effective: "Women have community ties. We knew that to make things happen in a community, you have to talk to people. It was a matter of tapping our networks."[92] Although some local programs, including SANYO and MACHOS, placed women in key roles, women's poverty and single parenting were for the most part not on the OEO's agenda.

Excluded from the OEO, women activists fought their own war on poverty. In 1966 University of Syracuse economist George Wiley created the National Welfare Rights Organization. The movement spread, and African American women comprised the majority of NWRO members and local leadership. Austin activist Velma Roberts began the first Texas chapter of the NWRO in 1967. Chapters also opened in Dallas, Houston, and San Antonio.[93] Roberts and fellow NWRO leaders organized protests against reductions in welfare payments and work requirements to get checks without adequate child care or job training. NWRO groups provided hot breakfasts and health care to schoolchildren in low-income neighborhoods. In San Antonio women organized a chapter of the independent Chicana National Welfare Rights Organization. Leaders of the Chicana NWRO in San Antonio had gained an education in activism with COPS or as SANYO workers in the sixties. The welfare rights movement provided Mexican American women in San Antonio with a cause and an organizational foundation to continue antipoverty activism. Along with pushing for welfare rights, the Chicana NWRO was credited with curbing gang violence in San Antonio's westside barrios in the late seventies and early eighties. The NWRO launched the political careers of many Mexican American women in San Antonio who had been excluded from politics by both the city's white establishment and the masculine focus of the Chicano movement.[94]

A final lesson the history of independent grassroots organizing teaches is patience. Before organizing in his native San Antonio, Ernesto Cortés spent 1971 to 1974 learning IAF tactics in Chicago. He spent another three years building COPS before that organization scored any measurable successes. The TMO and EPISO did not make any headway until the early eighties. Valley Interfaith did not open its doors until 1982. Each of these agencies continues to function more than a quarter of a century later. The OEO, on the other hand, was scaled back under political pressure within three years of starting. The agency ceased to exist just nine years after LBJ signed the Economic Opportunity Act.

Lyndon Johnson understood that the OEO would not single-handedly end poverty. LBJ and the antipoverty warriors designed the OEO to accompany and coordinate other government programs that, when combined with continued economic growth, would reduce poverty and welfare costs.[95] Moreover, Johnson understood that the OEO would have failures and problems. The president could not comprehend why the public and Congress remained unwilling to accept mistakes in poverty programs:

> I wish the public had seen the task of ending poverty the same way as they saw the task of getting to the moon, where they accepted mistakes as part of the scientific process. I wish they had let us experiment with different programs, admitting that some were working better than others. It would have made everything easier. But I knew that the moment we said out loud that this or that program was a failure, then the wolves would be down upon us at once, tearing away at every joint, killing our effort before we even had a chance.[96]

CONCLUSION   *Texans and the "Long War on Poverty"*

It seems mandatory in any study of the War on Poverty to repeat Ronald Reagan's notorious assessment of the effort, which he offered in his final state of the union address in 1988: "My friends, some years ago, the federal government declared war on poverty, and poverty won."[1] In response to Reagan's assessment, liberals concluded that the "War on Poverty didn't fail. It was called off."[2] Recent scholarship has made it clear that both assessments are wrong. The fact that poverty still exists does not mean poverty won the war, if for no other reason than the War on Poverty was not called off. The federal government began a retreat near the end of the Johnson administration, but the fight against poverty continued independently on the local level. Movements for economic justice have emerged with less federal assistance since the sixties. Historians have now begun to trace the contours of a "long war on poverty," just as Jacquelyn Dowd Hall introduced the concept of the "long civil rights movement."[3]

Early studies of the OEO more or less agreed with Reagan. Policy makers like Moynihan and historians like Matusow portrayed the agency as a failure, the product of noble ambitions but a fundamentally flawed policy that was ultimately crippled by the expense of the war in Vietnam. Recent research has revealed a much more complicated situation. While the OEO obviously did not resolve poverty, the new literature reveals a hidden history of success on the local level. Using OEO funds, local people in communities across the country built creative programs to provide health care, after-school activities and nutrition programs for children, education and job training for adults, and a variety of efforts to improve quality of life in some of the nation's poorest neighborhoods.

In Texas, examples of local success abound. MACHOS in El Paso convinced slumlords to improve conditions; SANYO in San Antonio provided jobs and services to tens of thousands of young people; the HCCAA helped prevent a full-scale riot in Houston; the Job Corps camps gave job training to thousands; and energetic small-town programs offered Head Start and adult education classes across the state. Most importantly, the OEO mobilized low-income citizens politically. Yet the answer to the question of whether the War on Poverty worked continues to rely more on statistics than on what actually happened at the grassroots.

The War on Poverty did coincide with a substantial reduction in poverty throughout the nation. The proportion of Americans living on incomes below the poverty line fell from 22 percent in 1959 to 11 percent in 1973.[4] Texas likewise experienced a notable decrease in poverty. Between 1960 and 1970 the percentage of families defined as poor in the state declined from approximately 30 percent to less than 17 percent. As Texas cities integrated into the economy of the Sunbelt, urban areas especially enjoyed economic growth and reductions in poverty. Urban poverty in Texas declined to 15 percent of families. In keeping with historical patterns, rural Texans remained poorer than their urban counterparts. One in four rural Texans lived on an income below the poverty line in 1970. However, the decline of the farm population effectively reduced the total number of rural poor in the state to record lows. In 1970 the overall rural population accounted for fewer than 2.4 million of the state's total population of 11.2 million people, and the number of rural poor decreased to fewer than one-half million.[5]

Some historians have concluded that the statistical reduction in poverty owed much to the War on Poverty. One college survey textbook goes so far as to state, "It is sometimes said that the United States declared war on poverty and lost. In fact, the nation came closer to winning the war on poverty than the war in Vietnam."[6] This conclusion has some merit, but the OEO played at best an indirect role in poverty reduction in relation to other factors. Poverty declined during the 1960s for the most part because of the general strength of the economy. Better jobs and higher wages through most economic sectors elevated millions out of poverty.[7]

Aside from economic growth, impressive reductions in poverty in the late 1960s and early 1970s owed much to increased social welfare spending. Nationally the number of Americans receiving assistance through Aid to Families with Dependent Children expanded from 3.1 million in 1960 to 9.7

million in 1970. During the same period, costs for AFDC increased from $2.8 billion to $14.5 billion.[8] In-kind benefits including public housing, Medicaid, and food stamps further reduced the statistical proportion of poor people in the United States to about 6.5 percent.[9] One study of AFDC in New York City found that the average welfare recipient received $6,088 worth of benefits. Cash payments from AFDC and other programs accounted for only 38 percent of this total, and the balance came from in-kind benefits. Excluding public assistance and in-kind benefit programs from income statistics, the number of poor people in the United States exceeded twenty million families. This so-called "pre-transfer" poor population represented one in four individual Americans in 1970.[10]

Texas conformed to the national trend in increased welfare and entitlement spending. The number of families in Texas receiving AFDC benefits grew from fewer than 19,700 in 1963 to nearly 120,000 in 1972, or about 443,000 people.[11] The number of Texas families receiving any form of public assistance income expanded to 142,000 in the same period. Assuming that these families would have been counted as poor without public assistance income, the pre-transfer poor population of the state exceeded two million families.[12] Population growth in Texas likely accounted for some of this increase. The state's population expanded from 9.5 million to more than 11.2 million in the 1960s.[13] Increased expenditures on Social Security benefits also contributed to the decline of poverty. The elderly, who ranked among the poorest Americans in 1960, rose from poverty largely because of these benefits. Social Security programs provided 20.8 million Americans with income in 1965, a number that expanded to nearly 30 million a decade later.[14] Despite a lengthening average life span that caused the elderly population to grow, national poverty rates among those over sixty-five declined from 40 percent in 1959 to about 25 percent at the end of the 1960s.[15] Social Security benefits in Texas expanded even more rapidly than in the nation as a whole. In 1963 Texas had 229,000 recipients of assistance from Social Security; by 1973 the number climbed to 857,000.[16] Statewide poverty among the elderly declined to 22.3 percent by 1970.[17] Again, much of this decline probably resulted from population growth as more Americans retired in Sunbelt states like Texas with warmer climes.

Along with a strong economy, increased welfare spending, and more benefits for the elderly, changes in the method for estimating the poverty line contributed to the statistical reduction in poverty in the late 1960s and early 1970s. The poverty line for a family of four rose from $3,000 in 1963 to $6,600 per annum in 1976, but the method for determining the poverty line changed.

Instead of a fixed poverty line at one-half the national median income, the method used in 1963, the U.S. Commerce Department developed a sliding scale for determining the "poverty threshold" based on income, occupation, family size, and urban or rural residence.[18] If the poverty line remained fixed at half the national median, which in the early 1970s stood at $7,500, the proportion of Americans falling below the poverty line would have been about 20 percent. Given these figures, an argument might be made that poverty defined as income inequality did not improve at all during the 1960s.[19]

Furthermore, poverty rates among African Americans, Mexican Americans, and unmarried women did not decrease relative to the rest of the population. In 1959 the national poverty rate of nonwhites stood at three times that of whites. By the mid-1970s, after the OEO shut its doors, the poverty rate among nonwhites rose to three and a half times that of whites.[20]

In Texas, poverty rates among Mexican Americans declined but remained nearly double that of whites. About 35 percent of Mexican American families in Texas lived on incomes below the poverty line in 1970. About 52 percent of rural Mexican American families in Texas at the end of the 1960s continued to suffer from poverty, though their numbers had dwindled to 142,000 families. Although the majority of urban Mexican Americans had moved out of poverty by the end of the 1960s, nearly a third lived on incomes below the poverty line.[21]

Approximately 36 percent of black Texans, about one-half million people, remained poor in 1970. While this represented a decline from 1960, African Americans continued to lag behind their white and Mexican American counterparts. The majority of blacks in the state had moved into the cities, where 33 percent lived below the poverty line. More than half of rural blacks remained poor in 1970, though their numbers had declined to just over 100,000 families.[22]

Single women and households headed by women only marginally improved their lot in the 1960s. More than 45 percent of all female-headed households in Texas and 60 percent of African American and Mexican American families headed by women earned incomes below poverty thresholds in 1970.[23] Having a combination of associated factors continued to almost guarantee poverty. For example, 92 percent of black women over sixty-five years of age in rural areas in Texas lived below the poverty line.[24] These explanations and qualifications for the reduction in poverty through the 1960s might lead one to discount the OEO as at best superfluous and at worst a miserable failure.

A statistical assessment, however, fails to take into account the focus of antipoverty warriors on community action. It was designed not to provide immediate results in the form of higher incomes but as a political tool to reform institutions within communities, such as education, infrastructure, housing conditions, and employment practices, that limited the opportunities of the poor. Even service-oriented CAP programs produced few measurable results. If a poor person received assistance finding a job or earned a high school diploma through programs sponsored by a CAA, no one followed that person to determine if his or her income rose as a result. Therefore, evidence of the effectiveness of community action in helping individuals move out of poverty remains largely anecdotal. VISTA, as an effort designed around the principles of community action, produced many individual success stories but few measurable results. With community action, then, the War on Poverty was waged around programs that could not satisfy what fiscally sensitive politicians demanded—absolute statistical proof that people moved out of poverty because of federal spending.

Statistical methods of determining the War on Poverty's worth fail to consider intangible benefits of the program. Head Start, the one CAP program that has generated reams of statistical evidence, produced few measurable benefits. Studies in 1985 and 1995 conducted by the Department of Health and Human Services found that Head Start did not lead to higher IQs or better grades. Both studies concluded that "in the long run, cognitive and emotional tests scores of former Head Start students do not remain superior to those of disadvantaged students who did not attend Head Start."[25] Nevertheless, Head Start remains one of the most popular programs of the Great Society. It has provided invaluable aid to parents in need of day care to keep working. Within two decades of its founding, more than eight million children attended Head Start programs.[26] A similar argument can be made for the Job Corps. While the statistics suggest that Job Corps training had at best a marginal benefit in producing higher incomes, even the harshest critics admit that the majority of enrollees benefited from the experience. The Job Corps took in people no one else wanted. Allen Matusow, who blasted the program as "unrealistic," admitted that the Job Corps deserved "everlasting credit [for recruiting] from a clientele that nearly every other institution in America had abandoned."[27]

The record of some individual programs in Texas indicates that regardless of income statistics or numbers showing people moving off welfare rolls, OEO programs helped many thousands of Texans in tangible ways. Undoubtedly, thousands of El Pasoans benefited from OEO funding through Project BRAVO's programs. Nearly 1,200 El Paso children enrolled in Head Start classes and 1,000 youths received pay and work experience through the NYC in 1968 alone.[28] Beyond this, however, most of the assistance went largely un-recorded, so Project BRAVO, like other CAAs, produced few objective mea-surements to gauge its effectiveness. Proactive, politically motivated groups like MACHOS clearly made a political impact in impoverished urban areas of El Paso and elsewhere. While housing in south El Paso remained substan-dard, protests organized by MACHOS encouraged the development of new public housing there in the early 1970s.

One interesting story from El Paso illustrates the type of achievement for which the OEO never received credit. The Tigua Indian community had mi-grated to the El Paso region from New Mexico as refugees from the Pueblo Revolt of 1680. Metropolitan El Paso gradually enveloped the Tigua com-munity as the city expanded southward along the Rio Grande. Few people recognized the Tiguas as a distinct people before, and as regional director Bill Crook put it, the OEO "stumbled on the Tigua Indian tribe." While the tribe had accepted Catholicism and spoke Spanish, the Tiguas' culture proved remarkably resilient as they "resisted absorption into the culture and the economic activities of the 20th century." While the Tiguas did not ask for OEO assistance, Crook said the OEO should devote some attention to them because they "live in poverty in adobe shacks without modern conveniences and many are in danger of losing even these homes through tax foreclosure." He contended that the OEO should reach out to the Tiguas because "not only is there terrific need . . . but also a real opportunity for the OEO to demon-strate what it can do for primitive poverty."[29] After the OEO's "discovery" of the Tiguas, LBJ issued a formal recognition of the tribe in 1968, placing the Tiguas under the jurisdiction of the Bureau of Indian Affairs.[30]

The ascension of poverty in the public discourse and the emergence of in-dependent, grassroots wars on poverty rank as the most significant long-term contributions of the OEO. It is likely that a connection existed between the skyrocketing cost of welfare in the 1960s and 1970s and the information that community action activists and VISTA volunteers provided to the poor on the availability of public assistance. Moreover, OEO workers encouraged the poor to demand their welfare benefits.[31] In this sense, the OEO not only in-formed the people of the availability of public assistance but instilled the idea that the poor were entitled to this assistance. The dramatic surge of the sec-ond phase of the War on Poverty, the independent movements of the 1970s, owed its inspiration to the OEO. If nothing else, the independent movements found in the OEO a basis of comparison. With the NWRO, it was as if the women who led the welfare rights struggle were saying to the government, "So you want to fight poverty? Let us show you how."

Beyond the OEO's influence on later antipoverty activism, the history of the agency provides a valuable resource for understanding broad trends in American political and social history in the late twentieth century. When coupled with the unquestioned triumph of the Johnson administration's civil rights legislation, the Economic Opportunity Act promised to realize the ultimate ambition of twentieth-century American liberalism—the establishment through progressive government of equality of opportunity for all Americans at birth, regardless of race or inherited wealth. The fact that a Texan proposed to both tear down the nation's racial inequities and eliminate poverty suggests a profound change in the nation's core values. Lyndon Johnson, as the standard-bearer of postwar liberalism, proposed to do nothing less than turn Thomas Jefferson's egalitarian rhetoric into reality.

A fundamental problem with the vision of postwar liberalism was the presumption that race minorities would forgive and forget the past and integrate with white America. As Chicanos in Texas made clear, America owed them a War on Poverty because of the legacy of racism and discrimination that kept the barrios poor. This recompense should not require them to abandon their Mexican heritage, language, and economic independence in order to integrate with white society. African Americans understood similarly that justice demanded that white America compensate for the legacy of slavery and Jim Crow. Black militants demanded compensation on their own terms for their communities, without qualification or evaluation by the white establishment. Postwar liberalism came to grips with the realities of racial disadvantage and made attempts to overcome them with civil rights legislation and the War on Poverty, but with a pervasive, unconscious ethnocentrism devalued nonwhite cultures by inviting them to integrate into the American mainstream.

Indeed, questioning the value of integration stands out as the primary influence of the militant movements on American political culture. While only a minority in Mexican American and African American communities identified themselves as militant or became involved in the movements directly, the cultural pride of the Chicanos and Black Power activists was central to life in these communities through the next generation. The militants also demanded recognition of the injustices that had defined life for nonwhites in American society. These two features of the militant agenda moved American liberalism itself away from integration as a worthwhile goal.

What Alan Matusow decried as the "unraveling of America" and Arthur Schlesinger Jr. condemned as the "disuniting of America" were in reality the birth pangs of the new liberalism, a political philosophy whose proponents still are working out its principles under the leadership of the nation's first black president. The militants revealed the failures of liberalism and forced the creation of a new vision of progressive government. Liberals since Johnson have sought to both overcome long-standing historical inequities and to show respect for cultural diversity. At the same time, racial minorities have recognized the folly of isolating their communities as the racial nationalist movements of the sixties era attempted. Affirmative action is the most obvious attempt to pull underrepresented minorities up economically and to diversify workplaces and colleges. The celebration of cultural diversity in education and government is further evidence that a new liberal value system emerged from the social revolution of the sixties.

Liberals no longer ask people of color to become white, no longer ask women to stay at home, and no longer ask gays to stay in the closet, but the urgency of fighting poverty has been lost in the scuffle over what liberalism ought to accomplish. The right has put liberals in check by mobilizing mostly white voters, including those who would benefit from progressive policies, with social issues like gay rights, gun rights, abortion, immigration, and religion in public life. Some working-class Americans might have voted against Bill Clinton because he smoked pot or John Kerry because he supported civil unions of same-sex couples, yet economic justice is hardly even discussed by major candidates on the campaign trail or considered in the voting booth. Modern liberals now face a danger of their own making. Inaugurating a black president is an unquestioned triumph in American race relations, but will Barack Obama, a black man raised by a single mother, be held as evidence that the need to confront black poverty no longer exists? The millions who remain in poverty may be forgotten as we celebrate the achievement of racial equality in American politics. As liberals move forward with optimism, enthusiastic about Americans choosing a black man to lead them out of the Bush morass, it is more important than ever to renew the fight against poverty.

NOTES

INTRODUCTION

1. Richard Goodwin, *Remembering America: A Voice from the Sixties* (New York: Harper and Row, 1988), 334.

2. Paul Conkin, *Big Daddy from the Pedernales: Lyndon Baines Johnson* (Boston: Twayne, 1986), 14.

3. Julie L. Pycior, *LBJ and Mexican Americans: The Paradox of Power* (Austin: University of Texas Press, 1997), 4.

4. *San Antonio News*, March 18, 1965, 1.

5. *San Antonio News*, March 21, 1965, 1A.

6. Ibid.

7. "Lesson Two: A Barrier," *VISTA Volunteer* 6, no. 3 (April–May 1970): 12–19.

8. Ibid.

9. Pycior, *LBJ and Mexican Americans*, 236–238.

10. Ignacio García, *United We Win: The Rise and Fall of La Raza Unida Party* (Tucson: University of Arizona Press, 1989), 22.

11. "Lesson Two," *VISTA Volunteer*, 17.

12. Martin Luther King Jr., interview by Tom Wicker, March 28, 1965, *Meet the Press*, transcript, Office of Economic Opportunity Records, RG 381 (hereafter cited as OEO Records), Office of Civil Rights, Records of the Director, Alphabetical File, National Archives, College Park, MD (hereafter NA).

13. Gareth Davies, *From Opportunity to Entitlement: The Transformation and Decline of Great Society Liberalism* (Lawrence: University of Kansas Press, 1996), 70–71.

14. In recent years able scholars from across the country have begun the painstaking task of tracing the OEO's activities on the state and local level: Susan Youngblood Ashmore, *Carry It On: The War on Poverty and the Civil Rights Movement in Alabama, 1964–1972* (Athens: University of Georgia Press, 2008) and "More Than a Head Start: The

War on Poverty, Catholic Charities, and Civil Rights in Mobile, Alabama, 1965–1970," in *The New Deal and Beyond: Social Welfare in the South since 1930*, ed. Elna C. Green (Athens: University of Georgia Press, 2003), 196–238; Robert Bauman, *Race and the War on Poverty: From Watts to East LA* (Norman: University of Oklahoma Press, 2008) and "The Black Power and Chicano Movements in the Poverty Wars in Los Angeles," *Journal of Urban History* 33, no. 2 (2007): 277–295; William Clayson, "'The Barrios and the Ghettos Have Organized!': Community Action, Political Acrimony, and the War on Poverty in San Antonio," *Journal of Urban History* 28, no. 2 (January 2002): 158–183; Kent Germany, *New Orleans after the Promises: Poverty, Citizenship, and the Search for the Great Society* (Athens: University of Georgia Press, 2007); Lisa Gayle Hazirijan, "Combating NEED: Urban Conflict and the Transformations of the War on Poverty and the African American Freedom Struggle in Rocky Mount, North Carolina," *Journal of Urban History* 34, no. 4 (May 2008): 639–664; Thomas J. Kiffmeyer, *Reformers to Radicals: The Appalachian Volunteers and the War on Poverty* (Lexington: University of Kentucky Press, 2008) and "From Self-Help to Sedition: The Appalachian Volunteers in Eastern Kentucky, 1964–1970," *Journal of Southern History* 64, no. 1 (1998): 65–94; Annelise Orleck, *Storming Caesar's Palace: How Black Mothers Fought Their Own War on Poverty* (Boston: Beacon, 2005); Marc Simon Rodriguez, "A Movement Made of 'Young Mexican Americans Seeking Change': Critical Citizenship, Migration, and the Chicano Movement in Texas and Wisconsin," *Western Historical Quarterly* 34, no. 3 (2003): 275–300.

15. Texas Office of Economic Opportunity (OEO), *The Texas Front in the Nation's War on Poverty: The Annual Report of the Texas Office of Economic Opportunity*, foreword by Governor John Connally (Austin: 1968).

16. James Patterson, *America's Struggle Against Poverty, 1900–1994* (Cambridge: Harvard University Press, 1994), 150.

17. The term "Chicano" will be used generically to refer to both Chicano and Chicana activists, but it is important to understand that women played an active role in the movement.

18. Davies, *From Opportunity to Entitlement*, 46, 62.

19. Allen Matusow, *The Unraveling of America: A History of Liberalism in the 1960s* (New York: Harper, 1984), 255.

CHAPTER ONE

1. Texas OEO, *Texas Front*.

2. U.S. Department of Commerce, *Statistical Abstract of the United States, 1960* (Washington, DC: GPO), 1961.

3. U.S. Census Bureau, *1960 Census of Population, General Population Characteristics* (Washington, DC: GPO, 1964), hereafter *1960 Census, General Population*.

4. U.S. Census Bureau, *1960 Census of Housing*, vol. 1, *States and Small Areas*, part 6, *Texas–Wyoming* (Washington, DC: GPO, 1963), hereafter *1960 Census, Housing, Texas–Wyoming*.

5. Harley L. Browning and S. Dale McLemore, "The Spanish Surname Population in Texas," *Public Affairs Comment* 10, no. 1 (January 1964).

6. U.S. Census Bureau, *1930 Census,* vol. 6, *Families* (Washington, DC: GPO, 1933), hereafter *1930 Census, Families; 1930 Census of Population, Occupations* (Washington, DC: GPO, 1933), hereafter *1930 Census, Occupations.* The *1930 Census of Population* was the last census to list Mexican Americans separately until the 1960 census created a special report titled *Persons of Spanish Surname, 1960* (Washington, DC: GPO, 1964). Most Mexican Americans were counted as white in 1940 and 1950.

7. Browning and McLemore, "Spanish Surname Population," 2–3.

8. U.S. Census Bureau, *Persons of Spanish Surname, 1960* (Washington, DC: GPO, 1964). Statistics from this source only include white persons with Spanish surnames.

9. U.S. Census Bureau, *1960 Census of Population and Housing, Detailed Characteristics of the Population, Texas* (Washington, DC: GPO, 1963), hereafter *1960 Census, Population Characteristics, Texas;* Alwyn Barr, *Black Texans: A History of African Americans in Texas, 1582–1995,* 2d edition (Norman: University of Oklahoma Press, 1996), 199.

10. Richard Griswold del Castillo and Arnoldo De León, *North to Aztlán: A History of Mexican Americans in the United States* (New York: Twayne, 1997), 106; David Montejano, *Anglos and Mexicans in the Making of Texas, 1836–1986* (Austin: University of Texas Press, 1987), 268, 274.

11. U.S. Department of Labor, *Subemployment in the Slums of San Antonio* (Washington, DC: GPO, 1967); Frances J. Woods, "The Model Cities Program in Perspective, the San Antonio, Texas Experience," presented to the House of Representatives, Hearings Before the Subcommittee on Housing and Development of the Committee on Banking, Finance, and Urban Affairs, 97th Congress, 1st Session (January 1972), 61.

12. In Richard A. García, *Political Ideology: A Comparative Study of Three Chicano Organizations* (San Francisco: R&E Research, 1977), 64.

13. Bill Crook to Bill Moyers, February 18, 1966, Office of Economic Opportunity Records, RG 381 (hereafter OEO Records), Regional Director's Records, Laredo Problems File, National Archives Southwest Region, Fort Worth (hereafter NASWR).

14. Saul Friedman, "Life in Black Houston," *Texas Observer,* June 9–23, 1967, 10.

15. U.S. Census Bureau, *1960 Census of Population and Housing, Detailed Housing Characteristics, Texas* (Washington, DC: GPO, 1963), hereafter *1960 Census, Housing Characteristics, Texas.* The census only differentiated between whites and nonwhites.

16. Rodolfo Acuña, *Occupied America: A History of Chicanos,* 3d edition (New York: HarperCollins, 1988), 281, 397.

17. U.S. Census Bureau, *1960 Census, Housing Characteristics, Texas.*

18. F. J. Pierce, *Hunger and Malnutrition: Citizens Board of Inquiry Preliminary Report, Food Intake Among Low Income Families in San Antonio* (San Antonio: Our Lady of the Lake University, 1969), 2, in Joe Bernal Papers, Box 6, Benson Latin American Collection, University of Texas, Austin (hereafter cited as BLAC-UT).

19. Mario T. Garcia, *The Making of a Mexican American Mayor: Raymond L. Telles of El Paso* (El Paso: Texas Western Press, 1998), 5.

20. Barr, *Black Texans,* 196–197; Montejano, *Anglos and Mexicans,* 274.

21. University of Texas at Dallas, *Windows on Urban Poverty,* School of Economic, Political, and Policy Sciences at the University of Texas at Dallas and Brookings In-

stitution on Urban and Metropolitan Policy (n.d.). http://templeton.utdallas.edu/poverty/index.htm. The website begins with data from the *1970 Census of Population and Housing* to track demographic trends in poverty over time. Odessa data in Barr, *Black Texans*, 220.

22. University of Texas at Dallas, *Windows on Urban Poverty.*

23. Ibid. The website ranks population density in quartiles, 1 being the least dense and 4 being the most dense. Nine of Dallas's 14 neighborhoods with populations of at least 95 percent black residents all ranked in the fourth quartile. Four of ten similar neighborhoods in Houston ranked in the fourth quartile. Almost all of the predominantly white neighborhoods in these cities ranked in the second quartile.

24. Acuña, *Occupied America*, 313.

25. R. U. Maddox to Sargent Shriver, April 1, 1964, John Connally Papers, Lyndon Baines Johnson Library and Archives, Austin (hereafter LBJL), War on Poverty Correspondence, Series 38d, Box 24.

26. Gary Gerstle, *American Crucible: Race and Nation in the Twentieth Century* (Princeton, NJ: Princeton University Press, 2001), 4.

27. Montejano, *Anglos and Mexicans*, 262.

28. Barr, *Black Texans*, 163.

29. In Pycior, *LBJ and Mexican Americans*, 60.

30. Griswold del Castillo and De León, *North to Aztlán*, 112.

31. Montejano, *Anglos and Mexicans*, 284.

32. Barr, *Black Texans*, 177–179; Thomas R. Cole, *No Color Is My Kind: The Life of Eldreway Stevens and the Integration of Houston* (Austin: University of Texas Press, 1997), 42.

33. George Norris Green, *The Establishment in Texas Politics* (Westport, CT: Greenwood Press, 1979), 17, 197.

34. Merle Black and Earl Black, *The Rise of Southern Republicans* (Cambridge: Harvard University Press, 2002), 56–57; Green, *The Establishment*, 46.

35. Black and Black, *Rise of Southern Republicans*, 56.

36. George Mowry, *Another Look at the Twentieth Century South* (Baton Rouge: Louisiana State University Press, 1973), 66.

37. Green, *The Establishment*, 113.

38. Patrick Cox, *Ralph W. Yarborough: The People's Senator* (Austin: University of Texas Press, 2001), 103.

39. Green, *The Establishment*, 113, 142–145, 156.

40. Barr, *Black Texans*, 178; Montejano, *Anglos and Mexicans*, 276.

41. Green, *The Establishment*, 197.

42. John Tower Papers, Austin Office Files, 1966 Senatorial Campaign, Box 715, File 4, John Tower Library, Southwestern University, Georgetown, TX.

CHAPTER TWO

1. Sean Willentz, *The Age of Reagan: A History, 1976–2006* (New York: Harper, 2008), 92, 136, 271.

2. Matusow, *Unraveling of America*, 11.

3. Peter Beinart, "The Rehabilitation of the Cold War Liberal," *New York Times Magazine*, April 30, 2006, 41–45.

4. Conkin, *Big Daddy*, 129.

5. Robert Mann, *The Walls of Jericho: Lyndon Johnson, Hubert Humphrey, Richard Russell, and the Struggle for Civil Rights* (New York: Houghton Mifflin, 1996), 164–165; Robert Dallek, *Lone Star Rising: Lyndon Johnson and His Times, 1908–1960* (London: Oxford University Press, 1992), 444–445; Bruce Schulman, *Lyndon B. Johnson and American Liberalism: A Brief Biography with Documents* (Boston: Bedford, 1995), 42–43.

6. In Patterson, *Grand Expectations: The United States, 1945–1974* (New York: Oxford University Press, 1996), 272.

7. Mann, *Walls of Jericho*, 222–224; Dallek, *Lone Star Rising*, 522–524.

8. In Mann, *Walls of Jericho*, 279.

9. Conkin, *Big Daddy*, 209.

10. Schulman, *Lyndon B. Johnson and American Liberalism*, 36, 63, 83.

11. Davies, *From Opportunity to Entitlement*, 21.

12. Michael Katz, *The Undeserving Poor: From the War on Poverty to the War on Welfare* (New York: Pantheon, 1990), 92.

13. Newt Gingrich, "Contract with America" speech, in his *To Renew America* (New York: HarperCollins, 1995), 9.

14. Matusow, *Unraveling of America*, 121.

15. Patterson, *America's Struggle*, 127–129.

16. Matusow, *Unraveling of America*, 117.

17. Ibid.; Patterson, *America's Struggle*, 139.

18. Matusow, *Unraveling of America*, 97, 121.

19. Eric C. Schneider, *Vampires, Dragons, and Egyptian Kings* (New York: Princeton University Press, 1999), 74–77, 219.

20. Matusow, *Unraveling of America*, 111.

21. In Robert Dallek, *Flawed Giant: Lyndon Johnson and His Times, 1961–1973* (New York: Oxford University Press, 1998), 61.

22. Matusow, *Unraveling of America*, 123.

23. Dallek, *Flawed Giant*, 61.

24. Ibid., 33.

25. Patterson, *America's Struggle*, 86.

26. Ibid., 135.

27. Matusow, *Unraveling of America*, 243.

28. Michael L. Beschloss, *Taking Charge: The Johnson White House Tapes, 1963–1964* (New York: Touchstone, 1997), 201–202, 208; Lyndon Johnson to Sargent Shriver, February 11, 1964, White House Central Files (hereafter cited as WHCF), Box 124, LBJL; Sargent Shriver, Statement to House Education and Labor Committee, undated, WHCF, Box 124, LBJL.

29. Dallek, *Flawed Giant*, 78.

30. Maurice Isserman and Michael Kazin, *America Divided: The Civil War of the 1960s* (New York: Oxford University Press, 2000), 109.

31. A. Philip Randolph Institute, "A Freedom Budget for All Americans: Budget-

ing Our Resources, 1966–1975, to Achieve 'Freedom from Want,'" pamphlet, October 1966, OEO Records, Records of the Office of Civil Rights, Director Alphabetical Files, 1964–1969, NA; Dallek, *Flawed Giant*, 78–79.

32. Matusow, *Unraveling of America*, 124.

33. Adam Cohen and Elizabeth Taylor, *American Pharaoh: Mayor Richard Daley— His Battle for Chicago and the Nation* (New York: Little, Brown, 2000), 317.

34. Daniel Moynihan, *Maximum Feasible Misunderstanding: Community Action in the War on Poverty* (New York: Free Press, 1970), 142.

35. Matusow, *Unraveling of America*, 125, 243.

36. Ibid., 243–246; John A. Andrew, *Lyndon Johnson and the Great Society* (Chicago: I. R. Dee, 1998), 64–65; John Morton Blum, *Years of Discord: American Politics and Society, 1961–1974* (New York: Norton, 1992), 150–152; Dallek, *Flawed Giant*, 111.

37. Andrew, *Lyndon Johnson and the Great Society*, 71.

38. Moynihan, *Maximum Feasible Misunderstanding*, xv.

39. Matusow, *Unraveling of America*, 244.

40. Moynihan, *Maximum Feasible Misunderstanding*, xviii.

41. Matusow, *Unraveling of America*, 126.

42. Davies, *From Opportunity to Entitlement*, 47; Patterson, *America's Struggle*, 134.

43. Davies, *From Opportunity to Entitlement*, 46–47.

44. Katz, *Undeserving Poor*, 85–86.

45. Dona Cooper Hamilton and Charles V. Hamilton, *The Dual Agenda: Race and Social Welfare Policies of Civil Rights Organizations* (New York: Columbia University Press, 1997), 157.

46. Dallek, *Flawed Giant*, 108.

47. Taylor Branch, *Pillar of Fire: America in the King Years, 1963–1965* (New York: Touchstone, 1998), 444.

48. Davies, *From Opportunity to Entitlement*, 46.

49. Sargent Shriver, Address before the Arkansas State Legislature, March 9, 1965, OEO Records, Office of Civil Rights, Director's Alphabetical Files, 1964–1969, NA.

50. Branch, *Pillar of Fire*, 445; Nick Kotz, *Judgment Days: Lyndon Baines Johnson, Martin Luther King Jr., and the Laws That Changed America* (Boston: Houghton Mifflin, 2005), 184.

51. Davies, *From Opportunity to Entitlement*, 47.

CHAPTER THREE

1. Green, *The Establishment*, 7.

2. Sar Levitan, *The Great Society's Poor Law: A New Approach to Poverty* (Baltimore: Johns Hopkins University Press, 1969), 60.

3. Ibid.

4. Terrell Blodgett to Terry Sanford, July 12, 1965, John Connally Papers, Box 25 Series 38, LBJL.

5. Ibid.

6. OEO, *Community Action Program Guide* (Washington, DC: 1965), 33.

7. Bill Moyers to Marvin Watson, June 9, 1965, WHCF, Confidential File (hereafter CF), Box 98, LBJL.

8. Ibid.

9. Dallek, *Lone Star Rising*, 186–187, 360–362.

10. James Reston, *The Lone Star: The Life of John Connally* (New York: Harper and Row, 1989), 202.

11. Ibid., 434.

12. Reston, *Lone Star*, 291.

13. Beschloss, *Taking Charge*, 206. The Shivercrats, in opposition to the growing liberalism of the Democratic Party, staged a Democrats for Eisenhower campaign to secure the state for the Republicans in the 1952 and 1956 presidential elections.

14. Memorandum, Sargent Shriver to Lyndon Johnson, May 4, 1965, WHCF, Executive Series, Box 124, LBJL.

15. Pycior, *LBJ and Mexican Americans*, 173.

16. Reston, *Lone Star*, 305.

17. John Connally to Lyndon Johnson, telegram, May 17, 1965, Connally Papers, Box 25, Series 38, Center for American History, University of Texas (hereafter CAH-UT).

18. Ibid.

19. Patterson, *America's Struggle*, 147.

20. Ashmore, *Carry It On*, 122.

21. Reston, *Lone Star*, 303. Reston left out the name of the city to protect the identity of the former felon.

22. Ibid., 304.

23. Ibid., 302.

24. Ibid., 303.

25. Ibid., 304.

26. Ibid., 306.

27. Walter Richter to John Connally, May 31, 1966, John Connally Papers, Box 25, Series 38, LBJL.

28. Levitan, *Great Society's Poor Law*, 61; OEO, *Community Action Program Guide*, 34.

29. Beschloss, *Taking Charge*, 205–206.

30. Montejano, *Anglos and Mexicans*, 276–277.

31. Pycior, *LBJ and Mexican Americans*, 51, 99.

32. Reston, *Lone Star*, 305.

33. Ibid.

34. Ibid., 302.

35. Ibid.

36. "Hope Seen for Poor and Jobless," *Houston Informer*, December 25, 1965.

37. "Job Corp[s]," *Houston Informer*, May 13, 1967, 3.

38. Ibid.

39. "Gary Job Corps Observes 2d Year of Service, Lauds Informer," *Houston Informer*, April 8, 1967, 4.

40. William Clayson, "Texas Poverty and Liberal Politics: The Office of Eco-

nomic Opportunity and the War on Poverty in the Lone Star State" (Ph.D. diss., Texas Tech University, 2001), 111–117.

41. Pycior, *LBJ and Mexican Americans*, 151.

42. Arnoldo De León, *Ethnicity in the Sunbelt: A History of Mexican Americans in Houston* (Houston: University of Houston Press, 1989), 152; also see William Clayson, "The War on Poverty and the Fear of Urban Violence in Houston, 1965–1968," *Gulf South Historical Review* 18, no. 2 (Spring 2003): 50–51.

43. Clayson, "Texas Poverty and Liberal Politics," 126, 162–163.

44. "Albert Peña of PASO [*sic*] Attacks Connally for Declaring War on the War on Poverty," *Houston Chronicle*, July 11, 1965, 1.

45. Reston, *Lone Star*, 10.

46. Ibid., 312–313.

47. Pycior, *LBJ and Mexican Americans*, 176.

48. Reston, *Lone Star*, 313.

49. In Pycior, *LBJ and Mexican Americans*, 200.

50. "Senator John Tower Calls Poverty War Unworkable," *Austin American-Statesman*, February 21, 1965, 1.

51. John Tower, *Washington Newsletter* 2, no. 1 (January 1, 1962), John G. Tower Papers, John G. Tower Library, Southwestern University, Georgetown, TX (hereafter cited as Tower Papers), Speeches (1961–1984), Box 25, File 12.

52. George T. Abell to John Tower, June 4, 1964, Tower Papers, General Correspondence, 1964, Box 287, File 1.

53. John Tower to D. H. Edge, n.d., Tower Papers, General Correspondence (1964), Box 290, File 2.

54. Ibid.

55. Ibid.

56. John Tower, Weekly Report, March 7, 1965, Tower Papers, Speeches (1961–1984), Box 25, File 13.

57. John Tower, news release, August 22, 1965, Tower Papers, Speeches (1961–1984), Box 25, File 12.

58. Ibid.

59. Ibid.

60. John Tower, Weekly Radio Report, June 5, 1964, Tower Papers, Speeches (1961–1984), Box 25, File 12.

61. John Tower, *Reports From Washington* 4, no. 7 (November 1965), Tower Papers, Speeches (1961–1984), Box 25, File 12.

62. Edge to Tower, n.d., Tower Papers, General Correspondence (1964), Box 290, File 2.

63. Chandler Davidson, *Race and Class in Texas Politics* (Princeton, NJ: Princeton University Press, 1990), 234.

64. Dan T. Carter, *From George Wallace to Newt Gingrich: Race in the Conservative Counterrevolution, 1963–1994* (Baton Rouge: Louisiana State University Press, 1996), x.

65. John Boles, *The South through Time: A History of an American Region* (Englewood Cliffs, NJ: Prentice Hall, 1995), 506.

CHAPTER FOUR

1. "Poverty Talk Ends Quietly," *Brownsville Herald*, January 27, 1965, 1.

2. Ibid.

3. Gillis Long to Wright Patman, March 5, 1965, OEO Records (microfilm), Alphabetical Correspondence, LBJL.

4. OEO Public Affairs Office, "The War on Poverty—A Hometown Fight," OEO Records, Director's Records, Subject Files, NA.

5. Ibid.

6. Matusow, *Unraveling of America*, 245.

7. Moynihan, *Maximum Feasible Misunderstanding*, xviii.

8. Matusow, *Unraveling of America*, 245–246.

9. Sargent Shriver, foreword to *Poverty in Plenty*, ed. George H. Dunne (New York: P. J. Kennedy and Sons, 1964), 10–11.

10. OEO, *The Quiet Revolution: OEO Annual Report, 1965* (Washington, DC: 1965), 11.

11. OEO, *The Quiet Revolution: OEO Annual Report, 1966* (Washington, DC: 1966), 90–91.

12. Levitan, *Great Society's Poor Law*, 58.

13. Proposal and Application for CAP Grant, November 4, 1965, Ralph Yarborough Papers, Senate Records, Legislative Files, Box 3w294, CAH-UT.

14. U.S. Census Bureau, *1960 Census of Population*, vol. 1, part 45, *Texas* (Washington, DC: GPO, 1964), hereafter *1960 Census of Population, Texas.*

15. Lubbock County CAA Board to OEO Regional Office, "The Community Action Board in Lubbock," memorandum, April 29, 1966, OEO Records, Director's Records, Regional Civil Rights Files, Box 32, NA.

16. Robstown CAP Application, n.d., Yarborough Papers, Senate Records, Legislative Files, Box 4ja11, CAH-UT.

17. Schulman, *Lyndon B. Johnson and American Liberalism*, 98.

18. Lubbock County CAA to OEO Regional Office, April 29, 1966.

19. Fort Worth Application for CAP Grant, November 4, 1965, Yarborough Papers, Senate Records, Legislative Files, Box 3w294, CAH-UT.

20. Texas Office of Economic Opportunity (Texas OEO), *The Texas Front in the Nation's War on Poverty, 1968* (Austin: Texas OEO, 1968).

21. Andy McCutchon to Walter Richter, February 8, 1968, WHCF-CF, Box 129, LBJL.

22. Sargent Shriver to Earle Cabell, March 6, 1968, WHCF-CF, Box 129, LBJL.

23. Sargent Shriver to Earle Cabell, March 6, 1968, OEO Records, City Economic Opportunity Boards Files, Dallas File, NASWR.

24. OEO, "Dallas Went 'Mad Ave.,'" *Communities in Action* 1, no. 4 (December 1966): 23.

25. Ibid.

26. Dallas County Community Action Committee (DCCAC), "A Family Tradition," poster, John Connally Papers, Box 35 Series 38, LBJL.

27. OEO, "Dallas Went 'Mad Ave.,'" 23.

28. OEO, *Communities in Action* 2, no. 3 (1967), 4–5; Matusow, *Unraveling of America*, 246.

29. Patterson, *America's Struggle*, 150.

30. Levitan, *Great Society's Poor Law*, 1.

31. "Preview Issues: Office of Economic Opportunity," memorandum, September 10, 1965, OEO Records, Evaluation File (microfilm), Reel 7 LBJL; Memorandum, Robert A. Levine to Walter W. Wilcox, August 3, 1967, OEO microfilm, Reel 14, LBJL; "OEO Instruction, Establishment of the Office of Rural Affairs," memorandum, December 6, 1968, OEO Records, Director's Records, Reference Correspondence, NA.

32. U.S. Census Bureau, *1960 Census of Population, Texas*.

33. *Alice Daily Echo*, February 3, 1965, 1.

34. *Alice Daily Echo*, March 19, 1965, 1.

35. Sargent Shriver to Charles Schultze, December 17, 1965, OEO Administrative History, Documentary Supplement, LBJL.

36. Deborah Wagner, "The Ten Biggest Myths About the OEO," *Communities in Action* 2, no. 3 (April–May 1967): 22–23.

37. Walter Richter to Fred Baldwin, February 2, 1968, OEO Records, Southwest Region Records, Regional Directors Records, NASWR.

38. OEO, *Quiet Revolution*, 1966, 107, 113; OEO, *As the Seed Is Sown: OEO Annual Report, 1968* (Washington, DC: OEO, 1968), 87. The title of the OEO annual report changed from *The Quiet Revolution* to *As the Seed Is Sown* in 1967.

39. Texas OEO, *Texas Front*, 1968. The 1968 annual report was the first to give a county-by-county summary of OEO expenditures.

40. Ibid.

41. Jerome Vacek to Ralph Yarborough, Yarborough Papers, Senate Records, Legislative Files, Box 3w294, CAH-UT.

42. Texas OEO, *Texas Front*, 1968.

43. Betty McNabb, "Busy in Beeville," *Communities in Action* 4, no. 3 (December 1968): 13–15.

44. Ibid.

45. *Alice Daily Echo*, April 9, 1965, 1.

46. U.S. Census Bureau, *1960 Census of Population, Texas*, 563.

47. Dimmit Application for CAP Grant, n.d., Yarborough Papers, Senate Records, Legislative Files, Box 4ja11, CAH-UT.

48. Ibid.

49. Zook Thomas to Ralph Yarborough, July 5, 1967, Yarborough Papers, Senate Records, Legislative Files, Box 3w294, CAH-UT.

50. Ibid.

51. Texas OEO, *Texas Front*, 1968.

52. OEO, *As the Seed Is Sown*, 1968, 91; Texas OEO, *Texas Front*, 1968. Because Local CAAs also controlled the NYC, Head Start, and other programs, more money was spent under CAP in Texas than the Job Corps. Nevertheless, the Job Corps remained the most expensive individual program.

53. Matusow, *Unraveling of America*, 237.

54. Ibid.

55. Toni Miller, "The History of Gary Job Corps" (master's thesis, Southwest Texas State University, 1970), 30.

56. OEO, *Quiet Revolution*, 1966, 95.

57. Texas OEO, *Texas Front*, 1966.

58. OEO, *Quiet Revolution*, 1966, 95; Sar A. Levitan and Benjamin H. Johnston, *The Job Corps: A Social Experiment That Works* (Baltimore: Johns Hopkins University Press, 1975), 33.

59. Levitan and Johnston, *Job Corps*, 33.

60. Sar Levitan, *Antipoverty Work and Training Efforts: Goals and Reality* (Washington, DC: National Manpower Policy Taskforce, 1967), 13.

61. James H. Quillen to Sargent Shriver, April 5, 1966, OEO Records, Records of the Office of Civil Rights, Director's Records, Alphabetical File, 1966–1969, NA.

62. Ibid.

63. Levitan and Johnston, *Job Corps*, 32.

64. Job Corps, "New Waverly Civilian Conservation Center," pamphlet (Washington, DC: 1968), OEO Records, Records of the Job Corps, State Files, New Waverly, TX, File, NA; Texas OEO, *Texas Front*, 1968.

65. Clarence La, "Few Leave Gary: Job Corps Center Students Look Eagerly to New Chance," *San Antonio Express-News*, March 20, 1965, 7A. The *Express-News* released this article very early in Camp Gary's history. Only twelve of the first two hundred enrollees dropped out, hence the title of the article. Dropout rates increased rapidly as the population of the center grew.

66. Blum, *Years of Discord*, 151.

67. Job Corps, "New Waverly."

68. Reston, *Lone Star*, 304.

69. Ibid., 301.

70. "Poverty Set Up Irks Connally," *Washington Post*, February 3, 1966, 4A.

71. Ibid. Reston argues that the governor never threatened to close the camp. Instead, Reston contends that the *Washington Star* misquoted Connally and other papers picked up the story; Reston, *Lone Star*, 304.

72. George Bush to O. J. Baker, September 11, 1967, OEO Records, Job Corps, Records of Congressional Liaison Staff, State Files, Box 7, NA.

73. Matusow, *Unraveling of America*, 238. In truth, in Matusow's critique of the relevance of the Job Corps program he fails to consider that much of the training involved skills that many employers were unwilling to teach entry-level employees.

74. Wagner, "Ten Biggest Myths," 22.

75. Miller, "History of Gary Job Corps," 43.

76. OEO, *Quiet Revolution*, 1966, 9; Texas OEO, *Texas Front*, 1966, 1968.

77. Marvin Schwarz, *In Service to America: A History of VISTA in Arkansas, 1965–1985* (Fayetteville: University of Arkansas Press, 1988), 10.

78. Ibid.; T. Zane Reeves, *The Politics of the Peace Corps and VISTA* (Tuscaloosa: University of Alabama Press, 1988), 37.

79. OEO, *As the Seed Is Sown*, 1969–1970, 78.

80. OEO, *As the Seed Is Sown*, 1968, 89. In 1968 Puerto Rico had more VISTA volunteers (256) than any of the fifty states.

81. Schwarz, *In Service to America*, 14.

82. Texas OEO, *Texas Front*, 1968.

83. William Crook to Robert E. Lucey, February 17, 1967, Robert E. Lucey Papers, SANYO File, Catholic Archives of San Antonio, TX (hereafter cited as CASA).

84. "Houston: Starting at the Bottom," *VISTA Volunteer* (March 1967): 17.

85. Ibid.

86. Ibid.

87. Ibid.

88. Pycior, *LBJ and Mexican Americans*, 190.

CHAPTER FIVE

1. See Ashmore, *Carry It On*; Bauman, *Race and the War on Poverty*; Hazirijan, "Combating NEED"; Orleck, *Storming Caesar's Palace*; Germany, *New Orleans After the Promises*; Rodriguez, "Movement Made of 'Young Mexican Americans.'"

2. Andrew, *Lyndon Johnson and the Great Society*, 68.

3. Ibid., 245.

4. Matusow, *Unraveling of America*, 245.

5. Ibid., 251–265.

6. Patterson, *America's Struggle*, 146.

7. In Cohen and Taylor, *American Pharaoh*, 343.

8. Ibid., 250; Patterson, *America's Struggle*, 146.

9. Blum, *Years of Discord*, 173.

10. *New York Times*, April 14, 1965, 25.

11. Matusow, *Unraveling of America*, 254.

12. Patterson, *America's Struggle*, 147.

13. David R. Johnson and John A. Booth, eds., *The Politics of San Antonio: Community, Progress, and Power* (Lincoln: University of Nebraska Press, 1983), 23.

14. Nelson Wolff, *Mayor: An Inside View of San Antonio Politics, 1981–1995* (San Antonio: Express News, 1997), 4.

15. Luther Lee Sanders, *How to Win Elections in San Antonio the Good Government Way, 1955–1971* (San Antonio: St. Mary's University Department of Urban Studies, 1975), 16.

16. Rodolfo Rosales, *The Illusion of Inclusion: The Untold Political Story of San Antonio* (Austin: University of Texas Press, 2000), 14.

17. Montejano, *Anglos and Mexicans*, 281.

18. Sanders, *How to Win Elections*, 16.

19. Ibid., 9–19.

20. Ibid., 76–77.

21. Rosales, *Illusion of Inclusion*, 63–65.

22. Ibid., 72.

23. "$1.25 Youth Corps Rejection Hit By Archbishop Lucey," *San Antonio Express-News*, June 26, 1965, 12A; "Albert Peña of PASO Attacks Connally," *Houston Chronicle*.

24. *San Antonio News*, March 5, 1965.

25. "San Antonio Mounts Concerted War on Poverty," *Alamo Messenger*, March 12, 1965, 1.

26. Matusow, *Unraveling of America*, 268.

27. Mario T. Garcia, *Mexican Americans: Leadership, Ideology, and Identity, 1930–1960* (New Haven, CT: Yale University Press, 1989), 61–83.

28. Andy Price, Mark Ray Hernandez, and David Coleman to Edgar May (CAP Inspectors), Report of Inspection of San Antonio EODC, July 18, 1968, OEO Records, Director's Office Files, NASWR. The NYC came into being under the EOA as an OEO delegate agency administered in conjunction with the Labor Department. During the Johnson administration, the NYC furnished two million youths between sixteen and twenty years of age with employment in low-paying, make-work jobs or as counselors in recreational programs; see Patterson, *America's Struggle*, 148.

29. John Yanta to Solomon Casseb (District Court Judge for Bexar County), July 29, 1965, Connally Papers, Texas OEO Files, Box 25, Series 38, LBJL. James L. Turbon, "Glory Be to the Father: The History of the San Antonio Neighborhood Youth Organization" (master's thesis, Trinity University, San Antonio, 1988), 14.

30. Yanta to Casseb, July 29, 1965; Archdiocese of San Antonio, *SANYO: Tenth Anniversary, 1965–1975*, pamphlet, SANYO File, CASA; *San Antonio News*, July 16, 1965; Woods, "Model Cities Program," 61. Bexar County received an NYC grant of $823,400. The balance remaining after SANYO's share was taken out was divided up among the county's school districts.

31. Employment through SANYO created some controversy because the wage that enrollees were paid was more than the wages of many of their parents; "$1.25 Youth Corps Rejection Hit by Archbishop Lucey," *San Antonio Express-News*, June 26, 1965, 12A; "Albert Peña of PASO Attacks Connally," *Houston Chronicle*.

32. Irma Mireles, phone interview by the author, September 5, 2000.

33. José Angel Gutiérrez, phone interview by the author, August 31, 2000.

34. Mireles, interview by the author; OEO, "The Emancipation of Janie Torres," *Communities in Action* 4, no. 3 (June–July 1968), 32.

35. *SANYO Reports* 2, no. 8 (November 4, 1968), newsletter, OEO Records, Southwest Regional Office Records, Director's Office Files, NASWR.

36. These included the Centers Policy Committee, Seminar Implementation Committee, Political Activities Committee, and Youth Programs Committee. SANYO Board of Directors, Meeting Minutes, August 28, 1968, OEO Records, Southwest Regional Office Records, San Antonio CAP Files, NASWR.

37. *San Antonio News*, July 17, 1965; Price, Hernandez, and Coleman to May, Report of Inspection of San Antonio EODC, NASWR.

38. Bob Emond (CAP inspector) to Bertrand Harding (OEO CAP director), memorandum, June 14, 1968, OEO Records, Records of CAP, Director's Correspondence, NA.

39. Archdiocese of San Antonio, *SANYO: Tenth Anniversary*, CASA.

40. Samuel Broder, *Social Justice and Church Authority: The Public Life of Archbishop Robert E. Lucey* (Philadelphia: Temple University Press, 1982), 104.

41. Pycior, *LBJ and Mexican Americans*, 151–153.

42. In Turbon, "Glory Be to the Father," 65.

43. Ibid.

44. *Austin American-Statesman*, June 27, 1965; Chancery Office, Archdiocese

of San Antonio, press release, "Yanta Appointed Bishop," 1994, Bishop Yanta News Article File, SANYO Files, CASA; Woods, "Model Cities Program," 61.

45. Bob Emond to Bertrand Harding, memorandum, June 14, 1968; Sal Tedesco to John McLean (Inspectors for Model Cities Program), memorandum, December 15, 1967, WHCF-CF, LBJL.

46. Price, Hernandez, and Coleman to May, Report of Inspection of San Antonio EODC, NASWR.

47. SANYO Board of Directors, meeting minutes, August 28, 1968, OEO Records, Southwest Regional Office Records, City Economic Opportunity Board Files (hereafter CEOB), San Antonio CAP Records, NASWR; Mireles, interview by the author.

48. Rodriguez, interview by the author.

49. Rosales, *Illusion of Inclusion*, 76.

50. Turbon, "Glory Be to the Father," 14.

51. *SANYO Reports*, newsletter, OEO Records, Southwest Regional Office Records, CEOB, San Antonio CAP Records, NASWR.

52. Kemper Diehl, "Poverty War $17 Million Bexar Business," *San Antonio Express-News*, August 26, 1967, 1+; Price, Hernandez, and Coleman to May, Report of Inspection of San Antonio EODC, NASWR; Woods, "Model Cities Program," 61.

53. Woods, "Model Cities Program," 61.

54. Stryker McGuire, "Keep 'N' in SANYO," *San Antonio Light*, October 22, 1975, 1.

55. Diehl, "Poverty War"; Price, Hernandez, and Coleman to May, Report of Inspection of San Antonio EODC, NASWR; Woods, "Model Cities Program," 61.

56. In Woods, "Model Cities Program," 61.

57. Ibid.

58. In Turbon, "Glory Be to the Father," 67.

59. Kemper Diehl, "Father Yanta and the SA Poverty War," *San Antonio Express-News*, August 28, 1967, 1+.

60. Paulette Washington, "EODC and the Neighborhood Corporations" (master's thesis, Trinity University, San Antonio, 1971), 35.

61. Ed Foster, "Catholic Leader Rips Board," January 24, 1966, clipping, OEO Records, Southwest Regional Office Records, Director's Correspondence, NASWR.

62. Don Mathis to Sargent Shriver, telegram, January 25, 1966, OEO Records, Director's Correspondence, NA.

63. William Crook (Austin Regional OEO Director) to Sargent Shriver, telegram, January 24, 1966, OEO Records, Southwest Regional Office Records, Director's Correspondence, NASWR.

64. Foster, "Catholic Leader Rips Board."

65. Ibid.

66. Ibid.

67. Ibid.

68. Don Mathis to Sargent Shriver, telegram, January 25, 1966, OEO Records, Director's Correspondence, NA.

69. Don Mathis to Leal Schurman, January 28, 1966, OEO Records, Southwest Regional Office Records, San Antonio Problems File, NASWR.

70. Mathis to Schurman, January 28, 1966.

71. Ibid.

72. Ibid.

73. Ibid.

74. Ibid.

75. Mathis to Shriver, January 25, 1966.

76. Ibid.

77. Bill Crook to Bill Moyers, "Situation Report, San Antonio," memorandum, January 27, 1966, OEO Records, Southwest Regional Office Records, San Antonio Problems File, NASWR.

78. Ibid.

79. Ibid.

80. Ralph C. Caserez to Henry B. Gonzalez, January 26, 1966, OEO Records, Southwest Regional Office Records, San Antonio Problems File, NASWR.

81. Donna McNeill, "EODC: Invoking the Green Amendment" (master's thesis, Trinity University, San Antonio, 1979), 39.

82. William Crook to Sargent Shriver, February 4, 1966, telegram, OEO Records, Southwest Regional Office Records, San Antonio Problems File, NASWR.

83. In 1960, 80 percent of El Pasoans lived in segregated neighborhoods; Alwyn Barr, *Black Texans*, 220.

84. Montejano, *Anglos and Mexicans*, 265.

85. Mario Garcia, *Making of a Mexican American Mayor*, 5.

86. Ibid., 76.

87. Ibid., 162.

88. Benjamin Marquez, *Power and Politics in a Chicano Barrio* (Lanham, MD: University Press of America, 1985), 116.

89. "BRAVO Starts Formal Operation," *El Paso Times*, May 24, 1965, 1A.

90. "Poverty Director to Be Named," *El Paso Times*, June 4, 1965, 1A.

91. Texas OEO, *Texas Front*, 1966, 1968.

92. Bill Crook to Bill Moyers, February 18, 1966, OEO Records, Regional Director's Records, Laredo Problems File, NASWR; Texas OEO, *Texas Front*, 1968. Because the OEO ranked Laredo as the "poorest [city] in the nation," the Laredo CAA received more money per poor person than anyplace in the United States (approximately $120 per poor person over the same period).

93. In Richard A. García, *Political Ideology*, 64.

94. Ibid.

95. In Marquez, *Power and Politics*, 98.

96. Ibid.

97. Ibid., 99. "100 March in Plaza over Fire," *El Paso Times*, August 1, 1966, 1A.

98. "100 March in Plaza," *El Paso Times*.

99. Marquez, *Power and Politics*, 99.

100. "100 March in Plaza," *El Paso Times*.

101. Ibid.

102. Ibid.

103. Loretta Overton, "Poverty Work Is Remedial Program," *El Paso Herald-Post*, October 23, 1967, 2A.

104. Dimas Chavez to José Aguilar, Annual Evaluation of MACHOS, March 26–29, 1968, OEO Records, CEOB, El Paso File, NASWR.

105. In "MACHOS Stages Protest," *El Paso Times,* May 21, 1968.

106. José Aguilar to Frank Curtis, August 13, 1968, OEO Records, CEOB, El Paso File, NASWR.

107. Frank Curtis to Hanah King, memorandum, "Thoughts on El Paso," December 18, 1968, OEO Records, CEOB, El Paso File, NASWR.

108. Ibid.

109. "BRAVO Gets $2,032,477 for Work," *El Paso Times,* September 17, 1968, 1A+; El Paso CAMPS Coordinating Committee, Meeting Minutes, September 17, 1968, OEO Records, CEOB, El Paso File, NASWR.

110. Frank Curtis to Barbara Craven, memorandum, September 20, 1968, OEO Records, CEOB, El Paso File, NASWR.

111. Texas OEO, *Texas Front,* 1966, 8; Howard Beeth and Cary Wintz, eds., *Black Dixie: Afro Texan History and Culture in Houston* (College Station: Texas A&M Press, 1992), 225.

112. "Kelly Named to Poverty Post," *Houston Informer,* August 14, 1965, 1.

113. "Hope Seen for Poor and Jobless," *Houston Informer,* December 25, 1965, 1.

114. "Houston Youth Project Opened," *Houston Informer,* December 25, 1965, 4.

115. "EOO, HAY Merger Almost Clinched," *Houston Informer,* May 20, 1967, 1.

116. Texas OEO, *Texas Front,* 1968.

117. "Hope Seen for Poor and Jobless," *Houston Informer,* 1.

118. Cole, *No Color Is My Kind,* 42.

119. Bill Helmer, "A Context for Tragedy," *Texas Observer,* June 9–23, 1967, 6.

120. Ibid.

121. Blair Justice, *Violence in the City* (Fort Worth: Texas Christian University Press, 1969), 221.

122. Helmer, "Context for Tragedy," 6.

123. Louis Welch to Sargent Shriver, May 25, 1967, Connally Papers, Box 25, Series 38, LBJL.

124. "Blueprint for HOPE," *Forward Times,* September 9, 1967, 16–17.

125. Barr, *Black Texans,* 201–202.

126. "Blueprint for HOPE," *Forward Times.*

127. Statement of Reverend Earl Allen presented to the Senate Permanent Subcommittee of the Committee on Government Operations, transcript, February 7, 1968, OEO Records, Southwest Regional Office Records, CEOB, Houston File, NASWR; "HOPE Conducts Fundraising Campaign," *Forward Times,* October 7, 1967, 9.

CHAPTER SIX

1. Sam Kindrick, "Hundreds March Downtown in SANYO-EODC Dispute," *San Antonio Express,* September 12, 1968, 1.

2. Ibid.

3. Ibid.

4. Ibid. In the end, the EODC board voted to deny SANYO's request, but the

demonstration achieved some success because SANYO received nearly 80 percent of the CEP funds. Rodriguez, interview by the author.

5. Nicolas Vaca, *The Presumed Alliance: The Unspoken Conflict Between Latinos and Blacks and What it Means for America* (New York: Rayo, 2004), ix, 62–84.

6. Barr, *Black Texans*, 183.

7. Matusow, *Unraveling of America*, 243–271.

8. Houston, San Antonio, and El Paso provide the most fruitful source material on local War on Poverty programs in the state. Due to the conservative political culture of the Dallas–Fort Worth area, OEO programs in the Metroplex started after most of the controversial features of CAP had been eliminated by the OEO bureaucracy and Congress.

9. Davies, *From Opportunity to Entitlement*, 45.

10. Thomas Jackson, *From Civil Rights to Human Rights: Martin Luther King Jr. and the Struggle for Economic Justice* (Philadelphia: University of Pennsylvania Press, 2007), 238.

11. Ben Seligman, *Permanent Poverty: An American Syndrome* (Chicago: Quadrangle, 1968), 165.

12. Sargent Shriver to A. Philip Randolph, March 10, 1965, OEO Records, Office of Civil Rights (hereafter OCR), Director's Records, Alphabetical File, NA.

13. OEO press release, February 16, 1966, OEO Records, OCR, Director's Records, Alphabetical File, NA.

14. "Civil Rights Clearance Screen for Community Action Programs," completed form for San Angelo Independent School District, March 14, 1965, OEO Records, OCR Records Relating to Civil Rights in the Regions (hereafter OCR-Regions), Box 30, NA.

15. In Dona Cooper Hamilton and Charles V. Hamilton, *The Dual Agenda: Race and Social Welfare Policies of Civil Rights Organizations* (New York: Columbia University Press, 1997), 157–158.

16. Patterson, *America's Struggle*, 150.

17. Jerome Vacek to Ralph Yarborough, May 19, 1967, Yarborough Papers, Senate Records, Legislative Files, Box 3w294, CAH-UT.

18. Clayson, "Texas Poverty and Liberal Politics," 143.

19. "Minority Gap Report," OEO Records, Director's Records, Reference Correspondence, NA.

20. Bill Crook to Hayes Redmon, Memorandum RE Personnel for Southwest Regional Office, August 18, 1965, WHCF-CF, LBJL.

21. Wagner, "Ten Biggest Myths," 22–23.

22. Harvey Friedman to Samuel Yette, August 3, 1966, OEO Records, OCR, Director's Records, Alphabetical File, 1964–1969, NA.

23. Carl Allsup, *The American GI Forum: Origins and Evolution* (Austin: Center for Mexican American Studies, University of Texas, 1986), 137.

24. Pycior, *LBJ and Mexican Americans*, 166.

25. "Bias, Indifference Charged: Mexican American Walkout Mars U.S. Job Conference," *Los Angeles Times*, March 29, 1966, in OEO Records, OCR, Director's Records, Alphabetical File, 1964–1969, NA.

26. Harman Bookbinder to David North (head of LBJ's task force on Mexican Americans), October 25, 1966, OEO Records, OCR, Director's Records, Alphabetical File, 1964–1969, NA.

27. Hector García to Sargent Shriver, July 7, 1966, OEO Records, OCR, Director's Records, Alphabetical File, 1964–1969, NA.

28. *Corpus Christi Caller,* September 29, 1966, n.p., in OEO Records, OCR, Director's Records, Alphabetical File, 1964–1969, NA.

29. Ibid.

30. Ibid., handwritten note dated July 11, 1966.

31. OEO, "The American GI Forum of Texas Supports War on Poverty," press release, July 10, 1967, OEO Records (microfilm, reel 8), LBJL.

32. OEO, "Project SER to Benefit Spanish Americans," press release, June 10, 1966, League of United Latin American Citizens (LULAC) Records, William Flores Papers, BLAC-UT.

33. Ibid.

34. Quoted by Senator Ralph Yarborough, *Congressional Record,* vol. 113, 90th Congress, 1st Session, Joint Resolution 128, "Request to the President to Authorize LULAC Week, February 11–17, 1968," December 12, 1967, 196.

35. Pycior, *LBJ and Mexican Americans,* 190.

36. Harman Bookbinder to David North (head of LBJ's task force on Mexican Americans), October 25, 1966, OEO Records, OCR, Director's Records, Alphabetical File, 1964–1969, NA.

37. Bob Allen to John Connally, March 31, 1967, John Connally Papers, Box 25, Series 38, LBJL.

38. Ibid.

39. Acuña, *Occupied America,* 309.

40. José Angel Gutiérrez, *The Making of a Chicano Militant: Lessons from Cristal* (Madison: University of Wisconsin Press, 1998), 112.

41. Ibid.

42. Shirley Anderson, *Mexican Americans in a Dallas Barrio* (Tucson: University of Arizona Press, 1978), 64.

43. Clayson, "'The Barrios and the Ghettos,'" 158–183.

44. Julian Rodriguez, interview by the author.

45. In Price to May, Report of Inspection of San Antonio EODC, July 18, 1968, NASWR.

46. Ibid. Don Politico, "Deal Splits Local NAACP," *San Antonio Light,* September 28, 1968, 8.

47. John Yanta to Archbishop Robert E. Lucey, December 15, 1967, Archbishop Robert E. Lucey Papers, SANYO file, CASA.

48. Washington, "EODC and the Neighborhood Corporations," 35.

49. Rodriguez, interview by the author.

50. "BRAVO Starts Formal Operation," *El Paso Times,* May 24, 1965, 1A.

51. "Poverty Director to Be Named," *El Paso Times,* June 4, 1965, 1A.

52. Morgan Groves to Jim Duck, March 20, 1968, OEO Records, CEOB, El Paso File, NASWR.

53. Charles W. Pankey to Jim Duck, March 25, 1968, OEO Records, CEOB, El Paso File, NASWR.

54. Ibid.

55. Ibid.

56. "Poverty Meeting Held," *El Paso Herald-Post*, May 6, 1965, 3.

57. Ibid.

58. Clayson, "War on Poverty and the Fear of Urban Violence."

59. De León, *Ethnicity in the Sunbelt*, 181–182.

60. A. D. Azios to Walter Richter, January 23, 1968, OEO Records, Southwest Regional Office Records, Director's Records, Correspondence Files, NASWR.

61. Hector del Castillo to Walter Richter, February 2, 1968, OEO Records, Southwest Regional Office Records, Director's Records, Correspondence Files, NASWR.

62. De León, *Ethnicity in the Sunbelt*, 152.

63. del Castillo to Richter, February 2, 1968.

64. Ibid.

65. Bauman, "Black Power and Chicano Movements," 277–295.

66. Black and Black, *Rise of Southern Republicans*, 56.

67. Bill Crook to Sargent Shriver, Weekly Activity Report, October 14, 1966, OEO Records, OCR-Regions, Director's Records, Region V File, 1965–1966, NA.

68. Black and Black, *Rise of Southern Republicans*, 56.

69. Mrs. C. O. Wade to Ralph Yarborough, n.d., Yarborough Papers, Senate Correspondence, Box 3w173, CAH-UT.

70. Ibid.

71. Wagner, "Ten Biggest Myths."

72. Ibid.

73. Ibid.

74. Conkin, *Big Daddy*, 225.

75. Shriver, Address to the Arkansas State Legislature, March 9, 1965, OEO Records, OCR, Director's Records, Alphabetical File, 1964–1969, NA.

76. Job Corps, "New Waverly," pamphlet.

77. David Gottlieb to Lewis Eigen, memorandum, December 12, 1964, OEO Records, Job Corps, Subject Files, Otis Singletary, 1964–1965, Box 735, NA.

78. Ibid.

79. Levitan and Johnston, *Job Corps*, 94.

80. Otis Singletary to Brewer, Cheston, White, and Wynne, memorandum, December 17, 1964, OEO Records, Job Corps, Director's Records, Subject Files, Otis Singletary, 1964–1965, Box 735, NA.

81. Ibid.

82. Miller, "History of Gary Job Corps," 61.

83. Luther E. Hall to John Connally, March 5, 1965, Connally Papers, New Waverly Job Corps File, Box 25, Series 28, LBJL.

84. Ibid.

85. Reeves, *Politics of the Peace Corps and VISTA*, 115.

86. Ibid.

87. Schwarz, *In Service to America*, 43.

88. Ibid., 46.

89. Ibid.

90. Pat Phillips, "An Introduction to Poverty," *Vista Volunteer* 2, no. 1 (May 1966): 10.

91. Pycior, *LBJ and Mexican Americans*, 171.

CHAPTER SEVEN

1. Ignacio M. García, *Chicanismo: The Forming of a Militant Ethos among Mexican Americans* (Tucson: University of Arizona Press, 1997), 35.

2. Harvard Sitkoff, *The Struggle for Black Equality, 1954–1980* (New York: Hill and Wang, 1981), 214.

3. Armando Rendon, *Chicano Manifesto* (New York: Macmillan, 1971), 87–88.

4. Bill Crook to Samuel Yette, April 6, 1966, OEO Records, OCR-Regions, Region V File, NA.

5. Bill Crook to Sargent Shriver, April 15, 1966, OEO Records, OCR-Regions, Region V File, NA.

6. W. Aster Kirk to Bill Crook, April 5, 1966, OEO Records, OCR-Regions, Region V File, NA.

7. Fred Baldwin to Bill Crook, April 5, 1966, OEO Records, OCR-Regions, Region V File, NA.

8. Mrs. D. G. Coronado to William Crook, December 20, 1965, OEO Records, OCR, Special Greg File, NA. The exchange of correspondence here was particularly frustrating for a researcher because Dominga Coronado did not use her first name in these exchanges. I finally discovered her first name in Julie L. Pycior's book *LBJ and Mexican Americans*.

9. Mike Garza to John Connally, April 7, 1966, and Bill Crook to Sam Yette, April 19, 1966, OEO Records, OCR, Special Greg File, NA.

10. Mrs. D. G. Coronado to John Connally, April 12, 1966, John Connally Papers, Box 25 Series 38, LBJL.

11. Walter Richter to D. G. Coronado, April 15, 1965, OEO Records, OCR, Special Greg File, NA.

12. In the Community Action Board in Lubbock memorandum to the OEO, April 29, 1966, OEO Records, OCR, Box 30, NA.

13. Crook to Yette, April 19, 1966.

14. Ibid. Shriver wrote this message by hand on the memo and rerouted it to Yette.

15. Sam Yette to Sargent Shriver, May 6, 1966, OEO Records, OCR, Special Greg File, NA.

16. U.S. Congress, House Committee on Education and Labor, Ad Hoc Hearing Task Force on Poverty (Washington, DC: GPO, 1969), 2042; Pycior, *LBJ and Mexican Americans*, 159.

17. Mario Garcia, *Mexican Americans*, 21.

18. Carl Allsup, "Hernández v. Texas," in *The Handbook of Texas Online* (Texas State Historical Association, n.d.), http://www.tshaonline.org/handbook/online/articles/HH/jrh1.html.

19. Ignacio García, *Chicanismo*, 24.

20. Ibid., 26.

21. Carlos Muñoz, *Youth, Identity, Power: The Chicano Movement* (New York: Verso, 1989), 58.

22. Ignacio García, *Chicanismo*, 34–36.

23. Teresa Palma Acosta, "Raza Unida Party," *The Handbook of Texas Online* (Texas State Historical Association, n.d.), http://www.tshaonline.org/handbook/online/articles/RR/war1.html.

24. Mireles, interview by the author.

25. Gutiérrez, interview by the author.

26. Gutiérrez, *Making of a Chicano Militant*, 104.

27. Schwarz, *In Service to America*, 10.

28. T. Zane Reeves, *The Politics of the Peace Corps and VISTA* (Tuscaloosa: University of Alabama Press, 1988), 31.

29. In García, *United We Win*, 22.

30. Rodriguez, "A Movement Made of 'Young Mexican Americans,'" 275–301.

31. Bauman, "Black Power and Chicano Movements," 277–295.

32. In Woods, "Model Cities Program," 124.

33. John Yanta to Robert E. Lucey, December 14, 1966, Lucey Papers, SANYO file, CASA.

34. "English Rule Out, SANYO Head Says," *Alamo Messenger,* December 15, 1966; the "big three" were Yanta (executive director), Ben A. Singleton (president of the board of directors), and Francis B. Roser (vice president).

35. Yanta to Lucey, "Enemies from Within," memorandum, December 14, 1966, CASA.

36. Ibid.

37. *San Antonio Express,* March 27, 1970, 1; Rodriguez, interview by the author. The extent of the group's militancy is somewhat questionable because one of the fired counselors was Frank Tejeda, who would enter the U.S. House of Representatives in 1992 for the 28th District of Texas.

38. Matt Ahmann and Joe Bernal to Monsignor Martin, April 1, 1970, Lucey Papers, Social Problems File, SANYO File, CASA.

39. Ibid.

40. Ibid.

41. Rodriguez, interview by the author.

42. Clayson, "'The Barrios and Ghettos,'" 171.

43. Frank Curtis to El Paso Files, memorandum, record of Phone Call from Sinclair, October 3, 1968, OEO Records, CEOB, El Paso File, NASWR.

44. Ibid.; Hanah R. King to Saul Paredes, October 8, 1968, OEO Records, CEOB, El Paso File, NASWR.

45. Gutiérrez, *Making of a Chicano Militant*, 112.

46. Ibid., 111.

47. Juliet Pycior, *LBJ and Mexican Americans*, 25–26; Gladys Gregory and Sheldon B. Liss, "Chamizal Dispute," in *The Handbook of Texas Online* (Texas State Historical Association, n.d.), http://www.tshaonline.org/handbook/online/articles/CC/nbc1.html.

48. Pycior, *LBJ and Mexican Americans*, 202–204, 206–214.

49. Gutiérrez, *Making of a Chicano Militant*, 112.

50. Ibid., 110–111.

51. In Kemper Diehl, "MAYO Leader Warns of Violence, Rioting," *San Antonio Express*, April 11, 1969, 1.

52. Ibid.

53. Ignacio García, *Chicanismo*, 38.

54. Gonzalo Barrientos, interview by José Angel Gutiérrez, January 6, 1998, Tejano Voices, University of Texas at Arlington Center for Mexican American Studies Oral History Project, http://libraries.uta.edu/tejanovoices.

55. Pycior, *LBJ and Mexican Americans*, 216.

56. Ibid.

57. Joe Bernal to Walter Richter, April 23, 1968, Joe Bernal Papers, Box 6, BLAC-UT.

58. Texas OEO, *Texas Front*, 1968, 60.

59. Pycior, *LBJ and Mexican Americans*, 216.

60. Ignacio García, *United We Win*, 24.

61. Ibid., 19.

62. Montejano, *Anglos and Mexicans*, 284.

63. "Judge Orders Students Readmitted," (Harlingen) *Valley Morning Star*, November 26, 1968, 1.

64. Ibid.

65. Melodie Bowsher, "VISTA in Turmoil," *Wall Street Journal*, November 5, 1969, 1.

66. Ibid.

67. Ibid.

68. Acuña, *Occupied America*, 339.

69. Pycior, *LBJ and Mexican Americans*, 238.

70. Ignacio García, *United We Win*, 27.

71. Terry Anderson, *The Movement and the Sixties* (New York: Oxford University Press, 1995), 308.

72. Rendon, *Chicano Manifesto*, 333.

73. Ibid., 334–335.

74. Ibid., 336.

75. Ibid.

76. Ibid.

77. Texas OEO, *Texas Front*, 1969.

78. In Pycior, *LBJ and Mexican Americans*, 217.

79. Mario Garcia, *Mexican Americans*, passim.

80. Gutiérrez, interview by the author.

81. In Ignacio García, *United We Win*, 27.

82. Pycior, *LBJ and Mexican Americans*, 217.

83. Bowsher, "VISTA in Turmoil," 1.

84. Griswold del Castillo and De León, *North to Aztlán*, 11.

85. Gutiérrez, *Making of a Chicano Militant*, 84.

86. Gutiérrez, interview by the author.

87. Henry B. Gonzalez, "This Is No Land of Cynics," in *Ripples of Hope: Great American Civil Rights Speeches*, ed. Josh Gettheimer (New York: Basic Books, 2003), 333.

88. Ibid., 334.

89. Rodriguez, "Movement Made of 'Young Mexican Americans,'" 284.

90. Neil Birnbaum and Doug Ruhe to William Crook, April 11, 1967, Yarborough Papers, Senate Records, Legislative Files, Box 3w294, CAH-UT.

91. Untitled newspaper clippings, n.d., Yarborough Papers, Senate Records, Legislative File, Doug Ruhe File, Box 3w294, CAH-UT.

CHAPTER EIGHT

1. Barr, *Black Texans*, 223.

2. Ibid., 1; Beeth and Wintz, *Black Dixie*, 225.

3. Justice, *Violence in the City*, 1.

4. Ibid.

5. Bill Crook to Sargent Shriver, Weekly Activities Report, March 18, 1966, OEO Records, Southwest Regional Office Records, Director's Correspondence, NASWR.

6. Ibid.

7. Barr, *Black Texans*, 214–215.

8. Texas OEO, *Texas Front*, 1966.

9. Ibid., 217.

10. Sitkoff, *Struggle for Black Equality*, 215.

11. "Fear of Violence, Loss of Credits Return Calm to TSU," *Houston Informer*, April 1, 1967, 1.

12. Ibid.

13. Sitkoff, *Struggle for Black Equality*, 217.

14. "UH Hall Crowded for Carmichael Talk: Black Power Advocate Gets Freedom of Speech," *Houston Informer*, April 15, 1967, 1.

15. Helmer, "A Context for Tragedy," 6.

16. Ibid.

17. Ibid.

18. Bill Helmer, "Nightmare in Houston," *Texas Observer*, June 9–23, 1967, 4.

19. Barr, *Black Texans*, 192–193.

20. Helmer, "Nightmare in Houston," 4.

21. "Students Describe Nightmare during All-Out Assault on TSU," May 20, 1967, *Houston Chronicle*, 1.

22. Justice, *Violence in the City*, 260.

23. Ibid; Helmer, "Nightmare in Houston," 1.

24. *Forward Times*, "Blueprint for HOPE."

25. Justice, *Violence in the City*, 3.

26. Clayson, "War on Poverty and the Fear of Urban Violence," 48–49.

27. Sargent Shriver to Ralph Yarborough, memorandum, August 16, 1967, Yarborough Papers, Senate Records, Legislative Files, Box 3w294, CAH-UT.

28. Davies, *From Opportunity to Entitlement*, 195. Ironically, Houston Congressman George Bush told his constituents to forget about the issue and "get on with the business of combating poverty."

29. Shriver to Yarborough, August 16, 1967.

30. Ibid.

31. Justice, *Violence in the City*, 244.

32. Ibid., 162.

33. George Gray to Lyndon Johnson, September 12, 1968, OEO Records, Southwest Regional Office Records, Director's Records, Correspondence Files, NASWR.

34. Ibid.

35. Ibid.

36. Sonny Wells, "The Whipping Post," *Forward Times*, March 9, 1968, 33.

37. Statement of Reverend Earl Allen presented to the Senate Permanent Subcommittee of the Committee on Government Operations, transcript, February 7, 1968, OEO Records, Southwest Regional Office Records, CEOB, Houston File, NASWR; "HOPE Conducts Fundraising Campaign," *Forward Times*, October 7, 1967, 9.

38. Ibid.

39. Justice, *Violence in the City*, 24.

40. Statement of Reverend Earl Allen, NASWR.

41. Ibid.

42. *Forward Times*, "Blueprint for HOPE."

43. Ibid.

44. "Black Is Beautiful," *Like It Is* (Marshall, TX), July 18, 1969, Yarborough Papers, Senate Correspondence (1968–1970), Box 3w173, CAH-UT.

45. Ibid.

46. "VISTA: To Be Used, Not Abused," *Like It Is*, July 18, 1969, Yarborough Papers, Senate Correspondence, 1968–1970, Box 3w173, CAH-UT.

47. Ibid.

48. Franklin Jones to Preston Smith, August 5, 1969, Yarborough Papers, Senate Correspondence, 1968–1970, Box 3w173, CAH-UT.

49. Ibid.

50. Franklin Jones to *Marshall News Messenger*, August 5, 1969, Yarborough Papers, Senate Correspondence, 1968–1970, Box 3w173, CAH-UT.

51. Ibid.

52. Ibid.

53. Gene Godley to Ralph Yarborough, August 6, 1969, Yarborough Papers, Senate Correspondence, 1968–1970, Box 3w173, CAH-UT.

54. Barr, *Black Texans*, 201.

55. Schwarz, *In Service to America*, 139.

56. Matusow, *Unraveling of America*, 238–239.

57. Statement of Representative Catherine May (Fourth District, Washington) before the Republican Planning and Research Committee Task Force on Economic Opportunity, OEO Records, Director's Records, Subject Files, Confidential Press File, FY 1966, NA.

58. Ibid.

59. Miller, "History of Gary Job Corps," 101.

60. Ibid., 102.

61. Ibid.

62. Anonymous report on activities at Gary Job Corps Center, n.d., OEO Records, Job Corps, Director's Subject Files, 1964–1965, NA.

63. Miller, "History of Gary Job Corps," 102.

64. Levitan and Johnston, *Job Corps*, 6–7.

65. Davies, *From Opportunity to Entitlement*, 196.

66. Hyman Bookbinder and Sam Yette to Sargent Shriver and Bernard Boutin, July 3, 1966, OEO Records, OCR, Director's Records, Alphabetical File, 1964–1969, NA.

67. Ibid.

68. Sargent Shriver to Lyndon Johnson, May 27, 1965, OEO Records (microfilm, reel 8), LBJL.

69. Sargent Shriver to Lyndon Johnson, memorandum, July 21, 1965, WHCF-CF, Box 124, LBJL; Davies, *From Opportunity to Entitlement*, 77.

70. Shriver to Schultze, December 17, 1965, LBJL.

71. Sargent Shriver, "Talking Points . . . Budget Bureau Appeal," 1965, OEO Administrative History, Documentary Supplement, LBJL.

72. Jackson, *From Civil Rights to Human Rights*, 238; Noel A. Cazenave, *Impossible Democracy: The Unlikely Success of the War on Poverty Community Action Programs* (Albany: State University of New York Press, 2007), 156.

73. Marjorie Graham, "Shriver Cites OEO Problem," *El Paso Times*, October 23, 1967, 1A+.

74. Ibid.

75. Ibid.

76. Handwritten notes attached to memorandum, Bookbinder and Yette to Shriver and Boutin, July 3, 1966.

77. Ibid.

78. Ibid.

79. Ibid.

80. Theodore Berry, "OEO and Cities Where There Were No Riots," *Communities in Action* 2, no. 5 (October–November 1967): 3.

81. Ibid.

82. Ibid.

83. Ibid.

84. Germany, *New Orleans after the Promises*, 140.

85. Sargent Shriver, "OEO and the Riots: A Summary," memorandum, 1967, OEO Administrative History, Documentary Supplement, Box 2, WHCF, LBJL.

86. Ibid.

87. Ibid.

88. Job Corps, "Riot Prevention: Job Corps Program," *Job Corps Reports*, 1968, 22–23.

89. Samuel Yette to Staff, undated memorandum, OEO Records, OCR, Director's Records, Alphabetical File, Operation Dixie File, 1964–1969, NA.

90. Samuel Yette to OEO Staff, Memorandum on "Operation Dixie," 1967, OEO Records, OCR, Director's Records, Alphabetical File, 1964–1969, NA.

91. Ibid.

92. *Austin American-Statesman*, September 8, 1966, in Ralph Yarborough Papers, Department Files, Executive Office of the President, 1967, Box 3w293, CAH-UT.

93. Ibid.

94. Ibid.

95. Ibid.

96. Ibid.

97. Ibid.

98. Ibid.

99. Davies, *From Opportunity to Entitlement*, 195.

100. Theodore M. Berry, "CAP Instruction, Responsibilities of Antipoverty Employees in Regard to Unlawful Demonstrations, Rioting, and Civil Disturbances," memorandum, April 12, 1968, OEO Records, Office of Operations, Training, and Technical Assistance, Subject File, NA.

101. Ibid.

102. Ibid.

CHAPTER NINE

1. King Papers Project, "Poor People's Campaign" (Martin Luther King Jr. Research and Education Institute, n.d.), http://mlk-kpp01.stanford.edu/index.php/kingpapers/article/poor_peoples_campaign/.

2. Bertrand Harding interview by Steve Goodell, November 25, 1968, transcript, Scripps Library, Miller Center for Public Affairs, University of Virginia.

3. Jeffrey A. Krames, *Rumsfeld's Way: Leadership Wisdom of a Battle-Hardened Maverick* (New York: McGraw Hill, 2002), 26.

4. Harding interview by Goodell.

5. Ibid.

6. In Davies, *From Opportunity to Entitlement*, 79.

7. Ray Pearson to John Connally, August 7, 1967, John Connally Papers, Box 25, Series 38, LBJL.

8. John Herbers, "Riot Inquiry Seeks Lawless Elements," *New York Times*, November 2, 1967, 1A.

9. Ibid.

10. "Houston Militants Took over Poverty Unit, Senators Told," *Baltimore Sun*, November 2, 1967.

11. T. L. (Tim) Parker to Francis Williams, June 27, 1968, OEO Records, Southwest Regional Office Records, CEOB, Houston File, NASWR.

12. Ibid.

13. Ibid.

14. Ibid.

15. Blum, *Years of Discord*, 173.

16. Dallek, *Flawed Giant*, 331.

17. Germany, *New Orleans after the Promises*, 8.

18. Joan Hoff, *Nixon Reconsidered* (New York: Basic Books, 1994), 62.

19. Krames, *Rumsfeld's Way*, 26.

20. Hoff, *Nixon Reconsidered*, 62.

21. Ibid., 63; Reeves, *Politics of the Peace Corps and VISTA*, 55.

22. Krames, *Rumsfeld's Way*, 26.

23. Hoff, *Nixon Reconsidered*, 65.

24. Germany, *New Orleans after the Promises*, 280-281.

25. Jeffrey M. Berry, Kent Portney, and Ken Thomson, *The Rebirth of Urban Democracy* (Washington: Brookings Institution, 1993), 22-30.

26. Davies, *From Opportunity to Entitlement*, 98, 103.

27. Stephen Ambrose, *Nixon*, vol. 2, *1962-1972* (New York: Simon and Schuster, 1987), 269.

28. Blum, *Years of Discord*, 344.

29. Davies, *From Opportunity to Entitlement*, 221.

30. Hoff, *Nixon Reconsidered*, 130.

31. Ibid.; Davies, *From Opportunity to Entitlement*, 229.

32. Davies, *From Opportunity to Entitlement*, 220.

33. San Antonio Archdiocese, *SANYO Tenth Anniversary, 1965-1975*.

34. Ibid.

35. Rodriguez, interview by the author.

36. Stryker McGuire, "Keep 'N' in SANYO," *San Antonio Light*, October 22, 1975, 1A+.

37. Rodriguez, interview by the author.

38. Ibid.

39. Veronica Flores, "Agency's Program Opened New Doors for Many Members," *San Antonio Express-News*, October 9, 1994, 1A+; Paulette Washington, "EODC and the Neighborhood Corporations" (master's thesis, Trinity University, San Antonio, 1971), 126.

40. Marquez, *Power and Politics*, 135.

41. Levitan and Johnston, *Job Corps*, 32.

42. Larry Howell, "A Job Corps Graduate's Testimonial," editorial, *Dallas Morning News*, January 22, 1969.

43. Ibid.

44. Ibid.

45. U.S. Senate, Closing of Job Corps Centers, Hearings before the Senate Subcommittee on Employment, Manpower, and Poverty of the Committee on Labor and Public Welfare, 1st Session, 91st Congress, April-May 1969, 216-217.

46. Ibid. Wilson's use of the term "Civilian Conservation Center," which was not the official name of the New Waverly center, suggests that he still viewed the Job Corps as a modern version of the CCC.

47. Levitan and Johnston, *Job Corps*, 6-7, 49.

48. "Penalizing a Failure," editorial, *Dallas Morning News*, April 26, 1969.

49. Reeves, *Politics of the Peace Corps and VISTA*, 56.

50. Texas OEO, *Texas Front*, 1970.

51. "About VISTA," *Vista Volunteer* 5, no. 1 (January 1969): 18.

52. Texas OEO, *Texas Front*, 1970.

53. Ibid.

54. In Bowsher, "VISTA in Turmoil," 1.

55. Robert D. Thomas and Richard W. Murray, "Applying the Voting Rights Act in Houston: Federal Intervention or Local Political Determination," *Publius: The Journal of Federalism* 16 (Fall 1986): 91.

56. Katz, *Undeserving Poor,* 46.

57. Davidson, *Race and Class,* 234.

58. Carter, *From George Wallace to Newt Gingrich,* x.

59. In Davidson, *Race and Class,* 232.

60. In Dan T. Carter, *The Politics of Rage: George Wallace, the Origins of the New Conservatism, and the Transformation of American Politics* (New York: Simon and Schuster, 1995), 377.

61. In Davidson, *Race and Class,* 248.

62. John Boles, *The South through Time,* 506; Pete Daniel, *Standing at the Crossroads: Southern Life in the Twentieth Century* (New York: Hill and Wang, 1986).

63. Jill Quadango, *The Color of Welfare: How Racism Undermined the War on Poverty* (New York: Oxford University Press, 1994), 196.

64. George Bush to William Flores, February 3, 1968, LULAC Records, William Flores Papers, Box 1, Folder G, BLAC-UT.

65. Ibid.

66. Ibid.

67. Gareth Davies, "The Great Society After Johnson: The Case of Bilingual Education," *Journal of American History* 88, no. 4 (March 2002): 1410–1412.

68. Jon Ford, "Viva Wallace Drive Launched in Texas," *San Antonio Express-News,* September 21, 1968, 9A.

69. Pycior, *LBJ and Mexican Americans,* 232.

70. National Archives and Records Administration (NARA), *Guide to Federal Records in the National Archives of the United States, Records of the Community Services Administration* (Washington, DC: N.d.), http://www.archives.gov/research/guide-fed-records (Go to Record Group #: 381); Germany, *New Orleans after the Promises,* 294.

71. James Sundquist, "The End of the Experiment," in *On Fighting Poverty: Perspectives from Experience,* ed. James Sundquist (New York: Basic Books, 1969), 239–240.

72. Robert Putnam and Lewis Feldstein, *Better Together: Restoring the American Community* (New York: Simon and Schuster, 2003), 14.

73. Rosales, *Illusion of Inclusion,* 142.

74. In McGuire, "Keep 'N' in SANYO," 1A.

75. Ernesto Cortés, "Justice at the Gates of the City: A Model for Shared Prosperity" (Dallas: Dallas Area Interfaith, n.d.), http://www.dallasareainterfaith.org/justice.htm.

76. Donald C. Reitzes and Dietrich C. Reitzes, *The Alinsky Legacy: Alive and Kicking* (Greenwich, CT: JAI Press, 1987), 119.

77. In Turbon, "Glory Be to the Father," 51.

78. Pycior, *LBJ and Mexican Americans,* 242.

79. In Turbon, "Glory be to the Father," 51.

80. Schwarz, *In Service to America,* 15.

81. Ibid.

82. Benjamin Marquez, "Organizing the Mexican American Community in Texas: The Legacy of Saul Alinsky," *Policy Studies Review* 9, no. 2 (Winter 1990): 355–373.

83. Benjamin Marquez, *Constructing Identities in Mexican American Political Organizations: Choosing Issues, Taking Sides* (Austin: University of Texas Press, 2003).

84. Cortés, "Justice at the Gates," 3.

85. Ibid.

86. Putnam and Feldstein, *Better Together*, 19.

87. Geoffrey Rips, "Organizing Neighborhood Clout," *Texas Observer*, September 27, 1985, 5–6.

88. In Putman, *Better Together*, 13.

89. Miriam Axel-Lute, "In Their Own Hands: Colonias Organize," (National Housing Institute) *Shelterforce Online*, no. 82 (July–August 1995), http://www.nhi.org/online/issues/82/colonias.html; "Colonias Projects," Texas State Energy Conservation Office, http://www.seco.cpa.state.tx.us/colonias.htm.

90. Maria-Cristina García, "Colonia," in *The Handbook of Texas Online*, http://www.tshaonline.org/handbook/online/articles/CC/poc3.html.

91. Teresa Amott and Julie Matthari, *Race, Gender, and Work: A Multicultural History of Women in the United States* (Cambridge, MA: South End Press, 1996), 84.

92. Vicki Ruíz, "Communities Organized for Public Service," in *Latinas in the United States*, ed. Vicki Ruíz and Virginia Sánchez Korrol (Bloomington: University of Indiana Press, 2006), 170.

93. Ruth Winegarten, *Black Texas Women: A Sourcebook* (Austin: University of Texas Press, 1996), 212.

94. Rosales, *Illusion of Inclusion*, 110–111; Gabriela F. Arredondo, *Chicana Feminisms: A Critical Reader* (Durham, NC: Duke University Press, 2003), 78.

95. "Draft Strategy Paper: Projected Reduction in Poverty," 1969, OEO Records, Southwest Regional Records, Director's Records, NASWR.

96. Doris Kearns, *Lyndon Johnson and the American Dream* (New York: Signet, 1976), 291.

CONCLUSION

1. Ronald Reagan, "State of the Union Address," January 25, 1988, *Public Papers of the Presidents: Ronald Reagan*, vol. 1 (Washington, DC: 1990), 8.

2. Randy Albelda and Nancy Folbre, *The War on the Poor: A Defense Manual* (New York: New Press, 1996), 10.

3. Jacquelyn Dowd Hall, "The Long Civil Rights Movement and the Political Uses of the Past," *Journal of American History* 91, no. 4 (March 2005): 1235; Bauman, *Race and the War on Poverty*, 9.

4. Patterson, *America's Struggle*, 161.

5. U.S. Census Bureau, *1970 Census of Population*, vol. 1, *Characteristics of the Population*, part 45, *Texas* (Washington, DC: GPO 1973), hereafter *1970 Census of Population, Characteristics, Texas*.

6. David Goldfield et al., *The American Journey: A History of the United States* (Upper Saddle River, NJ: Prentice Hall, 1998), 937.

7. Patterson, *America's Struggle*, 161.

8. Ibid., 165; Patterson, *Grand Expectations*, 672.

9. Patterson, *America's Struggle*, 161.

10. Ibid., 165–166.

11. U.S. Department of Commerce, *Statistical Abstract of the United States, 1963* and *1973* (Washington, DC: GPO, 1964 and 1974).

12. U.S. Census Bureau, *1970 Census of Population, Characteristics, Texas*.

13. U.S. Census Bureau, *Historical Annual Time Series of State Population Estimates and Demographic Components of Change, 1900–1990* (Washington, DC: GPO).

14. U.S. Department of Commerce, *Statistical Abstract, 1963* and *1973*.

15. Patterson, *America's Struggle*, 158.

16. U.S. Department of Commerce, *Statistical Abstract, 1963* and *1973*.

17. U.S. Census Bureau, *1970 Census of Population, Characteristics, Texas*.

18. Ibid., appendix. In Texas the poverty threshold for a family of four was $3,721.

19. Matusow, *Unraveling of America*, 240.

20. Patterson, *America's Struggle*, 165.

21. U.S. Census Bureau, *1970 Census of Population, Characteristics, Texas*.

22. Ibid.

23. Ibid.

24. Ibid.

25. James Traub, "What No School Can Do," *New York Times Magazine*, January 16, 2000, 55.

26. Schulman, *Lyndon B. Johnson and American Liberalism*, 179.

27. Matusow, *Unraveling of America*, 238.

28. Texas OEO, *Texas Front*, 1968.

29. Bill Crook to Sargent Shriver, Weekly Activities Report, March 4, 1966, OEO Records, OCR-Regions, Director's Records, Region V Files, 1965–1966, NA.

30. Bill Wright, *The Tiguas: Pueblo Indians of Texas* (El Paso: Texas Western Press, 1993), xv.

31. Davies, *From Opportunity to Entitlement*, 158.

BIBLIOGRAPHY

ARCHIVAL COLLECTIONS

Benson Latin American Collection, University of Texas, Austin (BLAC-UT). Joe Bernal Papers; William Flores Papers.

Catholic Archives of San Antonio (CASA). Robert E. Lucey Papers; San Antonio Neighborhood Youth Organization (SANYO) Records.

Center for American History, University of Texas, Austin (CAH-UT). Ralph Yarborough Papers.

John Tower Library, Southwestern University, Georgetown, TX. John Tower Papers.

Lyndon Baines Johnson Library, Austin (LBJL). John Connally Papers; Office of Economic Opportunity (OEO) Records (microfilm); White House Central Files, (WHCF), Confidential File (CF).

National Archives (NA). College Park, MD. RG 381, OEO Records.

National Archives Southwest Region (NASWR), Fort Worth. RG 381, OEO Records.

BOOKS, ARTICLES, AND ACADEMIC WORKS

Albelda, Randy, and Nancy Folbre. *The War on the Poor: A Defense Manual.* New York: New Press, 1996.

Acosta, Teresa Palma, "Raza Unida Party," *The Handbook of Texas Online.* Texas State Historical Association, n.d. http://www.tshaonline.org/handbook/online/articles/RR/war1.html.

Acuña, Rodolfo. *Occupied America: A History of Chicanos.* 3d edition. New York: Harper Collins, 1988.

Allsup, Carl. *The American GI Forum: Origins and Evolution.* Austin: Center for Mexican American Studies, University of Texas, 1986.

————. "Hernández v. Texas." In *The Handbook of Texas Online*. Texas State Historical Association, n.d. http://www.tshaonline.org/handbook/online/articles/HH/jrhl.html.

Ambrose, Stephen. *Nixon*. Vol. 2, *1962–1972*. New York: Simon and Schuster, 1987.

Amott, Teresa, and Julie Matthari. *Race, Gender, and Work: A Multicultural History of Women in the United States*. Cambridge, MA: South End Press, 1996.

Anderson, Shirley. *Mexican Americans in a Dallas Barrio*. Tucson: University of Arizona Press, 1978.

Anderson, Terry. *The Movement and the Sixties*. New York: Oxford University Press, 1995.

Andrew, John A. *Lyndon Johnson and the Great Society*. Chicago: I. R. Dee, 1998.

Arredondo, Gabriela F. *Chicana Feminisms: A Critical Reader*. Durham, NC: Duke University Press, 2003.

Ashmore, Susan Youngblood. *Carry It On: The War on Poverty and the Civil Rights Movement in Alabama, 1964–1972*. Athens: University of Georgia Press, 2008.

————. "More Than a Head Start: The War on Poverty, Catholic Charities, and Civil Rights in Mobile, Alabama, 1965–1970." In *The New Deal and Beyond: Social Welfare in the South since 1930*, ed. Elna C. Green. Athens: University of Georgia Press, 2003.

Axel-Lute, Miriam. "In Their Own Hands: Colonias Organize." (National Housing Institute) *Shelterforce Online*, no. 82 (July–August 1995), http://www.nhi.org/online/issues/82/colonias.html.

Barr, Alwyn. *Black Texans: A History of African Americans in Texas, 1582–1995*. 2d edition. Norman: University of Oklahoma Press, 1996.

Bauman, Robert. "The Black Power and Chicano Movements in the Poverty Wars in Los Angeles." *Journal of Urban History* 33, no. 2 (2007): 277–295.

————. *Race and the War on Poverty: From Watts to East LA*. Norman: University of Oklahoma Press, 2008.

Beeth, Howard, and Cary Wintz, eds. *Black Dixie: Afro Texan History and Culture in Houston*. College Station: Texas A&M University Press, 1992.

Beinart, Peter. "The Rehabilitation of the Cold War Liberal." *New York Times Magazine*, April 30, 2006, 41–45.

Berry, Jeffrey, Kent Portney, and Ken Thomson. *The Rebirth of Urban Democracy*. Washington, DC: Brookings Institution, 1993.

Beschloss, Michael L. *Taking Charge: The Johnson White House Tapes, 1963–1964*. New York: Touchstone, 1997.

Black, Earl, and Merle Black. *The Rise of Southern Republicans*. Cambridge: Harvard University Press, 2002.

Blum, John Morton. *Years of Discord: American Politics and Society, 1961–1974*. New York: Norton, 1992.

Boles, John. *The South through Time: A History of an American Region*. Englewood Cliffs, NJ: Prentice Hall, 1995.

Branch, Taylor. *Pillar of Fire: America in the King Years, 1963–1965*. New York: Touchstone, 1998.

Broder, Samuel. *Social Justice and Church Authority: The Public Life of Archbishop Robert E. Lucey.* Philadelphia: Temple University Press, 1982.

Browning, Harley L., and S. Dale McLemore. "The Spanish Surname Population in Texas." *Public Affairs Comment* 10, no. 1 (January 1964).

Carter, Dan. *From George Wallace to Newt Gingrich: Race in the Conservative Counterrevolution, 1963–1994.* Baton Rouge: Louisiana State University Press, 1996.

———. *The Politics of Rage: George Wallace, the Origins of the New Conservatism, and the Transformation of American Politics.* New York: Simon and Schuster, 1995.

Cazenave, Noel A. *Impossible Democracy: The Unlikely Success of the War on Poverty Community Action Programs.* Albany: State University of New York Press, 2007.

Clayson, William. "'The Barrios and the Ghettos Have Organized!': Community Action, Political Acrimony, and the War on Poverty in San Antonio." *Journal of Urban History* 28, no. 2 (January 2002): 158–183.

———. "Texas Poverty and Liberal Politics: The Office of Economic Opportunity and the War on Poverty in the Lone Star State." PhD diss., Texas Tech University, 2001.

———. "The War on Poverty and the Fear of Urban Violence in Houston, 1965–1968." *Gulf South Historical Review* 18, no. 2 (Spring 2003): 38–59.

Cohen, Adam, and Elizabeth Taylor. *American Pharaoh: Mayor Richard Daley—His Battle for Chicago and the Nation.* New York: Little, Brown, 2000.

Cole, Thomas R. *No Color Is My Kind: The Life of Eldrewey Stevens and the Integration of Houston.* Austin: University of Texas Press, 1997.

Conkin, Paul. *Big Daddy from the Pedernales: Lyndon Baines Johnson.* Boston: Twayne, 1986.

Cortés, Ernesto. "Justice at the Gates of the City: A Model for Shared Prosperity." Dallas: Dallas Area Interfaith, n.d. http://www.dallasareainterfaith.org/justice.htm.

Cox, Patrick. *Ralph W. Yarborough: The People's Senator.* Austin: University of Texas Press, 2001.

Dallek, Robert. *Flawed Giant: Lyndon Johnson and His Times, 1961–1973.* New York: Oxford University Press, 1998.

———. *Lone Star Rising: Lyndon Johnson and His Times, 1908–1960.* London: Oxford University Press, 1992.

Daniel, Pete. *Standing at the Crossroads: Southern Life in the Twentieth Century.* New York: Hill and Wang, 1986.

Davidson, Chandler. *Race and Class in Texas Politics.* Princeton, NJ: Princeton University Press, 1990.

Davies, Gareth. *From Opportunity to Entitlement: The Transformation and Decline of Great Society Liberalism.* Lawrence: University of Kansas Press, 1996.

———. "The Great Society after Johnson: The Case of Bilingual Education." *Journal of American History* 88, no. 4 (March 2002): 1405–1429.

De León, Arnoldo. *Ethnicity in the Sunbelt: A History of Mexican Americans in Houston.* Houston: University of Houston Press, 1989.

Dunne, George H., ed. *Poverty in Plenty.* New York: P. J. Kennedy and Sons, 1964.

Friedman, Saul. "Life in Black Houston." *Texas Observer,* June 9–23, 1967.

García, Ignacio. *Chicanismo: The Forming of a Militant Ethos among Mexican Americans.* Tucson: University of Arizona Press, 1997.

———. *United We Win: The Rise and Fall of La Raza Unida Party.* Tucson: University of Arizona Press, 1989.

García, Maria-Cristina. "Colonia." In *The Handbook of Texas Online.* Texas State Historical Association, n.d. http://www.tshaonline.org/handbook/online/articles/CC/poc3.html.

Garcia, Mario T. *The Making of a Mexican American Mayor: Raymond L. Telles of El Paso.* El Paso: Texas Western Press, 1998.

———. *Mexican Americans: Leadership, Ideology, and Identity, 1930–1960.* New Haven, CT: Yale University Press, 1989.

García, Richard A. *Political Ideology: A Comparative Study of Three Chicano Organizations.* San Francisco: R&E Research, 1977.

Germany, Kent. *New Orleans after the Promises: Poverty, Citizenship, and the Search for the Great Society.* Athens: University of Georgia Press, 2007.

Gerstle, Gary. *American Crucible: Race and Nation in the Twentieth Century.* Princeton, NJ: Princeton University Press, 2001.

Gettheimer, Josh, ed. *Ripples of Hope: Great American Civil Rights Speeches.* New York: Basic Books, 2003.

Gingrich, Newt. *To Renew America.* New York: HarperCollins, 1995.

Goldfield, David, Carl Abbott, Virginia DeJohn Anderson, Jo Ann E. Argersinger, Peter H. Argersinger, William Barney, and Robert Weir. *The American Journey: A History of the United States.* Upper Saddle River, NJ: Prentice Hall, 1998.

Goodwin, Richard. *Remembering America: A Voice from the Sixties.* New York: Harper and Row, 1988.

Green, George Norris. *The Establishment in Texas Politics.* Westport, CT: Greenwood Press, 1979.

Gregory, Gladys, and Sheldon B. Liss. "Chamizal Dispute." In *The Handbook of Texas Online.* Texas State Historical Association, n.d. http://www.tshaonline.org/handbook/online/articles/CC/nbc1.html.

Griswold del Castillo, Richard, and Arnoldo De León. *North to Aztlán: A History of Mexican Americans in the United States.* New York: Twayne, 1997.

Gutiérrez, José Angel. *The Making of a Chicano Militant: Lessons from Cristal.* Madison: University of Wisconsin Press, 1998.

Hall, Jacquelyn Dowd. "The Long Civil Rights Movement and the Political Uses of the Past." *Journal of American History* 91, no. 4 (March 2005).

Hamilton, Dona Cooper, and Charles V. Hamilton. *The Dual Agenda: Race and Social Welfare Policies of Civil Rights Organizations.* New York: Columbia University Press, 1997.

Hazirijan, Lisa Gayle. "Combating NEED: Urban Conflict and the Transformations of the War on Poverty and the African American Freedom Struggle in Rocky Mount, North Carolina." *Journal of Urban History* 34, no. 4 (May 2008): 639–664.

Helmer, Bill. "A Context for Tragedy." *Texas Observer,* June 9–23, 1967.

———. "Nightmare in Houston." *Texas Observer,* June 9–23, 1967.

Hoff, Joan. *Nixon Reconsidered*. New York: Basic Books, 1994.

Isserman, Maurice, and Michael Kazin. *America Divided: The Civil War of the 1960s*. New York: Oxford University Press, 2000.

Jackson, Thomas. *From Civil Rights to Human Rights: Martin Luther King Jr. and the Struggle for Economic Justice*. Philadelphia: University of Pennsylvania Press, 2007.

Johnson, David, and John A. Booth, eds. *The Politics of San Antonio: Community, Progress, and Power*. Lincoln: University of Nebraska Press, 1983.

Justice, Blair. *Violence in the City*. Fort Worth: Texas Christian University Press, 1969.

Katz, Michael. *The Undeserving Poor: From the War on Poverty to the War on Welfare*. New York: Pantheon, 1990.

Kearns, Doris. *Lyndon Johnson and the American Dream*. New York: Signet, 1976.

Kiffmeyer, Thomas J. "From Self-Help to Sedition: The Appalachian Volunteers in Eastern Kentucky, 1964–1970." *Journal of Southern History* 64, no. 1 (1998): 65–94.

———. *Reformers to Radicals: The Appalachian Volunteers and the War on Poverty*. Lexington: University of Kentucky Press, 2008.

King Papers Project. "Poor People's Campaign." Martin Luther King Jr. Research and Education Institute, n.d. http://mlk-kpp01.stanford.edu/index.php/kingpapers/article/poor_peoples_campaign/.

Kotz, Nick. *Judgment Days: Lyndon Baines Johnson, Martin Luther King Jr., and the Laws that Changed America*. Boston: Houghton Mifflin, 2005.

Krames, Jeffrey. *Rumsfeld's Way: Leadership Wisdom of a Battle-Hardened Maverick*. New York: McGraw Hill, 2002.

Levitan, Sar. *Antipoverty Work and Training Efforts: Goals and Reality*. Washington, DC: National Manpower Policy Taskforce, 1967.

———. *The Great Society's Poor Law: A New Approach to Poverty*. Baltimore: Johns Hopkins University Press, 1969.

Levitan, Sar, and Benjamin H. Johnston. *The Job Corps: A Social Experiment That Works*. Baltimore, MD: Johns Hopkins University Press, 1975.

Mann, Robert. *The Walls of Jericho: Lyndon Johnson, Hubert Humphrey, Richard Russell, and the Struggle for Civil Rights*. New York: Houghton Mifflin, 1996.

Marquez, Benjamin. *Constructing Identities in Mexican American Political Organizations: Choosing Issues, Taking Sides*. Austin: University of Texas Press, 2003.

———. "Organizing the Mexican American Community in Texas: The Legacy of Saul Alinsky." *Policy Studies Review* 9, no. 2 (Winter 1990): 355–373.

———. *Power and Politics in a Chicano Barrio*. Lanham, MD: University Press of America, 1985.

Matusow, Allen. *The Unraveling of America: A History of Liberalism in the 1960s*. New York: Harper, 1984.

McNeill, Donna. "EODC: Invoking the Green Amendment." Master's thesis, Trinity University, San Antonio, 1979.

Miller, Toni. "The History of Gary Job Corps." Master's thesis, Southwest Texas State University, 1970.

Montejano, David. *Anglos and Mexicans in the Making of Texas, 1836–1986*. Austin: University of Texas Press, 1987.

Mowry, George. *Another Look at the Twentieth Century South*. Baton Rouge: Louisiana State University Press, 1973.

Moynihan, Daniel. *Maximum Feasible Misunderstanding: Community Action in the War on Poverty*. New York: Free Press, 1970.

Muñoz, Carlos. *Youth, Identity, Power: The Chicano Movement*. New York: Verso, 1989.

Orleck, Annelise. *Storming Caesar's Palace: How Black Mothers Fought Their Own War on Poverty*. Boston: Beacon, 2005.

Patterson, James. *America's Struggle Against Poverty, 1900–1994*. Cambridge: Harvard University Press, 1994.

———. *Grand Expectations: The United States, 1945–1974*. New York: Oxford University Press, 1996.

Pierce, F. J. *Hunger and Malnutrition: Citizens Board of Inquiry Preliminary Report, Food Intake Among Low Income Families in San Antonio*. San Antonio: Our Lady of the Lake University, 1969.

Putnam, Robert, and Lewis Feldstein. *Better Together: Restoring the American Community*. New York: Simon and Schuster, 2003.

Pycior, Julie L. *LBJ and Mexican Americans: The Paradox of Power*. Austin: University of Texas Press, 1997.

Quadango, Jill. *The Color of Welfare: How Racism Undermined the War on Poverty*. New York: Oxford University Press, 1994.

Reeves, T. Zane. *The Politics of the Peace Corps and VISTA*. Tuscaloosa: University of Alabama Press, 1988.

Reitzes, Donald C., and Dietrich C. Reitzes. *The Alinsky Legacy: Alive and Kicking*. Greenwich, CT: JAI Press, 1987.

Rendon, Armando. *Chicano Manifesto*. New York: Macmillan, 1971.

Reston, James. *The Lone Star: The Life of John Connally*. New York: Harper and Row, 1989.

Rips, Geoffrey. "Organizing Neighborhood Clout." *Texas Observer*, September 27, 1985, 5–6.

Rodriguez, Marc Simon. "A Movement Made of 'Young Mexican Americans Seeking Change': Critical Citizenship, Migration, and the Chicano Movement in Texas and Wisconsin." *Western Historical Quarterly* 34, no. 3 (2003): 275–300.

Rosales, Rodolfo. *The Illusion of Inclusion: The Untold Political Story of San Antonio*. Austin: University of Texas Press, 2000.

Ruíz, Vicki. "Communities Organized for Public Service." In *Latinas in the United States*, ed. Vicki Ruíz and Virginia Sánchez Korrol. Bloomington: University of Indiana Press, 2006.

Sanders, Luther Lee. *How to Win Elections in San Antonio the Good Government Way, 1955–1971*. San Antonio: Department of Urban Studies, St. Mary's University, 1975.

Schneider, Eric C. *Vampires, Dragons, and Egyptian Kings*. New York: Princeton University Press, 1999.

Schulman, Bruce J. *Lyndon B. Johnson and American Liberalism: A Brief Biography with Documents*. Boston: Bedford, 1995.

Schwarz, Marvin. *In Service to America: A History of VISTA in Arkansas, 1965–1985*. Fayetteville: University of Arkansas Press, 1988.

Seligman, Ben. *Permanent Poverty: An American Syndrome*. Chicago: Quadrangle, 1968.

Shriver, Sargent. Foreword to *Poverty in Plenty*, George H. Dunne. New York: P. J. Kennedy and Sons, 1964.

Sitkoff, Harvard. *The Struggle for Black Equality, 1954–1980*. New York: Hill and Wang, 1981.

Sundquist, James. "The End of the Experiment." In *On Fighting Poverty: Perspectives from Experience*, ed. James Sundquist. New York: Basic Books, 1969.

Thomas, Robert D., and Richard W. Murray. "Applying the Voting Rights Act in Houston: Federal Intervention or Local Political Determination." *Publius: The Journal of Federalism* 16 (Fall 1986): 81–96.

Traub, James. "What No School Can Do." *New York Times Magazine*, January 16, 2000, 55.

Turbon, James L. "Glory Be to the Father: The History of the San Antonio Neighborhood Youth Organization." Master's thesis, Trinity University, San Antonio, 1988.

Vaca, Nicolas. *The Presumed Alliance: The Unspoken Conflict Between Latinos and Blacks and What It Means for America*. New York: Rayo, 2004.

Wagner, Deborah. "The Ten Biggest Myths about the OEO." (OEO) *Communities in Action* 2, no. 3 (April–May 1967).

Washington, Paulette. "EODC and the Neighborhood Corporations." Master's thesis, Trinity University, San Antonio, 1971.

Willentz, Sean. *The Age of Reagan: A History, 1976–2006*. New York: Harper, 2008.

Winegarten, Ruth. *Black Texas Women: A Sourcebook*. Austin: University of Texas Press, 1996.

Wolff, Nelson. *Mayor: An Inside View of San Antonio Politics, 1981–1995*. San Antonio: Express-News, 1997.

Wright, Bill. *The Tiguas: Pueblo Indians of Texas*. El Paso: Texas Western Press, 1993.

GOVERNMENT DOCUMENTS

National Archives and Records Administration (NARA). *Guide to Federal Records in the National Archives of the United States, Records of the Community Services Administration*. Washington, DC: N.d. http://www.archives.gov/research/guide-fed-records (Go to Record Group #: 381).

Reagan, Ronald. State of the Union Address. January 25, 1988. *Public Papers of the Presidents: Ronald Reagan*, vol. 1. Washington, DC: 1990.

University of Texas at Dallas. *Windows on Urban Poverty*. School of Economic, Political, and Policy Sciences at the University of Texas at Dallas and Brookings Institution on Urban and Metropolitan Policy, n.d. http://templeton.utdallas.edu/poverty/index.htm.

U.S. Census Bureau. *1930 Census*. Vol. 6, *Families*. Washington, DC: Government Printing Office (GPO), 1933.

———. *1930 Census of Population, Occupations*. Washington, DC: GPO, 1933.

———. *1960 Census of Housing*. Vol. 1, *States and Small Areas*, part 6, *Texas–Wyoming*. Washington, DC: GPO, 1963.

———. *1960 Census of Population.* Vol. 1, part 45, *Texas.* Washington, DC: GPO, 1964.

———. *1960 Census of Population and Housing, Detailed Characteristics of the Population, Texas.* Washington, DC: GPO, 1964.

———. *1960 Census of Population, General Population Characteristics.* Washington, DC: GPO, 1963.

———. *1960 Census of Population and Housing, Detailed Housing Characteristics, Texas.* Washington, DC: GPO, 1963.

———. *1970 Census of Population.* Vol. 1, *Characteristics of the Population,* part 45, *Texas.* Washington, DC: GPO, 1973.

———. *Historical Annual Time Series of State Population Estimates and Demographic Components of Change, 1900–1990.* Washington, DC: GPO.

———. *Persons of Spanish Surname, 1960.* Washington, DC: GPO, 1964.

U.S. Congress. House Committee on Education and Labor, Ad Hoc Hearing Task Force on Poverty. Washington, DC: GPO, 1969.

U.S. Department of Commerce. *Statistical Abstract of the United States, 1960.* Washington, DC: GPO, 1961.

———. *Statistical Abstract of the United States, 1963.* Washington, DC: GPO, 1964.

———. *Statistical Abstract of the United States, 1973.* Washington, DC: GPO, 1974.

U.S. Department of Labor. *Subemployment in the Slums of San Antonio.* Washington, DC: GPO, 1967.

U.S. Office of Economic Opportunity (OEO). *As the Seed Is Sown: OEO Annual Report.* Washington, DC: 1968, 1969–1970.

———. *Community Action Program Guide.* Washington, DC: 1965.

———. *The Quiet Revolution: OEO Annual Report.* Washington, DC: 1965, 1966.

———. *The Texas Front in the Nation's War on Poverty.* Austin: Texas OEO, 1966, 1968, 1970.

U.S. Senate. Committee on Labor and Public Welfare, Subcommittee on Employment, Manpower, and Poverty. Hearings on Closing of Job Corps Centers, 1st Session, 91st Congress. April–May 1969.

Woods, Frances J. "The Model Cities Program in Perspective, the San Antonio, Texas Experience." Presented to the House of Representatives, Hearings before the Subcommittee on Housing and Development of the Committee on Banking, Finance, and Urban Affairs, 97th Congress, 1st Session. January 1972. Washington, DC.

NEWSPAPERS

Alamo Messenger (San Antonio)
Alice Daily Echo
Austin American-Statesman
Baltimore Sun
Brownsville Herald
Corpus Christi Caller
El Paso Herald-Post
El Paso Times

Forward Times (Houston)
Houston Chronicle
Houston Informer
Like It Is (Marshall, TX)
Los Angeles Times
New York Herald Tribune
New York Times
San Antonio Express
San Antonio Express-News
San Antonio Light
San Antonio News
Valley Morning Star (Harlingen, TX)
Wall Street Journal
Washington Post

INTERVIEWS

Barrientos, Gonazalo. Interview by José Angel Gutiérrez, 6 January 1998. In Tejano Voices series, Center for Mexican American Studies Oral History Project, University of Texas at Arlington. Transcript, http://libraries.uta.edu/tejanovoices.

Gutiérrez, José Angel. Phone interview by the author. 31 August 2000.

Harding, Bertrand. Interview by Steve Goodell, 25 November 1968. Scripps Library, University of Virginia Miller Center for Public Affairs. Transcript, webstoreage4 .mcpa.virginia.edu/lbj/oralhistory/harding_bertrand_1968_1125.pdf.

King, Martin Luther Jr. Interview by Tom Wicker, 28 March 1965. *Meet the Press*, transcript, OEO Records, NARA.

Mireles, Irma. Phone interview by the author, 5 September 2000.

Rodriguez, Julian. Phone interview by the author, 28 August 2000.

INDEX

CPSIA information can be obtained at www.ICGtesting.com
Printed in the USA
LVOW040246240512

283085LV00002B/3/P